The Wise Woman's Guide to Erotic Videos

D0953991

ANGELA
COHEN

AND

SARAH
GARDNER
FOX

Broadway Books

New York

The Wise Woman's Guide to Erotic Videos

300 SEXY VIDEOS

FOR EVERY WOMAN—

AND HER LOVER

BROADWAY

Broadway Books titles may be purchased for business or promotional use
or for special sales. For information, please write to: Special Markets
Department, Bantam Doubleday Dell Publishing Group, Inc., 1540
Broadway, New York, NY 10036.

BROADWAY BOOKS and its logo, a letter B bisected on the diagonal,
are trademarks of Broadway Books, a division of Bantam Doubleday Dell
Publishing Group, Inc.

Library of Congress Cataloging-in-Publication Data
Cohen, Angela.
    The wise woman's guide to erotic videos : 300 sexy videos for
every woman—and her lover / Angela Cohen and Sarah Gardner Fox.
        p.   cm.
    Includes bibliographical references and index.
    ISBN 0-553-06784-2 (pbk.)
    1. Erotic films—Catalogs.   2. Video recordings—Catalogs.
3. Erotic films—Reviews.   4. Video recordings—Reviews.   I. Fox,
Sarah Gardner.   II. Title.
PN1995.9.S45C65   1997
791.43'6538—dc20   96-27548
                                                              CIP

FIRST EDITION

Designed by Claire Vaccaro

97 98 99 00 10 9 8 7 6 5 4 3 2 1

To Caroline Herter, Bill Shinker,
Dawn Low, and John Owen—who were there
when it mattered.

A.C.

To Mark. Quite a guy.

S.G.F.

Contents

Sidebars

Acknowledgments

We are grateful to all the wise women and men who lent their time and enthusiasm to the development of this book. We are particularly indebted to those who watched dozens of videos and remained generous with their reactions and points of view: Lynn, Monica, Nancy A., Larry, Bob, Bonnie, Christa, David C., Judith, Jorge, George, George C., Lissa, Maria, David B., Marcelo, Samantha, Nancy, Laura, Melissa, Matthew G., Barbara, Dan, John, Caroline, Kathy, Mike M., Susan, Brenda K., Jane, Matthew L., Dawn, Joseph, Mike, Joan, Jerry, Allan, Deanne, George N., Kazui, Susan N., John, Susan R., Andy, Ed, Leslie, Carla, Brenda S., Belinda, Scott, Mary, Jay, Eugene, Joan V., Hazel, Donna R., Tony, Brian, Robert, Gay, Lisa, Jill, Mark and Betsy.

An appreciative thank-you to all those video store clerks who didn't even blink when we rented eight or more videos a day, day after day. To Janet Goldstein, our editor, and Betsy Thorpe, her assistant, many thanks for the patience and trust they gave us.

Finally, very special thank-yous to Nina Hartley, Porsche Lynn, Bernie Oakley, Candida Royalle, Mike Horner, and Jane Alexander for their good-will and openness in the interviews they gave us.

Introduction

Books about erotica tend to be earnest—full of theories, statistics, and logically defended opinions, as if soberness made the subject of sex less controversial. This is not one of those books. We have our serious moments but, in general, we're into having a good time. After all, that's why we—and millions of other women—watch erotic videos.

We want to rev up our fantasies, find out what everyone else is up to, learn a thing or two, give the man we love a new sexual thrill, or maybe have a laugh while we both get turned on. All these things are fun. We're talking about sex here, not mortgage rates, corporate downsizing, or saving the rain forest. Life is full of such difficult issues, but having a sensuous time in bed shouldn't have to be one of them. (If it is, don't despair. Go directly to the section "Instructional Videos and How-to Series," which starts on page 233.

This helpful section comes in the last third of the book and includes thorough reviews of the mail-order series advertised in the *New York Times Book Review* and national magazines. In the first two thirds you'll find a mix of reviews for every kind of erotic video, from Hollywood favorites and foreign movies to explicit adult videos. We have concentrated on the explicit, and the majority of the videos fall into that category, though there are many suggestions for those who don't feel ready to take the plunge into the world of adult movies.

Until now, good, woman-friendly erotic videos haven't been all that easy to find. Most of the more than five thousand adult videos made in the last year alone are intended for a murky group who apparently want to see plenty of enhanced T & bare A, no-frills action, and lurid genital close-ups. Movies like these can put you off sex for weeks.

Before we embarked on this project, we loved to network our discoveries of hot new adult videos along with recipes, good books, stock market tips, new vacation spots, and strategies for getting along with those we cherish. The two of us and our friends aren't the only women who throw an adults-only video into the VCR now and then. Statistics from diverse sources say that women (alone or with men) make up between 23 percent and 40 percent of the $2.5 billion erotic video market. Those are impressive numbers, but whether you're a regular in the adult section or cautiously curious, you know how difficult it is to find well-told stories, attractive settings, wit, romance, or anything resembling character development.

The *New York Times* article "Science Is Finding Out What Women Really Want" (August 13, 1995) reported on a Dutch study that scientifically measured the responses of both men and women as they viewed two different erotic film clips—the first from a popular video at the local rental store, the other from a Femme Productions video, made by filmmaker Candida Royalle with women in mind. Both clips had the same effect physiologically: men and women showed aroused physical responses. The difference was in how they felt about the videos. Men simply reported themselves as feeling "turned on." Women said the first video repulsed and disgusted them but the Femme Productions video turned them on; they needed to have a positive emotional response before they could have a positive sexual experience.

We're going to skip discussing how cultural and environmental factors might influence women and how the scientific study caught up with common sense. We'll cut right to the chase. The scientists proved what we know—women find some movies sexually exciting. Our mission has been to find these movies. In researching *The Wise Woman's Guide* we happily entertained many erotic tastes and practices, but at a minimum we looked for consensual sex, women portrayed as people (not inflatable sex toys), and a good outcome. After that we sought out videos with a polished style and healthy respect for our fantasies, finding mysteries, comedies, and even a few musicals. In instances where we have included a few films that are edgier and less "politically correct"—such as noir, S/M, and rape fantasies—our goal has been to give you enough information about the plot, point of view, and sexual content to help you make your personal choice. Sexuality can have a wild side, and what safer way to explore your fantasies than with a video.

What we tell you is the stuff you won't find on the box or in traditional reviews (mostly by men, for men), and we'll tell it from our point of view for women like us—smart, busy women who work, have families, date (and break up), and feel guilty when we watch Martha Stewart on Sunday mornings instead of going to exercise class. We're fans, not scholars, but we know what we and our friends like, even when we don't always agree with each other. Some of those friends took the time to share their opinions with us, and we incorporated their thinking into the reviews.

On one thing we certainly agree. Making sure the video you watch is one you might like often means stepping up to the plate and renting the movies yourself. Nobody knows better than us that taking an erotic movie to the checkout counter has the potential for embarrassment. It's sadly true that men have been given implied permission to consume erotica, but the cultural assumption is that women are too fine and sensitive to be interested in these movies. We'd like to say loud and clear that thanks to the '70s (when we focused on making love, not war) and writers like Lonnie Barbach and Nancy Friday (among others), our sexuality has been outed.

Many of our friends were as fascinated by the performers we talked about as they were by the videos. To share a little of that information we have written some brief sidebars along with the reviews. In addition to tips on renting and safe sex, the sidebars include interviews with people in several aspects of the business. We spoke with three who began as performers and now are making names for themselves as filmmakers (Nina Hartley, Candida Royalle, and Mike Horner), one who dances and runs a phone sex business (Porsche Lynn), and one who works for the most successful marketer of explicit videos, how-to tapes, sex toys, and condoms in the United States (Bernie Oakley, head of new business development at PHE).

By now we have watched more erotic videos than anyone else we know, so we'd like to offer a few tips to make your viewing happier. Keep in mind what these videos are for and subdue that hypercritical part of your brain. The explicit erotic video universe doesn't hold itself to the same standards as feature movies (in general, budgets are smaller, good acting is a side benefit, and plot serves the erotic action). Fast-forward the free-speech message (after you've seen it once) and the trailers, many of which are ads for phone sex. If you're watching for the first time, check out our sidebar notes on renting ("Losing Your Virginity," page 14).

Wherever available we've included the performers, producers, directors, writers, music, distributors, year of production (or copyright), and length. In spite of our best efforts, we weren't able to find some of this information, especially in regard to length. Also, those of you who notice such things may run across words in titles you won't find in your dictionary. *Exstasy* is such a word (probably created to distinguish the film from another, called *Ecstasy*). These are the inventions of the filmmakers. You may also perceive inconsistencies in the spelling of given names. Our efforts to be consistent were sabotaged by an industrywide indifference to such nitpicking. It is not unusual for a given name to be spelled one way on the box, another way in the opening credits, and a third in the closing credits. Performers, few of whom use their own names, frequently have more than one stage name and change the spelling at will.

As you explore the world of erotic videos we hope you'll share your discoveries, good and bad, with us. After all, we wise women have to stick together. Let us know about your movie favorites we've missed, videos that let you down, and those you like. You can reach us on e-mail at angelcohen@aol.com. Happy viewing and joyous sex.

Give Me One Good Reason...

If you've never seen an adult movie, here are some good reasons why you should march boldly into your video store and rent one today:

- Your fantasy life will improve. Where do you think Madonna comes up with all the ideas for her hot videos?
- You'll find out what's in those video series that promise to improve your sex life—the ones you see advertised in the *New York Times Book Review*, *Redbook*, *Esquire*, and other magazines—before you place an order.
- You'll probably buy some sexy new underwear. And get motivated to work out.
- You might find a new slant on an old technique or be energized to try some of what you already know but have been too shy to initiate.
- You can introduce new ideas to your partner in a non-threatening way and find out what it is he or she has been dying to try.
- Your libido will get a jump start when fatigue, medication, or illness has short-circuited your sex life. (Antidepressants, high-blood-pressure pills, and other medications can save your life but ruin your marriage.)
- You'll have a few laughs.
- You won't catch anything but attitude from your television set. It's the ultimate safe sex. And it can be very satisfying.
- At last you'll know for sure you're doing it right.

How to Use This Book

This book is the essential access guide for women to the adult section of video stores and sexy movies in general. Those of you who already rent erotic videos will find detailed summaries of movies you might enjoy. And those who have been hesitating will have enough information to confidently select titles that will entertain, inform, amuse, and turn you on. The reviews of erotic movies in *The Wise Woman's Guide* are arranged alphabetically in two categories. The first covers adult, Hollywood, and foreign videos. The second covers instructional and how-to videos, from the Kama Sutra to how to choose a vibrator to the many popular mail-order "how to have a better sex life" series.

Because tastes differ, we have tried to give enough information for readers to make informed personal selections, whether renting or buying.

- ⓦ indicates a Wise Woman's choice, videos at the top of our shopping list to rent or buy.
- **Highly recommended** indicates videos we both agree are excellent.
- **Recommended** indicates videos at least one of us thinks is excellent.
- **Recommended as a rental** indicates videos that are above average, but read the review carefully if you're buying, not renting, the video.
- **Highly recommended with caveat** or **Recommended with caveat** indicates videos that we enjoy but that might have areas of sensitivity for some viewers. The reasons for caution are spelled out in the review.
- Videos that appear without a recommendation have been included for a variety of reasons. Most of them are above average for the industry and a good evening's entertainment depending on your taste, preferences, and the selection available. Some are classics (e.g., *Debbie Does Dallas*) that captured the collective imagination. Others, like *John Wayne Bobbitt Uncut*, attained such notoriety that they could not be

ignored. And a few videos that are not so positively reviewed are included for reader information because they are recommended in other places (such as mail-order catalogs that we respect) or are part of a popular series.

- Simulated and explicit content is indicated, and separate ratings are given for degree of explicitness and sensuality quotient. The range for each is 1–10. Videos with an explicitness rating below 6 will have full-body nudity but no in-your-face genital focus; videos with a rating of 7 have some close-up of genitalia but are not likely to have anal sex; ratings of 8, 9, and 10 incorporate anal shots and anal sex and are progressively more explicit. These ratings are based on the versions we viewed. Soft, or cable, cuts of explicit movies are available in some communities and catalogs (see sidebar "Hard and Soft"). The sensuality rating is our personal, subjective assessment on the effectiveness of the video. We end the reviews with a list of detailed sexual content according to the Key of Abbreviations below.

Hollywood and foreign feature releases are not rated for explicitness or sensuality. Nor is their sexual content indicated. Their inclusion presupposes a high sensuality content. The sex in these movies, with the exception of the Japanese movie *In the Realm of the Senses,* is simulated.

The second section of reviews includes instructional videos on topics from the Kama Sutra to Tantric sex and massage. We describe the contents of many of the most popular mail-order series on improving your sex life. We have not rated these tapes because we think the choice of a particular tape is subjective, depending on your needs and preferences.

Following the reviews you will find an Index of Videos by Category (e.g., Over 40, Sci Fi) that will guide you to the right videos for every mood and occasion. You'll also find a list of mail-order sources and suggestions for further reading.

KEY TO ABBREVIATIONS

A	anal
B	light bondage (e.g., hands tied with silk scarves)
C	man comes outside woman (cascades of sperm on face, chest, etc.)
DP	double penetration
M	masturbation
M/M	man/man
2M/W	two men and one woman (numbers change with the variation)
O	orgy

S	spanking
S/M	leather stuff
SS	safe sex
T	sex toys, vibrators, beads, etc.
2W	woman/woman
2W/M	two women and one man (numbers change with the variation)

Adult,

Hollywood,

and

Foreign

Videos

Alexandra

STYLISH SEX IN THE SUBURBS

Starring: Eve Sternberg, Lauren Wilde, Joanna Storm, Ashley Summer, Eric Edwards, Red Willson, R. Bolla, Michael Gaunt, Steve Douglas. Producer/writer: Daniel Walker. Director: Robert Freeman. Card Productions VCA, 1983.

Meet three very nervous wives. Diana's (Joanna Storm) whirlwind courtship with new husband Cliff (Steve Douglas) left him in the dark about how she learned so many ways to please him. Jennifer persuaded discount electronic king Foster (R. Bolla) that she was strictly a net-no-discount woman so that he would come up with a wedding ring, while behind his back she was giving away free samples. Patricia (Ashley Summer) hasn't let marriage to her childhood sweetheart, Martin (Eric Edwards), stop her from undressing for success with her kinky boss at the ad agency. The three unsuspecting husbands are boyhood friends. And they have one other thing in common—they each once loved Alexandra, the golden girl from their high school class, a woman who retains her grasp on their imaginations.

Alexandra's more than a little possessive of her three old flames, and she has the mean low-down dirt on their wives. Now this irresistible seductress has vowed to tell their husbands everything and invite one lucky man to go away with her. And there's nothing the wives can do except wait, wonder, and examine their consciences in libidinous detail.

A sleek, sudsy drama with sophisticated dialogue and expensive, up-scale settings, this film also has plenty of hotly convincing sex, most of it in the context of the marriages. There is one slightly rough scene when a twosome turns into an unwilling threesome, but it still rates as a good selection for new viewers of explicit films. *Best scene:* Patricia

comes home late. Eric Edwards, who plays her husband, is a tall preppy-looking fellow often featured in "sensitive" roles. He can rock and roll with the best and comes across as a man who genuinely enjoys his work.
Highly recommended.

Explicitness: 7;   Sensuality: 8   O (film within a film),   2W/M

Alice in Wonderland

A VERY ADULT MUSICAL

Starring: Kristine de Bell, Bradford Arndexter, Teri Hall, Juliet Graham, Angel Barrett, Nancy Dare, Bree Anthony, Tony Richards, Allan Novack, John Lawrence, Ron Nelson, Larry Gelmann. Producer: Bill Osco. Director: Bud Townsend. Music: Bucky Searles. Caballero, 1976. 88 minutes.

Alice in Wonderland, the erotic musical? Is nothing sacred? We're not talking about an occasional song here and a dance there. This is an elaborately costumed and choreographed full-blown extravaganza with original show tunes. *Our favorite song:* "What's a Nice Girl Like You Doing on a Knight Like This?"

We meet prim Alice aboveground, where she's defending her virtue from her long-suffering boyfriend when, whoops—a sudden trip down the rabbit hole catapults her from nineteenth-century prudery to the hello-let's-get-naked sexual revolution of the '70s. Her adventures are nothing like what Lewis Carroll told us they were, though you might remember that his hobby was taking seminude photographs of prepubescent girls. Perhaps our Alice's adventures are what that respectable Victorian mathematician imagined but didn't dare record. You'll find all the characters of Alice, plus Humpty Dumpty, looking quite different from the last time you saw them. The poor fellow cannot get his ding-a-ling up after suffering his fall.

With an interracial cast and devilish dialogue, this ribald version of what goes on down the rabbit hole has a captivating innocence and delightful sense of merriment. Kristine de Bell, who went on to become a Playboy Playmate, had a career in *The Young and the Restless*. *Our favorite line:* "If it feels good there's a chance that it must be bad."
Highly recommended.

Explicitness: 7;   Sensuality: 6   M

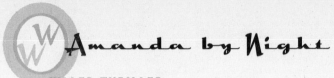

Amanda by Night

KILLER THRILLER

Starring: Veronica Hart, Samantha Fox, Lisa De Leeuw, Brook West, Nicole Noir, R. Bolla, Jamie Gillis, Ron Jeremy. Producer: Harold Lime. Director: Robert McCallum. Music: Ronnie Romonovich. Caballero, 1980. 95 minutes.

Dazzling Amanda (Veronica Hart), blessed with those famous twin assets—"a head for business and a bod for sin"—uses them to stop hooking for pimp Friday (Jamie Gillis) and go into business for herself. When Friday telephones with a "big-shot" client's request for two women, one a skilled dominatrix, Amanda tells him she can't take the job personally but for old times' sake (and a $1,000 fee) sends two of her girls—Gwen (Samantha Fox) and Beth (Lisa De Leeuw).

Several days later, Beth's body surfaces in the river, and within hours Gwen is dead of a heroin overdose. Lieutenant Ambrose (R. Bolla) is assigned to the case and goes to question Amanda. She saw the killer's face though she doesn't know his identity, but she isn't about to share this or any other information with a cop, even one who says he wants to protect her. Lieutenant Ambrose stays close, ostensibly trying to win Amanda's confidence so she can help him find the killer—before she's the killer's next victim. Of course, Amanda doesn't plan to be anybody's victim, and she has more than a few tricks up her silky sleeve.

This suspenseful drama tells an engrossing story along with the steamy sex. Because it's a murder mystery there is obviously some violence in the plot, but it is discreetly portrayed. We've seen much worse on prime-time television. Here, the director aims to thrill you with explicit sex not gore. *Best scene:* The slightly balding mensch R. Bolla proves again that when he gets a chance to stretch his rough-diamond persona to show his soft heart and sexy ways, he's more than equal to the task. Another **Highly recommended** survivor from adult films' good old days.

Explicitness: 6;   Sensuality: 7   B,   M,   O,   S/M,   2W

6

Veronica Hart, aka Jane Hamilton

The good news is that many of the women involved in the adult movie business are feminists. Believe it. An articulate, smart, and thoughtful lot, these women use the power of their authority and success to influence the industry's sometimes-sexist attitudes and practices. Nina Hartley, Annie Sprinkle, Gloria Leonard, Candida Royalle, and Veronica Hart are among the small group of women who function as the feminist conscience of the industry. As Jane Hamilton, Veronica Hart produces and directs the VCA's House Party Series for Adam and Eve. VCA has been in the business since 1979 and is known for its outstanding collection of classics (The Opening of Misty Beethoven, Barbara Broadcast, Cafe Flesh) and groundbreaking technological advancement in award-winning movies like Latex, Sex 1994, and Sex 2: Fate.

American Blonde

UNHAPPILY EVER AFTER

Starring: Janine, Kaitlyn Ashley, Rasha, Misty Rain, Veronica Lake, Colt Steele, Tony Tedeschi, Alex Sanders, Rasha Ramona. Producer: Bud Lee. Director: Paul Thomas. Writer: Raven Touchstone. Music: London Underground. Cinnamon Productions/Vivid, 1994. 84 minutes.

Does being blonde improve your love life? Not if you're Kaitlyn Ashley or Janine. Kaitlyn feels no chemistry for Tony Tedeschi, and Janine's marriage to Colt Steele is a sex-free zone unless he picks up a girl and brings her home so Janine can make love in a three-way. And the girl better be quality goods or Janine won't play. These blonde charmers cross

The child of what she describes as a normal upbringing, Jane was precocious sexually and academically. She lost her virginity at fifteen, a year before graduating from high school and four years before graduating at nineteen from the University of Nevada (we told you they were an intelligent lot). Hamilton moved to New York at twenty-two and loved getting paid for doing sex. When it wasn't fun anymore, she quit. Married for fourteen years to a man in the "straight" movie business, she's the mother of two young sons. Among her community activities she has also taught vacation Bible school. The one thing she's unequivocal about is her belief that only girls over the age of twenty-one should become performers. Before that age, "they're not emotionally or psychologically ready to make that kind of decision about their lives," she says.

Jane has played both sides of the street in tinsel town, having appeared in twenty-five R-rated films, most recently as a judge in New Line Cinema's Boogie Nights, *done voice-overs for* Electric Blue, *a movie produced for Playboy, and written a book* (Hot Spots) *with Ava Cadell.* Roommates *and* Amanda by Night *are her favorites of the adult movies she's performed in. You can also see her in* American Garter, Foxtrot, Outlaw Ladies, *and a cameo in the hugely successful award winner* Latex, *which she also produced. Of her writing and directorial efforts, our favorite is "Pickup," the second vignette in Candida Royalle's* A Taste of Ambrosia.

paths at a bar, where Janine finds Kaitlyn looking for a thrilling new change of pace. Can two dissatisfied women solve their problems in a three-way relationship? *Best scene:* Tony Tedeschi's sexy staircase seduction, with hot talk and a blindfold. In our opinion, it's all downhill after that.

Janine, a former Penthouse Pet, is one of the assertive generation of erotic women stars who, as of this writing, has on-screen sex only with women. It's not clear whether it's because of sexual preference, personal morality, or worry about disease. Whatever the reason, Janine's attitude doesn't make her unemployable, though it certainly leaves male reviewers carping about each new film, disappointed that once again some valiant warrior failed to sweep her off her feet and show her what's what in the lust department. Perhaps that's the suspense that keeps them coming back.

Explicitness: 8; Sensuality: 4 A, T, 2W/M, 3W

American Garter

FASHION FARCE

Starring: Seka, Selena Steele, Sierra, Ona Zee, Tifanny Million, Nicole London, Melanie Moore, Brittany O'Connell, Heather Hart, Steve Drake, Mike Horner, Tim Lake, Veronica Hart, Randy West, Jonathan Morgan, Nick E., Joey Silvera, Joe Verducci, Tony Tedeschi. Producer: Henri Pachard. Director: Henri Pachard/Gloria Leonard. Writers: Nicky Orleans, Henri Pachard, Raven Touchstone. Based on an original story by Nicky Orleans. Undergarments designed by Raven Touchstone and Simi Danse. VCA Platinum, 1993. 85 minutes.

Long, long ago, before pantyhose were invented, when Victoria still had secrets and the birth control pill was big news, the garter, girdle, and bullet bra were at the top of the undergarment heap. Set in 1961, *American Garter* celebrates a day in the life of the American Girdle Company and an ambitious designer who sets her sisters free. The episodic story moves from the executive suite and the sewing room to the bathroom (Producer/Director Pachard's jokey signature) and ends with a huge fashion show of retro undergarments.

We love the attitude of the Fran Drescher soundalike narrator and the amiable, fresh, and funny story line. To the producers we would like to say, "Have mercy." Explicit films starring mature women should not be lit up like a night game at Candlestick Park and would benefit from fewer lingering genital close-ups. Never mind. What *American Garter* sometimes lacks in pure turn-on it more than makes up for in a wonderful sense of fun. It's full of laughs and **Highly recommended** for its entertainment value.

Explicitness: 8;   Sensuality: 5   2M/W,   2W/M

American Pie

WHO'S ZOOMING WHOM?

Starring: Nikki Tyler, Jeanna Fine, Jenteal, Melissa Hill, Amber Woods, Marc Wallice, Tom Byron, Mark Davis, Frank Towers. Producer: Toni Brooks. Director/writer: Paul Norman. Music: Buster Gonads. Vivid/Paul Norman Productions, 1995.

Mrs. Carrington is a regular she-devil of a widow. Maybe she's so mean because she knows that her very rich husband was carrying on with the very young and buxom Julia. Or, as we suspect, she was born nasty, a terminal misanthrope. Claiming that her seventy-year-old husband left no will, she can't wait to get her hands on his money. The butler and maid, harboring no love in their hearts for their abusive mistress, know better.

Accused of being a gold digger when the terms of the will are revealed, Julia demurs and whispers, "It's not the money." Nasty (but no pervert), dirty old man Carrington was an incredible lover who knew how to really satisfy a woman. He taught Julia a few things, which she happily shares with her girlfriend and you. So what if he had to resort to the toys in his great big old chest? He was seventy, after all, and needed a little help every now and then.

To settle their differences, Mrs. Carrington and Julia reach an unusual rapprochement in the toilet of the lawyer's office in a cat-fight sequence that by turns shocked us and made us laugh. There's plenty of dirty talk and a fair amount of nasty sex between these two "ladies."

Explicitness: 9; Sensuality: 4   M,   S,   T,   2W

Angels

NOIR MORALITY TAKE

Starring: Savannah, Peter North, Angela Summers, Alicyn Sterling, Joey Silvera, Tom Byron, T.T. Boy, Brigette Aime, Missy Warner, James Lewis, Jake Steed, Joey Murphy, Jamie Gillis, Jerk-Off Sam. Producer: Louie T. Beagle. Director: John Leslie. Writer: Dominic Ruth. Music: Bill Heid. VCA Platinum, 1992. 80 minutes.

Trying to follow the narrative thread of this complicated story taxed our patience. It's Christmastime, and Caesar and Vito, owners of a strip bar, have had a lot of crooked deals between them. Caesar is depressed and suspicious that Vito is double-crossing him. His friend Dominic (Tom Byron) tells him he has no choice but to kill himself. Caesar puts a bullet in his own head only to discover that Dominic is no mere mortal but rather a good Angel who will make him invisible so he can see what his treacherous partner is really up to—not just with the business but with Caesar's wife as well.

The strip bar setting offers plenty of opportunity for some very raunchy (though mechanical and uninspired) sex, along with heavy doses of posturing by men with testosterone to spare. To his credit, director John Leslie succeeds in getting the performers to express just the right amount of grunge to make you feel like one of the barflies.

If you get lost in the intricacies of the plot or don't feel like raunch is what's going to make your bells ring, fast-forward to the strip scene two-thirds into the video. The dancer mesmerized us and her one-man audience by performing a deliciously sensuous and seductive strip, all the more effective because she never once takes her eyes away from her audience.
Recommended.

Explicitness: 7;   Sensuality: 6 (except for strip scene, which we rate a 9)   2M/W,   2W

Anna Obsessed (some catalogs and retailers list this as *Obsessed,* its title at time of release)

BAD GIRL SUSPENSE THRILLER

Starring: Constance Money, Annette Haven, John Leslie, Susanne McBaine, Jamie Gillis. Producer: The Strangers. Directors: Martin and Martin. Writer: Piastro Cruso. Music: The Avenger. VCA, 1977. 82 minutes.

Anna Obsessed is a video you won't be tempted to fast-forward. It's a classic suspense thriller in which the violence isn't gratuitous and sex happens in the context of a narrative. Completely plot driven, it's the story of Anna (Constance Money) and David (John Leslie) Carson, whose marriage has lost its zip, at least for Anna. She complains to David that she no longer gets off, to which he responds that she would if she didn't just lie there. There is some truth to his retort. It's clear from what we see of David's lovemaking to Anna and to his secretary that the inadequacy is not on his part.

Sex isn't the Carsons' only problem. Their neighborhood is being terrorized by a rapist who's just killed his fifth victim. While getting into her car late one night Anna is raped at gunpoint. This scene is graphic, violent, and scary and is one of the few sex-video rapes we've seen that treats rape appropriately—as inexcusable violence that can in no way be mistaken for consensual sex.

Anna falls apart after the rape and is befriended by the beautiful Maggie (Annette Haven), to whose comfort and seduction she succumbs in some of the best lesbian footage we've ever seen. The unexpected surprise ending startled us, and though we couldn't pinpoint

the psychological motivation of some of the characters, we found the story original and fully developed. If you're a child of the '60s, you'll get a chuckle out of some of the anachronisms in *Anna Obsessed*, like the fondue dinner Maggie feeds Anna and David.
Recommended.

Explicitness: 7;   Sensuality: 7   M,   2W,   2W/M

Another Woman's Lipstick

(see entry under *Red Shoes Diaries*)

Anything That Moves

FEMALE BUDDY FILM NOIR

Starring: Selena Steele, Tracey Winn, Cassidy, Heidi Kcat, Randy Spears, Tim Lake, Joel Clupper, Nick Santeoro, Nick E., Steve Drake, Tony Tedeschi, Randy Spears. Producers: Louie T. Beagle, John Leslie. Director: John Leslie. Writers: John Leslie, Henri Pachard. Music: Bill Heid, Howling Diablos. VCA Platinum, 1992. 94 minutes.

Lucky (Selena Steele) sits in the police station telling two police officers her version of what happened. In flashback we are introduced to the San Francisco sex club scene, where the small, feisty Lucky is a star who befriends and protects a fellow performer, the fetching, vulnerable, clueless Ronnie (Tracey Winn). Ronnie has split up with skeezoid lowlife Joey (Tim Lake), but she can't break the chains on her heart, not even when he has sex with another woman performer (Cassidy) while she's in the same dressing room.

Lucky gets the distraught Ronnie onstage for their act and even takes her along afterward when she goes out to make a little extra money by helping a bridegroom say good-bye to the single life. When Rachel sweetly lets two of the bachelors at the party con her into a freebie, Lucky hands over the money she earned and tells Ronnie to save it toward their dream—a hair salon they plan to open together. But even this small dream doesn't have a chance with Joey around.

He's the kind of loser who won't stay lost, until the night he finally pushes someone too far.

This is a well-acted, gritty, handsomely photographed film about the dark side of strip clubs and the dancers' lives. There is some violence (someone dies, someone gets broken ribs), but most of the action takes place off-screen, possibly for the pragmatic reason that special effects, gore, and stunt doubles are expensive. In one scene, Lucky bloodies the face of a woman who has made racist remarks. These remarks are uglier than the punch in the face with which she answers them, and they could ruin a mellow mood the way the murder doesn't, so view accordingly.

The sex is very explicit and wall-to-wall. The friendship between the women is the only tender relationship. Men, except for the understanding policeman, are strictly business. *Best scene:* A creepy couple sexually taunts Ronnie through her car window. *Moment of relief:* Ronnie and Lucky hit the stage with a clear plastic tub and soap bubbles. **Highly recommended.**

Explicitness: 8;   Sensuality: 7   M,   2M/W,   2W

Autobiography of a Flea

RAVISHING COSTUME SATIRE

Starring: Jean Jennings, John Holmes, Paul Thomas, Annette Haven, Joanna Hilden, John Leslie, Dale Meador, Mitch Mandell. Narrator: Warren Pierce. Producers: Jim and Artie Mitchell. Director: Sharon McKnight. Based on the anonymously written Victorian novel with the same title. VCA, 1976. 96 minutes.

Turn the concupiscent calendar back to 1810 and listen to a voyeuristic flea narrate the goings-on he witnessed from his perch in the pubic hair of the giddy young heiress Belle. After she and her suitor make love on a churchyard bench, her erotic future is appropriated by Father Ambrose (Paul Thomas), described by the flea as the "living personification of lust."

The other priests spy Belle's divine form through the keyhole of Father Ambrose's study, hike up their robes, and remind the pious Father of his religious obligation to share nicely. To keep control of his sexual prize, Father Ambrose offers Belle's uncle and guardian a guaranteed, sin-free chance to get in on the action. Belle, far from being upset, luxuriates in their attentions and helps them plot the seduction of her best friend, Julia. The cynically corrupt tale embraces "rape," sacrilege, death, betrayal, incest, and clerical orgies, spun as lightly as cotton candy and meant to be taken as seriously. Licentious priests, a respected taboo in adult films, cavort here because the story is based on a famous nineteenth-century erotic novel. The attitude toward women as chattels mirrors the historical period, something some viewers find a real turn-off, though for others the gorgeous production carries the day. **Highly recommended** with this caveat.

Explicitness: 7;   Sensuality: 5   M,   3M/W,   2W

Autoerotica

(see entry under *Red Shoes Diaries*)

Baby Face

STUDS FOR SALE

Starring: Lynn (Cuddles) Malone, Amber Hunt, Linda Wong, Dan Roberts, Paul Thomas, Joey Silvera, Ken Scudder. VCA, 1977.

The centerpiece of this controversial video is the Training Camp, a deluxe accommodation where successful women can hire their male sexual partners. The male employees understand that women and their desires rule. We like that. This also features an amazing scene in which a woman exuberantly sexes every man in the place and has a fine time doing it. We like that, too.

On the other hand, hulking Dan Roberts arrives at the Training Camp seeking a place to hide after having been caught flagrante delicto with an underage girl. Since he helped the more-than-willing fifteen-year-old take off a school uniform before they got down to business, he knew the girl was legally and morally off limits. That's not so good.

Our viewers enjoyed the first aspect of this film, but feelings ran high about the second, even though by U.S. federal law the actress playing the schoolgirl was at least eighteen. We almost dropped it from the list but thought that other women might want to make up their own minds, since the way we respond to the fantasy of teenage sex in the naughty-schoolgirl genre seems to depend partly on our own teenage sexual history. We also found that it made a difference whether we identified the girl in the film with ourselves or our daughters. Further, there's the guilty worry that getting turned on by a movie fantasy means giving tacit approval to something that in real life you don't support. If you are wavering, be warned that the girl comes to the Training Camp to warn Dan that her mother is looking for him and takes on three or four men in her personal happy ending. *Funniest scene:* Vengeful Mom immobilizes Dan in a cocoon of plastic wrap. To watch or not to watch—decide for yourself.

Explicitness: 8;   Sensuality: 7   A,   B,   2M/W,   O,   T (2), 2W

Losing Your Virginity

If you feel hesitant about watching an explicit video with your partner, or if you've tried and had a Bad Rental Experience, here are a few strategies for getting past the jitters and feeling in control of the situation.

- Rent the video yourself. That way, if the one you want isn't available, you decide on the alternatives.
- Read the box carefully. When a video is successful and well received, other producers will immediately try to copy the look of the packaging or give their effort a similar title. We can't tell you how many times we brought home the wrong tape until we learned to double-check cast lists and dates.
- Start with a simulated sex video or one from the For Beginners list in the "Index of Videos by Category."
- Not wanting to expose their lovers to the sight of all those tight, firm, young women is the one reason everyone mentions for fearing erotic videos. Be aware that unless your partner is significantly well endowed and ever ready, he's at

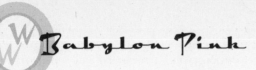

Babylon Pink

DAYDREAMS CAN COME TRUE

Starring: Samantha Fox, Vanessa Del Rio, Arcadia Blue, Merle Michaels, Debbie Revenge, Georgette Sanders, Bobby Astyr, Richard Bolla, David Morris, Georgina Spelvin, Dave Ruby, Eric Edwards. Producer: Cecil Howard. Writer/director: Henri Pachard. Music: Tanzelbrek & Cloud. Win Van Production/Command, 1979. 77 minutes. (Best Film, 1979 Erotic Film Award; Screw's Best 10 for 1978)

least as likely to worry about the comparisons you'll be making as he is to notice the ten pounds you think you need to lose. If that isn't reassurance enough, choose your video from the Womanly Bodies list in the "Index of Videos by Category."

- Rent at least two at a time, so if one disappoints, you have an option.
- Screen the movie by yourself, then decide if you want to share it with your significant other. You'll enjoy yourself more if you aren't worried about being turned off or grossed out. You might tease by telling what you did and (tantalizingly volunteer to) demonstrate something you saw.
- Set clear, loving boundaries before you watch. You don't have to do anything you don't want to do, no matter what's happening on the screen. The same goes for your partner. No nagging allowed.
- If you're planning a romantic evening, cue the tape beforehand so you don't have to confront all the trailers and phone sex advertisements—unless you want to see them.
- Remember that even the best tape can have a bad scene or one that doesn't appeal to you. The video police can't see you, and there's no rule that says you have to watch the whole thing. Negotiate control of that fast-forward button.

Henri Pachard, in his first video of vignettes, reveals the very original and exciting fantasies of a high-powered businesswoman, a socialite, a hormonal teenager, a housewife, a secretary, and a pair of female roommates. In the opening shots, the camera goes from apartment to apartment getting us acquainted with the cast, all of whom will interact with each other in the course of an ordinary day.

In our favorite scene, a rugged greengrocer catches the glance of mother and wife Vanessa Del Rio as she's straightening her living room. Before you can say ratatouille, he's looking into her eyes, undressing her with exquisite deliberation, and, as if in a slow-burning dance, turning on her switches and making her tingly all over. Playing this scene in complete silence makes it that much more riveting. You bet she's forgotten about those dust bunnies. The other stories, ranging from the bawdy to the comic, will supply you with fresh new material for your own day or nighttime reveries.

Vignettes can sometimes make for lazy filmmaking. Not in *Babylon Pink*. Characters are expertly and thoroughly developed, the dialogue is full of nuance, the performances are impressive, and the fantasies are original.
Highly recommended.

Explicitness: 8;   Sensuality: 7 (except for the scene described above, which gets a 9)   M,   O,   S/M (verbal)

Bad Habits

PSYCHO DRAMA

Starring: Diedre Holland, Tiffany Minx, Randy Spears, Mark Davis, Tom Byron, Debrah Wells, Sasha Strange, Angel Ash, Tom Byron, T.T. Boy, Jon Dough, Ted Craig, Dyanna Lauren. Producer: Kathleen Lucas. Director: John Leslie. Story/screenplay: Martin Brimmer. VCA, 1993.

Diedre Holland plays a best-selling writer with an addiction to sex clubs and a predilection for inviting home unknown men with tattoos and nipple rings. She's smart enough to know that her act is dangerous, yet she can't stop. Her therapist (Randy Spears) pushes the idea of controlled hypnotic regression. Since regular therapy sessions haven't put a dent in her compulsion, perhaps the answer lies in a previous life. After Diedre leaves her therapist's office, he acts out his arousal from her erotic adventures with his secretary (Tiffany Minx). Tiffany does a sexy cat thing, but Randy confuses getting wood with being wooden.

The skeptical and reluctant Diedre agrees to try regression—once.

The experience produces a hot fantasy with a woman from her past, but when Randy offers an interpretation of her experience, she says that both he and his ridiculous theories are history. He's fired. Randy's faults include greed and a total lack of scruples, but he understands his former client's taste in men. He hires a shady character (Mark Davis) to insinuate himself into Diedre's life. Armed by Dr. Randy with all the right things to say and do, Mark scores big time, even convincing Diedre he's not just a disposable stud muffin. Is it all an act?

There was enough plot to hold our interest, and two of the sex scenes were above average. The people and backgrounds look convincingly expensive. Sadly, the chemistry among the players has low voltage—only occasionally does the director coax a flicker of human connection out of his stars.

Recommended as a rental.

Explicitness: 9;   Sensuality: 6+   A,   2M/W,   2W

Barbara Broadcast

WE'LL HAVE OUR SALAD UNDRESSED . . .

Starring: Annette Haven, C.J. Laing, Susan McBain, Sharon Mitchell, Wade Nichols, Constance Money, Jamie Gillis, Bobby Astyr, Alan Marlow, Shirley Peters, Loren Michaels. Producer: L. Santana. Director: Henry Paris. Writer: Jake Barnes. VCA/Crescent Films, 1977. 87 minutes.

Picture an upscale, marble-walled restaurant right out of a decadent last-days-of-New York fantasy where the menu offers sex du jour along with the entrées and desserts. The flirtatious waitress takes your order and hops up on your table if you want her for an appetizer, women wearing designer suits and pearls elegantly go down on men in pinstripes, and obliging waiters ejaculate "to order" on the salads—all as background against which Barbara Broadcast answers questions about life as the world's most famous call girl. Occasionally someone stops by her table to request an autograph, or "a little head . . . [my brother] doesn't want to *come* or anything." Without removing her picture hat and with a Strauss waltz playing in the background, she obliges.

Perhaps because the people are well dressed with modulated voices and formal manners, the restaurant scene left us more startled than grossed out. (To think we sometimes wonder how frequently our local deli man washes his hands.) In the older rental videos you'll see a semidiscreet example of micturation and an S/M insert featuring a

woman trussed up in leather being "taught a lesson." Micturation is now a film taboo, and under the new laws (after July 1995) no scene with S/M content may include penetration, so we assume future copies of the video will have these scenes removed. If you want the full bizarre flavor, find an older rental.
Recommended.

Explicitness: 8;   Sensuality: 6   B

Barbara Dare's True Love

COMING OUT OF THE CLOSET—ALL THE WAY

Starring: Barbara Dare, April West, Brett True, Eric Price, Claire Tyler, Judy Blue, Nick Random. Producer/director: Paul Thomas. Writers: Marc Cushman, Jake Jacobs. Vivid Video, 1989.

April West wants to move in with her lover, Barbara Dare. Barbara, in a piece of well-written and authentic dialogue, is full of excuses. The truth turns out to be the secret Barbara is keeping from her parents. They don't know she's gay, and cowardly Barbara is unwilling to take the grief she expects Mom and Dad will give her during their upcoming visit. Barbara further complicates things by asking Brett, a musician friend, to be the beard for a dinner date with her parents. He's such a nice guy, Mom says she'd go for him if she were younger.

What events will encourage Barbara to find the courage to come out? How will Mom and Dad, who are looking forward to grandchildren, respond to the big news? The value of this video is the treatment of a delicate real-life situation that many face—and its resolution to everyone's satisfaction.

Explicitness: 6;   Sensuality: 7

Bare Market

STOCK MARKET GROUP SWINGS

Starring: Nicole London, Alex Jordan, P.J. Sparxx, Sunset Thomas, Francesca Le, Woody Long, Tom Byron, Peter North, Jake Steed, Kris Newz. Producer: Lucas Black. Director: John Leslie. VCA, 1993.

This begins promisingly with Dan (Woody Long) sitting beside a swimming pool while his plaintive voice-over tells us how threatened he feels by his wife Rachel's (Nicole London) stock market discussion group. He does admit that since the meetings started, their sex life has been hotter than ever, and soon Rachel comes home and proves it in a tender, loving scene.

When we see the next meeting of the group for ourselves, it's apparent that while Rachel wants to continue investigating bonds and mutual funds, her old college roommate Diane (Alex Jordan) wants to take the group in a new direction, starting with phone sex and a stud show. Diane taunts Rachel for being a "good girl," and Rachel herself wonders if her friendship with the racy Diane doesn't show that deep down she, too, yearns to be more sexually adventuresome. How you feel about the rest depends on whether you consider it progress when Rachel changes from a faithful wife to a woman who can enjoy grunge sex with a stranger before she goes home to a happy marriage and unsuspecting husband.

Sunset Thomas, whose name and glamorous photograph decorate the video package, appears in one three-way lavatory scene. In industry terms she's the "box girl," the person whose face and figure sell videos; she's not the star, only the most marketable image.

Explicitness: 9; Sensuality: 6 A, M, O, 2W, 3W, 2W/M

Beauty

MORE BEASTLY THAN BEAST

Starring: Loni Sanders, Jamie Gillis, Laurien Domonique, Nicole Noir, Vanessa Del Rio, Veronica Hart, Paul Thomas, Mai Lin, Michael Morrison, Herschel Savage, George Payne, Ron Hudd, Blair Harris, Sara Cruz,

Frederic Foster, Kathy Harcourt. Producer/director/writer: Warren Evans. VCA/Lesser Productions, 1983. 87 minutes.

You know the story. The good (too good, some might say), dutiful, self-sacrificing daughter forfeits her freedom for the sake of her undeserving father and ungrateful sisters. Set in contemporary San Francisco and New York, in this version Beauty's (Loni Sanders) freedom is lost in a high-stakes poker game by her careless father to Martin "The Animal" Gross (Jamie Gillis), whose taste for cigars and voracious appetite for women is unchallenged. Pure as the driven snow and virginal as an angel, Beauty becomes Martin's chaste consort as he satisfies his prurient tastes around town. Like other would-be princesses who preceded her, Beauty is yearning for (not to mention having major, hot fantasies about) her prince. Who is the sexy gentleman in the flashy uniform whose face we don't see? Will Beauty's goodness be victorious over her sisters' manipulations and Martin's grossness?

OK, so you know the ending too, but you don't know how it's going to happen. There isn't a thing we didn't love about this movie. Great writing, super sets, music creatively incorporated into the action, a lovely Beauty, and lots of hot, hot, sensuous sex. So if there's a special occasion in your life, grab hold of this video and celebrate. **Highly recommended.** (Warning: Don't confuse this movie with *Beauty and the Beast*, the next entry.)

Explicitness: 7; Sensuality: 9 O, S/M, T, 2W/M

Beauty and the Beast

BAWDY FAIRY TALE

Starring: Tracy Adams, Mike Horner, John Leslie, Niki Knights, Jerry Butler. Writer/director: Paul Thomas. Everything else: Mike Cates. VCA, 1988.

The traditional fairy tale in a fractured retelling offers an amazing number of opportunities for costumed foolin' around (e.g., Beauty and her fairy godmother, the two wicked stepsisters, Daddy and the scullery maid). If director Paul Thomas had granted us three wishes, we would have told Mike Horner to cool the doofus quality and to pick up the pace (two wishes). Since he didn't, you'll have to fast-forward when it drags. If you're in a hurry, go directly to Beauty's scene with the ultrahairy beast, a tryst that gets our unqualified approval. Do ap-

pearance-challenged guys try harder, or is it just that foxy pro John Leslie lurks under all that fur? *Best line* is Beauty's: "I guess sometimes being a self-sacrificing, guilt-ridden ninny pays off."
Recommended.

Explicitness: 8;   Sensuality: 6

Behind the Green Door

PENULTIMATE ORGY (THE DRAMA)

Starring: Marilyn Chambers, George S. McDonald, Johnnie Keye, Lisa Grant, Yank Levine, Toad Attell. Producers/directors: James Mitchell and Artie Mitchell. Music: Daniel LeBlanc. Adapted from the story Jartech. *Mitchell Brothers, 1972.*

This movie is considered a controversial classic, one of the two that even our friends who don't watch erotica usually have seen (the other is *Deep Throat*). Here, a radiant young girl (Marilyn Chambers), minding her own business, is kidnapped in broad daylight. The kidnappers bring her to a secret sex club, where she is tenderly prepared to be raped on-stage, not just once but many times in every orifice, watched by an enthralled audience of orgying sexual deviants. She loves it.

Obviously, the nonconsensual sex is a big issue. That Marilyn Chambers's character seems to thoroughly enjoy the experience fuels the arguments on both sides. Our position is that real-life nonconsensual sex is totally unacceptable but that fantasy is a private matter. If being coerced to perform prodigious sexual feats to rapt, admiring applause fits your fantasy, go ahead and rent it. If you find the very idea repugnant, outrageous, and kowtowing to men's lowest impulses, not yours, don't even take a peek. We know women who feel both ways, others who aren't thrilled about the costume Johnnie Keye wears, and a few who hate the mime. As we said, controversial. Some feminist mail-order video sources refuse to list or sell it.

While we didn't like the kidnapping or the nonconsensual sex, the real problem for us was that the elaborate fantasy and attitudes look old-fashioned in spite of pretty, perky Marilyn Chambers's heartfelt effort. To see why, compare it with the side-splitting safe-sex sequel made fourteen years later by the very same Mitchell brothers.

Explicitness: 8;   Sensuality: 6   A,   B,   C,   2M,   O,   2W, 3W

Behind the Green Door: The Sequel

ULTIMATE ORGY (THE SATIRE)

Starring: Missy, James Martin, Lulu Reed, Maria Fallon, Candi, Friday Jones, Danny Daniels, Aubec Kane, Ja Kinncade, Susie Bright (in the orgy scene). Directors: James and Artie Mitchell. Mitchell Brothers, 1986.

Fourteen years after the first *Green Door*, the Mitchell brothers made a sequel. Instead of kidnapping and rape, they showcased the kinky fantasy of a wheelchair-bound veteran and his unconventional airline stewardess neighbor. The almost-ordinary beginning (sex in the skies and Peeping Tom next door) gives no hint of the eye-widening events behind the entrance to the Green Door, the club where the stewardess goes to perform and her neighbor goes to watch.

Your first clue that life has changed since 1972 are the condoms thrust at the vet by the doorman/bouncer—wear triple condoms or no entry. After that, it's déjà vu all over again—the woman on a swing with men on trapezes hanging around her, the audience full of people starting an orgy even more uninhibited than what's happening on stage. But wait! The men on the trapezes have spotted satyrs' legs, hoofs, substantial tails, and sport condoms on their jaunty members, and the motherly Dr. Ruth look-alike with the cigarette tray solicitously offers condoms, dams, jelly, latex gloves—the whole deal—to the orgying, who use them. There is also a cross-dressing chanteuse whose original songs offer a witty commentary on the action, in the unmistakable styles of Barbra, Judy, and Mae West.

This *Green Door* sequel, while explicit, is more funny than hot, and it's full of sly jokes at the expense of its famous predecessor. It delivers a serious safe-sex message with a belly laugh and a wink. **Highly recommended.**

Explicitness: 8;   Sensuality: 7   A,   B,   C,   S/M,   SS,   T, 2W

Belle de Jour

FRENCH CLASSIC

Starring: Catherine Deneuve, Jean Sorel, Genevieve Page, Michel Piccoli, Pierre Clementi, François Fabian, Macha Meril, Muni, Maria Latour, Claude Cerval, Michel Charrel, Iska Khan, Bernard Musson, Marcel Charvey, François Maistre, Francisco Raban. Producers: Robert Hakim, Raymond Hakim. Director: Luis Buñuel. Writers: Luis Buñuel, Jean-Claude Carriere. Music: Rene Longuet. Paris Film/Five Film, 1967. 102 minutes.

The film event of the year on its 1968 American release, *Belle de Jour* was reissued in 1995 to a nearly equal flurry of press. Thirty years of shifting attitudes about sex hasn't dulled the impact of this jewel. It's a must-see.

In the post–*Pretty Woman* '90s a story line about a middle-class woman who moonlights as a prostitute can hardly seem provocative, so why do we remain intrigued? From the opening sequence of Severine's (Catherine Deneuve) humiliation in a park to the surprise ending, what keeps our attention is the perfection of Buñuel's filmmaking genius in both direction and writing.

At its heart, *Belle de Jour* is about bourgeois hypocrisy. Severine is well-to-do, stunningly beautiful, and suffering from a monumental case of ennui as only the French know how to suffer. Her mild-mannered husband couldn't be nicer. A busy surgeon, he's solicitous, even managing to take her on a ski vacation. At first out of curiosity but later out of a compulsion having to do with traumatic childhood memories, Severine joins Mme Anais' brothel, taking on the name Belle de Jour. Reluctant, nervous, and shy at the outset, it doesn't take Severine long to become the house favorite.

In a recent interview with Mal Vincent of *The Virginian-Pilot*, Deneuve said, "I don't think the film is shocking today, but, then, I didn't think it should have shocked anyone in 1968. I do think that it still says a lot about fantasies. Women's sexual fantasies."

Simulated

Safe Sex 1

Does the word condom *stick in your throat when negotiating with a new lover? Is he likely to be resistant even to the latest fashions in condom color, taste, and texture? Or maybe he tries that old taking-a-shower-in-a-raincoat chestnut. Next time you find yourself in such a discomforting spot don't even breathe the* c *word. Ask him if he'd like to take possession of a French letter or slip his dipper in a slipper or maybe he'd like to park his pecker in a parka. We have a little something to suit up every profession. Before you know it you'll have his woody in its own surge protector and be on your way to making America safe for sex. With the help of the list below you'll never have to say* condom *again.*

IF HE'S AN:	OFFER HIM A:
accountant	**conceivable receivable**
auto mechanic	**hood ornament**
aviator	**ground crew**
baseball fan	**batting glove**
Beatle's fan	**yellow submarine**
biologist	**chromosome dome**
blue blood	**gent tent**
bum	**paternaway**
burglar	**cell block**
comedian	**DNA lounge**
computer programmer	**surge protector**
couch potato	**mask for the Lone Ranger**
deep-sea diver	**SCUBA (Self Contained Undercover Boning Apparatus)**
doctor	**embryno**

Englishman	willy wrap
fashion victim	haute couture
foodie	sugar cone
forest ranger	wood hood
geographer	Coney Island whitefish
hero	Purple Warrior Armor
jet setter	French letter
ladies' man	lover cover
literary critic (D. H. Lawrence fan)	John Thomas' overcoat
mechanic	nub cap
military officer	Major Woody's uniform
motorcycle cop	crash helmet
nutritionist	protein packet
plastics worker	full latex jacket
psychiatrist	security blanket
nerd	weenie beanie
nuclear protester	anti proliferation device
politician	party favor
pharmacist	child proof lid
race car driver	emergency brake
sailor	mast head
'70's boy	Johnson jacket
skeptic	inconceivable
spy	cloak for dagger
surfer dude	dong sarong
traditionalist	sheath

And remember, insisting on safe sex means you care for yourself as much as you care for your partner.

Beyond the Valley of the Dolls

HOLLYWOOD B PICTURE

Starring: Dolly Reed, Cynthia Myers, Marcia McBroom, Edy Williams, Erica Gavin, John Lazar, Michael Blodgett, David Gorsia, Duncan McLeod. Producer: Russ Meyer. Writers: Roger Ebert, Russ Meyer. 20th Century Fox, 1970. 109 minutes.

A long movie about a girl group of singers and the corrupting influence of success, having absolutely nothing to do with the Jacqueline Susann best-seller *Valley of the Dolls*. Bosoms are Russ Meyer's proud obsession, and there are plenty of those, as well as vivaciously smiling young women saying, "Groovy." To be fair, we don't find that Mr. Meyer's attitude toward women lives up to its Neanderthal reputation; the callow pretty girl lead learns from her experience and grows as a person, just like in television's *Beverly Hills, 90210*. That doesn't keep it from making our list of movies that haven't survived the test of time. Some people claim it a camp classic, not us. And yes, that cutie-pie thumbs up/thumbs down critic Roger Ebert shared the writing credit.

Simulated; Sensuality: 4

Bi Coastal

SMALL-TOWN GIRL IN LA LA LAND

Starring: Cara Lott, Tico Paterson, Sheri St. Clair, Michael Mann, Diedre Hopkins, Troy Ramsey, Tic Patterson, Rickey Turner, Chris Allen, David Ashfield, Pat Manning (as Vanessa). Producer/director: Lancer Brooks. Catalina, 1985.

We fear for Jill Harrington (Cara Lott) when she gets off the bus in LA expecting to meet a lover who never shows up. She has no money and no friends, and of course we all know what happens to the pretty blonde next door who goes to LA with no money and no friends.

Jill looks for a job and ends up, as many desperate women before her, answering an ad for figure modeling. Vanessa, a well-preserved fortyish beauty who runs the agency, tells Jill that she can be a star but that more (much more) than nude modeling is expected. She invites the young woman out on a date to "try out what I am selling." The date takes place at Vanessa's expensive-looking house, and she makes a point of telling Jill that she, too, started out modeling. Obviously, there's money to be made in this business. She instructs Jill in stripping for the camera, presenting the most alluring angles, teasing, turning the camera on . . . —beauty tips your mother probably never thought to share.

Jill's career in sex modeling takes off. The tough and basic sex includes three ways—two men and one woman, for a change—which use every orifice and camera angle. Hard core and athletic, not romantic. On the other hand, the participants have a satisfactory time, and the wages of sin for Jill are a red convertible and two men (not very attractive ones) in her bed. One of the few films we have seen that presents bisexuality positively and shows three-way sex with men having sex with each other as well as the woman.
Recommended.

Explicitness: 9;   Sensuality: 7   2M,   2M/W,   2W

The Big Easy

THOSE STEAMY BAYOU NIGHTS

Starring: Dennis Quaid, Ellen Barkin, Ned Beatty, John Goodman, Ebbe Roe Smith, Lisa Jane Persky, Charles Ludlam. Director: Jim McBride. Writer: Daniel Petrie Jr. Music: Brad Fiedel. Kings Road, 1986. 108 minutes.

Ellen Barkin manages to make her sexy self look like an all-business assistant DA, but Dennis Quaid's cop eyes see right through her masquerade. The romantic plot has something to do with Dennis having a relaxed moral code and Ellen belonging to a more upright new regime determined to get rid of New Orleans corruption. The real reason we watch it is for the scene on the bed. Even if you aren't a Dennis Quaid fan (hard to imagine, but we suppose it's possible) you don't want to miss it. The music is great, too.

Simulated

28

Bittersweet

LESBIAN EXTREME DOMINANT RELATIONSHIP WITH
LATEX AND LEATHER

Starring: Michaela and Gabriella. Producer/director/writer: Alice B. Brave. Music: Valerie. House o' Chicks/Brave Production, copyright 1993. About 15 minutes.

Generally we would pass this by without an annotation, but since it appears on several mail-order lists recommended for women and the content took us by surprise, we think it's worth noting. The subject is an extremely dominant S/M relationship between two consenting women that features piercing with long needles as part of the love-making. Your call.

Explicitness: 9;   Sensuality: N/A   B,   S/M,   T,   2W

Black and White in Living Color

MADONNA NOT

Starring: Carolyn Monroe, Dominique Simone, Daphne, Chirsy Anne, Peter North, Ron Jeremy. Producer: Hector Castaneda. Director: Robert McCallum. Screenplay: Robert McCallum. Writer: Steven Katz: Western Visuals, 1992. 90 minutes.

Donna (Carolyn Monroe) looks more like Anna Nicole Smith than Our Lady of Perpetual Lust, but that aside, the film is clearly a homage to the documentary *Truth or Dare*. It shows what Madonna insinuates. Unfortunately for us, these filmmakers mimicked the in-your-face quality of the original while leaving out the flirt, tease, and driving music. A few telling moments can't save it. Too bad. As usual, it's up to Madonna to top herself.

Explicitness: 8;   Sensuality: 4   A

Black Orchid

MTV SEX

Starring: Ona Zee, Ariana, Alana, Lacy Rose, Kimberly Kupps, Veronica Hart (cameo), Sunset Thomas, Marrelle de Keigh, Jonathon Morgan, T.T. Boy, Cal Jammer, Zack Thomas, Steve Drake. Producer: Hector Castaneda. Director/writer: Michael Ninn. Music: Dino Ninn. A Michael Ninn Film, Western Visuals Gold, 1993. 107 minutes.

Rich man Steve Drake hires Ona Zee to find the writer of a book titled *Black Orchid*. Ona then arranges to bring the chapters to life. Her character narrates some of the action in a voice-over, and the dialogue gets very pretentious about what amounts to intercut scenes of high-tech android sex. If you've never seen a Michael Ninn or Andrew Blake film or if you have and they take you to viewers' nirvana, this is worth a look, since it is above average for the genre. We just aren't big fans of the genre. *Suggestion for optimal enjoyment:* put in a lavender-blue light, rent a fog machine, and stage your own home video while you watch. *Best line:* "This film is dedicated to the brokenhearted who know the words 'I love you but I'm not in love with you.'"

Explicitness: 8;   Sensuality: 6

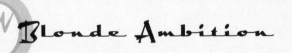

Blonde Ambition

ROMANTIC MUSICAL EXTRAVAGANZA

Starring: Suzy Mandel, Dory Devon, Eric Edwards, Jamie Gillis, George Payne, Kurt Mann, Wade Parker, Molly Malone, Richard Bolla, David Morris, Jeanne Joseph, W.P. Dremak, Patricia Dale, John Kovaks, Adam de Haven, Erica Eaton, Ronald Taylor, Ken Gable. Producers/directors: John and Lem Amero. Quality, 1981.

English stars Candy and Sugar Kane (Suzy Mandel and Dory Devon) may be the worst singing-and-dancing act ever to appear on the American stage (even the undemanding stage of Coyote Falls, Wyoming), but their humble talents don't stop them from having dreams of greatness. With the aid of Stephen Carlyle III (Eric Edwards), a millionaire dizzily smitten with Candy, the sisters fly off to New York for the career-making club date promised by their agent. Unhappily for them, the agent proves to be a low-rent weasel who left town with no forwarding address. The two women must scramble to survive, finding employment at last with Miracle Pictures, an adult film company that lives up to its motto: "If it's a good picture, it's a miracle."

Candy and Sugar's movie career culminates in a Miracle big-budget production with main characters named Miss Harlot and Brett and a bevy of hoop-skirted sweeties intent on welcoming the Yankees with open legs. Meantime, a priceless diamond brooch has been switched for a nearly worthless look-alike, and Stephen Carlyle's very rich English aunt has decided that the girls are gold diggers and must be exposed before her besotted nephew marries one of them. This naturally leads to Candy and Sugar crashing a gay review in Greenwich Village

The Golden Age

Pornographic films began to be made at the dawn of the movie business. Eadweard Muybridge's 1887 Animal Locomotion *fetishized women's bodies. The first so-called erotic movie was made in 1915, and there wasn't much progress after that until the short exploitation loops of the '50s and '60s. For a taste of what used to pass as erotica, see the review of* History of the Blue Movie *(page 114), a compilation of what were called "stag" (as in "a social affair for men only") films. These early offerings are mostly silly and whimsical, with women batting their eyes while exposing their behinds and men licking their lips and dangling their things.*

The sexual revolution of the late sixties changed everything. The business of explicitly sexual movies caught up with the changing social disorder in the early seventies, by which time "it" had already been done in the road, in the parks, and in many other public places where two or three were gathered. The enormous commercial success of Deep Throat *(1972) in-*

and becoming the toast of New York. If this sounds confusing, take our word for it, all does become clear. We loved it!

One-of-a-kind scene: sex in an ice skating rink. *Favorite quote* comes from the occasional narrator: "Looking back I see I've forgotten to mention pluck. Good old pluck. Pluck the adjective of course but also pluck the verb, knowing how to pluck and when to pluck and most of all who to pluck."

Highly recommended. (Note: Benny Hill fans may recognize Suzy Mandel as one of the bosomy blondes who decorated his show.)

Explicitness: 7.5;　　Sensuality: 8　　O

---

troduced a flood of a completely new kind of moviegoing experience.

Jim Holliday, the éminence grise of adult video, dates the golden age of celluloid pornography from 1975 to 1981. Fortunately, a surprising number of films has survived from this period. We don't know what was lost from these early days, but the films that continue to be available are, by any standard, of an exceptionally good quality. Perhaps because moviemaking was a costly enterprise and not every fool with a video camera could be considered a filmmaker, attention was paid to the details of character, plot, and good writing. Budgets for costumes, locations, and music contributed to high-quality productions. Directors of the seventies and eighties also show a high degree of cleverness, ingenuity, and creativity, and a big dose of humor. Which is not to say that the darker side of human nature is neglected—some of the finest movies from this period are overtly dark and can be categorized only as noir. Directors like Henry Paris, Alex deRenzy, Radley Metzger, Cecil Howard, Jim and Artie Mitchell, and Robert McCallum did some of their best work during these years. For a complete list of the Golden Age of Porn videos reviewed in this book, see the Classic Erotica list in the "Index of Videos by Category."

Blue Movie

CROSS-DRESSING COMEDY

Starring: Jenna Jameson, Stephan St. Croix, Jeanna Fine, Tera Heart, Jordan St. James, Rebecca Lord, Lana Sands, Dallas, Alex Sanders, Tony Tedeschi, T.T. Boy, Jackie Beat (as Dulcinea). Director: Michael Zen. Story: Michael Zen, Carl Esser. Screenplay: James Stark, Dan Thomas, B. Dawson. Music: Michelangelo. Wicked Pictures, 1995. 83 minutes.

Everything about famous director Peter Bent (Stephan St. Croix) is a deep, dark secret—whether he'll ever make another movie, what he's doing late at night in the studio, and what his sexual orientation is. To get the lowdown, Dulcinea, the ogress-in-chief of *Sleaze* magazine, sends Alice (Jenna Jameson)—her pretty, bright-eyed cub reporter—to get past the "diesel dyke" who guards Peter Bent. No story by tomorrow's deadline, no job by tomorrow night.

Thus motivated, the spunky Alice sneaks into the set where the manly bodyguard (Jeanna Fine in pinstripes) threatens to throw her out until the elusive filmmaker himself intervenes. He needs someone to play the barmaid, and presto!, our girl reporter's in show business. If Alice doesn't realize the carnal nature of her role in Bent's film, *The Golden Oyster*, perhaps she's dazed by the Carmen Miranda's-oldest-uglyiest-sister turban and electric blue housedress sported by the cross-dressing director. The rest of the movie is equally goofy, including a comic if gross flashback scene from "Anal Snow Bunnies," a band of enraged nymphomaniac lesbian Amazonian natives, and a bed fantasy about a talking blue ball that becomes an improbable sex toy. Is there anyone the film hasn't offended? Stick around.

The women have inflated boobs, and most of the in-your-face fornication is of the athletic pound-away type, notably the lengthy encounter between Alice and the great white hunter, played by T.T. Boy. T.T. isn't one of your new sensitive men, but here he vividly confirms his amazing powers of recovery, which are making him a legend in the business. On the other hand, St. Croix demonstrates a talent formerly unnoticed by us for slow, luscious oral sex, and his first scene (with a psychiatrist) and special last scene (with Jeanna Fine) make the film worth renting by themselves. Could it be that the wardrobe put him in touch with his inner woman? Something for everyone. ***Highly recommended.***

Explicitness: 9;   Sensuality: 7   A,   O,   T

Blue Sky

EXPRESSIONS OF LOVE AMONG THE VERY MARRIED

Starring: Jessica Lange, Tommy Lee Jones, Powers Boothe, Carrie Snodgress, Amy Locane, Chris O'Donnell. Producer: Robert Solo. Director: Tony Richardson. Writers: Rama Laurie Stagner, Arlene Sarner, Jerry Leichtling. Music: Jack Nitzsche. Orion Pictures, 1994. 101 minutes.

Made in 1991, *Blue Sky* is Tony Richardson's (*Tom Jones, Charge of the Light Brigade, A Delicate Balance*) last movie. It was shelved for three years because of Orion's financial woes and regarded as a "small" movie. Jessica Lange won both a Golden Globe and an Oscar for her dazzling performance as the manic-depressive wife of a military officer.

Neither her craziness nor their years of marriage has dulled the sexual passion Carly and Hank (Tommy Lee Jones) have for each other. "He's blind and she's crazy," says their daughter Alex (Amy Locane). His desire for her burns so bright it's blinded him to the havoc ensuing her manic-depressive mood swings. One of those women who creates her reality from fashion and movie magazines, Carly models herself after Marilyn Monroe and Brigitte Bardot. Wearing tight, strapless dresses, she vamps and plays the slut, making a spectacle of herself, testing the limits of Hank's long-suffering patience, and outraging the military community they live in.

Blue Sky is the magnificent expression of a fierce, emotionally and erotically powerful intimacy between two people who, no matter how bad things are, cannot get enough of each other. Their passion oozes, covers, and surrounds them, enclosing them like a hot, dense, fragrant mist. Dangerous and touching, their erotic fervor reaches the top and bottom registers of Carly's craziness, transcending time and space. "Through all the ups and downs," says Hank, "I've come to realize that what we call love is really the exchange of energy over time." Lange and Jones hold nothing back. Deserving of every award it got, *Blue Sky* is destined to become a Hollywood classic.

Simulated

Blue Velvet

SLIGHTLY SKEWED SMALL-TOWN U.S.A.

Starring: Kyle MacLachlan, Isabella Rossellini, Dennis Hopper, Laura Dern, Hope Lange, Dean Stockwell, Jack Nance, Brad Dourif. Producer: Richard Roth. Director/writer: David Lynch. Di Laurentis, 1986. Unrated version. 120 minutes.

An ear found in a field, a murder, a kidnapping, a masochistic nightclub singer who likes to sing "Blue Velvet," and a college boy too curious for his own good add up to a fascinating and bizarre but to us not very erotic movie. Isabella Rossellini sheds her clothes and makes love to the hero. She has looked better. When we asked a large number of people what Hollywood movies are a turn-on, most of them mentioned this and *9¹/₂ Weeks*. We say whatever floats your boat, but if an afternoon of delight is uppermost in your mind there are more interesting choices to be considered.

Simulated

Bodies in Heat

MARITAL DRAMA

Starring: Annette Haven, Herschel Savage, Eric Edwards, Lisa De Leeuw, Starr Wetherly, Crystal Fire, Billy De, Raysheena, Janey Robbins, with Christi Kaye, Shasa King, Desire Lane, Candy Kiss, Lacy Jay Waldeman, Jackie Jackson, Kissy Squeeze. Producer/writer: Jerry Ross. Title song "Sparks" words and music: Roger Stone and Chris Alan, performed by Remote Control. Caballero, 1983.

Annette Haven wants to do away with her rich husband, Eric Edwards, before he divorces her, which you'll figure out quickly because of the parallels to the movie *Body Heat*. Of course, she doesn't want to go to jail, so it all must look accidental. Her chosen chump is Herschel Savage, a corrupt policeman so in love with himself that he assumes it's part of nature's perfect plan that a beautiful, married socialite keeps calling 911 to report a fictitious burglar so he'll come over. Why would he doubt that she finds him irresistibly attractive? She's a woman.

Haven, the double-crossing siren, is ravishing but, we feel, only moderately enthusiastic.

Explicitness: 7;   Sensuality: 5   2W

Body of Evidence

HOLLYWOOD COURTROOM DRAMA

Starring: Madonna, Willem Defoe, Joe Mantegna, Anne Archer, Jurgen Prochnow, Julianne Moore, Frank Langella. Director: Uli Edel. 1993. 99 minutes.

Madonna is accused of killing her very rich lover with too much rough sex—seems he had a heart condition and she stood to inherit several million dollars. Joe Mantegna wants a conviction, and Madonna hires hot-shot lawyer Willem Defoe to handle her defense. The plot lacks believability, and Madonna's clothes look like what a modern nun would wear if she could afford a really good designer, but who cares. What mesmerized us were the scenes between Madonna and Willem Defoe. Hot wax, broken glass, handcuffs. He shows his back, not his front, but she doesn't keep many secrets, and if she used a body double in the kinky sex scenes, we couldn't tell. The movie exists in video stores in R and NC17; the latter includes footage cut in your local movie theater to keep an R rating. Look for the one rated NC17 (or unrated). It gives you the most Madonna for your buck.

Simulated (very hot)

Bonnie and Clyde 1: Outlaws of Love

RAUNCHY DRAMA

Starring: Randy West, Ashlyn Gere, Racquel Darian, Nikki Dial, Francesca Le, Alex Jordan, Derrick Lane, Nick E., Mickey Ray, Jonathan Morgan, T.T. Boy, Tom Chapman. Vivid, 1992.

This is a brightly lit period piece set in the '30s with tight close-ups of the usual hard-core activities. It ends with Bonnie, Clyde, and the gang hiding in a rural retreat, a hint of the general flavor telegraphed by the overalls-with-one-strap-off-the-shoulder (hayseed) the men wear when they aren't dressed in pinstripes (gangster). More expensively produced than usual, the rambling, unfocused story was well reviewed in the world of adult films and proved popular enough so that it has been extended to four parts, with no end in sight. We found it to be fairly standard, but there's equal opportunity for men and women to use each other, so if you like raw sex it might appeal.

Explicitness: 8;   Sensuality: 5   M,   2W,   2W/M

Bonnie and Clyde 2: Desperado

RAUNCHIER DRAMA

Starring: Ashlyn Gere, Randy West, Racquel Darian, Derrick Lane, Francesca Le, Nikki Dial, Alex Jordan, Mickey Ray, Nick E, T.T. Boy, Jonathan Morgan, Tom Chapman. Producer/director: Paul Thomas. Writer: Ariel Hart. Music: Double Vision. Vivid, 1992.

Life continues in Bonnie and Clyde's rural hideaway. The sheriff and deputy sniff around; a pretty blonde distracts them to win a bet from Clyde. One or two of the sex scenes manage to work up some energy; the rest of the video ambles aimlessly without plot or resolution of the story begun in part I. Bonnie and Clyde III and IV are available, but they're about making an adult movie called *Bonnie and Clyde,* so this is as much of the original story as you'll get. Unless people having standard video sex is all the content you require, you'll find this snooze material.

Explicitness: 9;   Sensuality: 5

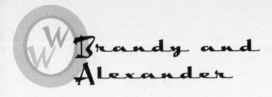 Brandy and Alexander

DOES MA BELL KNOW WHAT YOU DID WITH HER PHONE?

Starring: Jeanna Fine, Britt Morgan, K.C. Williams, Allycn Sterling, Heather Hart, Jon Dough, Mick Ray, Tom Byron, Edward Penishands. Writer/director: Paul Thomas. VCA.

Alexander (Jon Dough) wears the "full yuppie"—dark suit, white shirt, tie, and suspenders. He washes all the breakfast dishes before he leaves his immaculate house to go to work in an art gallery, where he formally addresses the female employees as Ms.

Brandy (Jeanna Fine) works in the same gallery. She's the chaotic, free-spirited secretary whose brief mini imperfectly conceals her lack of panties. Are these two made for each other or what?

They meet in the halls half a dozen times a day, but he doesn't suspect that she is the woman whose slinky red underwear turned up in his laundry bag any more than she guesses that he is the owner of the "hug me" sweatshirt that the laundry sent her. When the mischievous proprietress of this full-service laundry gives Brandy's telephone number to Alexander so he can track down his missing garments, Brandy impulsively treats him to telephone sex. Alexander's uptight attitude hits meltdown, and he begs her to meet him the next evening. She agrees, forgetting to correct her telephone description of herself as a languorous blonde.

This is a sweetly bawdy tale of urban love and lust. To our pleasure producer/director Paul Thomas takes the time and trouble to introduce the characters before letting them get down to business. After about ten minutes of setting the stage, the action is nearly nonstop. Brandy is a shouter, whose vocalizing leaves us in no doubt that she is having a better time than anyone else in the history of sex. She's the uninhibited one of the couple. Alexander's use of his hands is unusually tentative, as if he can't quite figure out what to do with such a live wire, but the rest of his well-muscled body is in excellent working order. *Best scene:* The phone sex is the clear winner here, but we also loved the funky take off on Michelle Pfeiffer on the baby-grand piano. **Highly recommended.**

Explicitness: 8;   Sensuality: 8   O,   A,   2M/W,   2W/M

Bull Durham

HOLLYWOOD ROMANTIC BASEBALL DRAMA/COMEDY

Starring: Kevin Costner, Susan Sarandon, Tim Robbins. Director/writer: Ron Shelton. Music: Michael Convertino. A Mount Company production, Orion, 1988. 108 minutes. Rated R.

A witty, sweet-natured movie, rather frank for Hollywood, which means there's sex but it happens mostly to people rolled up in sheets or covered with bubbles. The plot revolves around the triangle of Annie Savoy (an English teacher who every year selects a baseball player on her town's triple-A team to groom for greatness), Nuke LaLoosh (a pitcher on his way up), and Crash Davis (a catcher at the end of his undistinguished career). What could be sexier than a movie that brings a smile to your face when you think about it? *Best scene:* Crash Davis polishes Annie Savoy's toenails. *Best quote:* It's hard to choose a best quote in a movie so full of good talk, but we give the nod to one of the less often quoted ones that echoes our feelings: Annie Savoy: "You did not get lured, women do not get lured, they are too strong and powerful for that. Now say it. 'I did not get lured.' "

Simulated

Burgundy Blues

NIGHTCLUB REVIEW

Starring: Hypatia Lee, Debbie Diamond, Melanie Moore, Crystal Wilder, Roxanne Blaze, Marc Wallice, Tom Byron, Mike Horner, Tony Montana, Nick East, Terry Speed. Director: Thomas Paine. Producer: Thomas Paine Film. Music: Hypatia, G. G. Steel. Cal Vista/Metro Home Video, 1993. 89 minutes.

Singing her own songs to a nightclub audience, Hypatia Lee confronts and relives her past through song and story. Using flashbacks, the video switches between Hypatia's performance at the club and her past relationships with former lovers, who are in the audience. She acknowledges each of them one by one as she sings and talks about how they fell in and out of love. She tells these stories with a generous spirit of compassion and understanding, minus the hard edges of bitterness associated with lost love. The stories, songs, and lovemaking are all of a piece.

The many messages—anticensorship, safe sex, monogamy, sobriety—are sung and spoken as part of Hypatia's hard-won experience, and she doesn't shove them down our throats. Virtue may be its own reward, but we were pleased when Hypatia introduced us and the club audience to her true love, Adam. A good video for couples, *Burgundy Blues* values fidelity and affectionate, loving sex. *Best quote:* Mike Horner has his face in Hypatia's privates in a doctor's office. The doctor walks in and asks, "What the hell do you think you're doing?" "Just looking for a cure for cancer," Mike says, with a big grin and without skipping a beat.

Highly recommended.

Explicitness: 8;   Sensuality: 8   A,   SS,   2W,   2W/M

Cabin Fever

ARTIST MEETS HANDYMAN

Starring: Belinda Farrell, Judd Dunning. Director/writer: Deborah Shames. Based on Lonnie Barbach's Erotic Interludes. *Music: Vivaldi, Tschaikovsky, Wagner, Debussy, and other greats. Focal Point Productions, 1992.*

> "*Cabin Fever* . . . may well be the Behind the Green Door of the nearly virgin field of women's erotica." Gerald Nachman, *San Francisco Chronicle*

Belinda Farrell plays a woman of a certain age who has rented an isolated cabin in order to paint, undisturbed by her children and significant other. Suddenly through the window, past the row of dainty laundry, she sees a young and handsome stranger sniffing the crotch of a pair of her bikini pants. Under similar circumstances we would call 911, and so should you; since this is a movie, Belinda chats sternly with him. The landlord has thoughtfully sent this well-muscled cupcake to do some work in the yard.

The man takes off his shirt and turns on his radio, with the volume high enough to disturb Belinda's concentration. At least he's playing Vivaldi as he rakes, proving that he has a sensitive side, and the music isn't the only thing that disturbs her. When the inevitable happens, however, it doesn't live up to the erotic charge of the fantasy she had about him (he throws her down on the floor and has his way with her), but it's both romantic and politically correct, with the added plus of great composers on the soundtrack.

This is the first of the videos made by filmmaker Deborah Shames in consultation with Dr. Lonnie Barbach, a therapist and teacher who also is a best-selling writer on sex and relationships. The plots are centered on women and their fantasies, and the sex scenes show plenty of hot foreplay with simulated penetration, often making use of gauze curtains and other softening devices. Those who hesitate to go explicit find this and the other Shames tapes appealing. We wish star Belinda Farrell had left her breasts as the goddess made them, but the movie still rates a **Highly recommended.**

Simulated

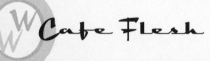

Cafe Flesh

FUTURISTIC SCI-FI CULT FILM

Starring: Andrew Nichols, Paul McGibonney, Joey Lennon, Neil Podorecki, Robert Dennis, Jay Kevin, Pia Snow, Marie Sharp, Darcy Nichols, Tantala, Becky Salvage, Terri Copeland, Kevin James, Ken Starbuck, Eric Nile, Pez D. Spencer, Dondi Bastone, Richard Beizer. Producer: Rinse Dream. Director: F.X. Pope. VCA, 1982. 78 minutes.

A little like the triple-X version of *The Rocky Horror Picture Show* cabaret style, *Cafe Flesh* reached cult status and very quickly became a staple in adult sections, as well as reaching a crossover audience at midnight showings in mainstream theaters. A CD-ROM of *Cafe Flesh* was introduced in 1995. Not bad for a fourteen-year-old video.

What, we asked ourselves, was going on in 1981–1982 to provide such fertile ground for this weirdly engaging film? Jimmy Carter (of the lustful thoughts) was president, and David Letterman had just launched the unconventional and offbeat *Late Night with David Letterman Show.* Fear of the cold war turning nuclear was the vibe of the times.

Cafe Flesh is set in post–WW III America. Though we don't know if there was physical damage to the planet, the people have mutated and are definitely not what they used to be. With the exception of about 10 percent of the population, Americans have lost their desire for sex and have become "sex negatives." "Moms" run clubs in which the vital 10 percent, the "sex positives," must perform for the gratification of the negatives, their less fortunate citizens. With the exception of a few subtle moments, but in accordance with the premise of the story, the sex scenes performed on and offstage are mechanical, impersonal, or cold, though they're seductive in an eerily bizarre way. The sets, art direction, and especially the music also work well with the concept of the story.

Andrew Nichols, who plays Max Mellow Dramatic, the emcee of Cafe Flesh, is a skilled and natural performer. His impressions reminded us at times of Max Headroom with soul. He loves the sex negatives, whose "desire is in chains, could anything be sweeter. Need is my fix. Recapture the smack of flesh on flesh. Panic in the loins that tells you yes, yes, yes." He delivers lines like "I don't want to say he's hung but he's the only guy I know whose skivvies need valet parking" with a perfect blend of borscht-belt humor and cynicism. The rest of the cast is equal to Nichols's performance, especially Tantala as the Moms of Cafe Flesh and Pia Snow and Paul McGibboney as a couple seeking the salvation that sex promises.

With lots of surreal images and sounds of war, *Cafe Flesh* sometimes seemed more like social commentary about sex than a sex video. Could the filmmakers have intuited that a drug like Prozac would come along, offering a whole generation the choice between reduced libido and suppressed depression? Original, entertaining, and **Highly recommended.**

Explicitness: 7;   Sensuality: 7

Candy Stripers

HOSPITAL FREE-FOR-ALL

Starring: Amber Hunt, Montana, Nancy Hoffman, Paul Thomas, Mimi Morgan, Rock Steadie, Lauren Black, Joey Nassivera, Marc Howard, Phaedra Grant, Eileen Welles, Sharon Thorpe (as "Sarge"); Cris Cassidy, Richard Pacheco, David Clark, Don Fernando, Bron White. Producer: Joseph A. Silver. Director: Bob Chinn. Writer: Dean Rogers. Music: Jonathan Long. Pacific Coast Film/Arrow, 1978. 84 minutes.

"Candy, magazines, vibrators?" announce the Candy Stripers as they navigate the hallways of a big city hospital. There to make your hospital stay as pleasant as possible, the young volunteers, nicknamed Candy Stripers because of their red-and-white striped aprons, run errands and lift patients' spirits. Chronicling the exploits of three of these cute and sassy volunteers, this 1978 video is worth seeing for attitude and hilarity.

Beds, examining tables, cool-looking instruments, horny doctors and nurses—if hospitals hadn't existed, erotic videos would have had to invent them. Think what good use a hospital full of beds can be put to in a sex video, not to mention the odd contortions bodies can be made to go into on all those unusual examining tables!

Besides the usual routine of distributing candy, magazines, and good cheer, these effervescent angels of mercy freely donate sexual favors to each other, nurses, patients, and doctors. Whether encouraging one patient toward better masturbating technique or exchanging a pathetic woman's banana for a vibrator, these lusty cherubs do Florence Nightingale one better.

The Stripers' bedside manner is refreshingly lighthearted and boisterous, with the sex bawdy and unabashedly lewd. With terrific music and funny lines, *Candy Stripers* could be just the right dose of medicine for a friend in the hospital.
Highly recommended.

Explicitness: 8; Sensuality: 6 O, 2W

Cat and Mouse

SUSPENSE GAME

Starring: Jeanna Fine, Cassidy, Scott Irish, Brandy Alexander, Chrissy Ann, Mike Horner, Sikki Nixx. Producer/director: Michael Craig. Writers: Leslie Black, Michael Craig. X-Citment Video, 1992.

Turn off the logical, reasoning part of your mind if you rent this video. Watch with the attitude that motivations do not have to make sense if the intimate relationships sizzle and you'll enjoy the goings-on without the distraction we had of arguing with the screen (e.g., "What kind of a dorky guy would. . . ."). The first scenes between the man and his wife and then wife with intruders are so erotically charged that you may not make it to the end of the film. Some of the action gets nasty, but notice that no one holds a gun to anyone's head. Dialogue banal—sex talk above average. Worth a look.
Recommended.

Explicitness: 8; Sensuality: 7 A, O, T

The Cathouse

BORDELLO ON THE BAYOU

Starring: Dyanna Lauren, Asia Carrera, Tina Tyler, Anna Malle, Loni, Colt Steele, Marc Wallice, Nick East, Steven St. Croix, Chi Chi La Rue, Dee Gordon. Producer/director: Toni English. Vivid, 1994.

Miss Wills (Chi Chi La Rue, a well-known transvestite of huge proportions) runs the coolest cathouse in New Orleans. Friendly to the call of true love, she has the proverbial heart of gold—and a big heart it is in Chi Chi's voluminous, lovable body. The bluesy music of Tinker (Dee Gordon) sets just the right sexy mood for telling an assortment of love stories.

A young man has fallen in love with one of Miss Wills's girls, and instead of breaking the girl's legs as you would expect, Miss Wills lets them visit under her roof until they're ready to tie the knot. Their loving is carried on in the kitchen with the help of strawberries and the juice of an orange. Yummy! Next, two sailors bring a still-virgin friend for a marriage-preparedness lesson. Determined to bring him up to speed for his nuptials, they tease and coax him into the delights of the flesh. With their long, flowing hair these sailors look more like surfer dudes and not at all like America's men in uniform. You didn't ask, and we won't tell. Finally, Tim brings his shy and reluctant wife, Ruth, to Miss Wills for instruction because they can't seem to hit a home run. It turns out that he's the one needing the tutoring, having not figured out how to put his mouth to good use. He's a quick study, and so is Ruth, and there may be a lesson or two for you and your honey. It all ends happily to the tune of "I'm Going to Love You Come Rain or Come Shine."

In true vignette style, all the characters end up in one way or another enjoying each other in Chi Chi's cathouse.
Recommended.

Explicitness: 7; Sensuality: 7 C, 2M/W, SS

The Catwoman

ROMANTIC NOIR FANTASY

Starring: Kathleen Gentry, John Leslie, Joey Silvera, Alexa Parks, Lauryl Canyon, Veronica Hall, Megan Leigh, Nikki Knights, Derek Lane, Ray Victory, Peter North, Buddy Love. Producer: Louis T. Beagle. Director: John Leslie (who also plays blues harmonica with the band). Music: Bill Heid. VCA, 1988. 90 minutes.

Jennifer (Kathleen Gentry) is taking pictures of a girl wearing scanty underwear when boyfriend Stefan (Joey Silvera) stops by to say good-bye. He's decided the chance to gamble at a big game in Reno is more important than their long-planned special date—after all, he supported himself by gambling for many years and he's only known Jennifer a few months. Unimpressed by this guy logic, Jennifer threatens she might not be waiting when he gets home.

Later, walking through the park, she gets the uncanny feeling that she's in danger, and since we see alternately through her eyes and the eyes of some unknown creature watching her and snarling, we think she's right. She begins to run and bumps into John Leslie, who reassures her and offers to buy her a drink. Over glasses of white wine, he tells her that she's a cat with a special cat's destiny. He points out other people from the group at the bar and asks if she can't see their animal kinships to hyenas, monkeys, and so on. This sounds to us like a pick-up line on a level with "What's your sign?" which doesn't stop her from going home with him and doing the sex thing. Leslie usually has a good line of bed talk, but here the growling and biting let us know that something truly animalistic is afoot.

Next day, Jennifer's eyes slant, and she returns snarling to the same saloon. She feels compelled to dance naked (she has some good moves) while another couple gets down to basics on the bar. Fate is calling, and John Leslie is on hand to lead her into the den of the future.

This missed the mark for us, though we kept rooting for John Leslie to turn it into magic. We hate to say it, but if he's going to take his clothes off for the camera it's time for him to play a more domesticated cat. He looks too worn to convince us in the mad, bad, and dangerous-to-know roles. For a while, in the park, we thought he'd pull it off, but not quite. *Best scene:* Kathleen Gentry shows Joey Silvera what he'll be missing from now on. The music is bluesy and fine, as it often is in the multitalented Mr. Leslie's films—here he plays lowdown harmonica with the band.
Recommended for rental.

Explicitness: 8;   Sensuality: 7   O,   2W,   2W/M

The Chameleon

A MORPH A MINUTE

Starring: Tori Wells, April West, Victoria Paris, Selena Steel, Debi Hansen, Tom Byron, Lynn Francis, Buck Adams, Scott Irish, Joey Silvera, Ray Victory, Peter North, Axel Horn. Director: John Leslie. Writers: John Leslie, Nick Hunter. VCA, 1989.

The sexually insatiable Diana (Tori Wells) can morph herself into other bodies, so her character also is played by Victoria Paris, Debi Hansen, and Selena Steel. Confusing. It confuses her husband, Marcus (Tom Byron), too, since with her new look she leaves him waiting at restaurant tables while she waltzes off with whatever man, woman, or group has taken her fancy. He understandably acts miffed when she gets home. Her therapist can't seem to help her come to grips with her problem, perhaps because when she can't seduce him she flounces out of the office. (Remember the old joke: Q. How many shrinks does it take to change a lightbulb? A. One, but it has to *want* to change.)

This ambiguous fantasy looks polished, and the sex, while emotionally cold, is in character. We might be more enthusiastic if *Chameleons: Not the Sequel* didn't leave this looking like a tryout for the real thing.

Explicitness: 8;   Sensuality: 7   SS

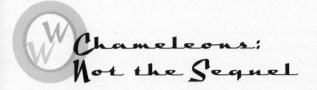

Chameleons: Not the Sequel

SHAPE SHIFTERS DWELL AMONG US

Starring: Diedre Holland, Ashlyn Gere, Rocco Sifreddi, John Dough, P.J. Sparx, Fawn Miller, Tim Lake, Mickey Ray. Director/writer: John Leslie. Music: Bill Heid. VCA, 1991. 96 minutes.

This video began with such an unappealing encounter that only duty made us keep watching. Were we glad we did! Stick with it until the scene in the ladies' room and probably you will be as hooked as we were. These are vampires with a difference—it's not your blood they want. The plot gets confusing because clarity of narrative is sacrificed for the sake of intense sex scenes, but eventually all is more or less made clear.

In an October 1995 article in the *New Yorker* ("The Money Shot"), Susan Faludi suggested that this movie, with its characters who shift sex as easily as they shift bodies, was a "futuristic male nightmare of where the 'feminization' of porn might lead." Whatever the root cause, director John Leslie has made the most intriguing so far of his explorations of shifting sexual roles, power, and the uncivilized animal that lies beneath our skins.

The backgrounds look as superb as the people. Ashlyn Gere's fierce quality works for her, and so does Diedre Holland's sophisticated remoteness. Rocco Sifreddi, a tawny-haired Italian with an intriguing accent, has never been better. He not only has sex, he makes love. **Highly recommended.**

Explicitness: 9;   Sensuality: 9   M/M,   2M/W,   T,   2W

Chinatown

SEX, DRUGS, NO ROCK AND ROLL

Starring: Asia Carrera, Steven St. Croix, Randy West, Sierra, Melinda Masglow, Jonathan Morgan, Bridgitte Amie, Jace Rocker, Sahara Sands, Don Nelson, T.T. Boy, Nikki Sinn, Jim Enright, Sydney Dance. Producer/director: Jim Enright. Writer: Jonathan Morgan. Sin City, 1994. 90 minutes.

A disappointing and unsuccessful attempt at a murder mystery, adult video style. In spite of a larger than usual budget, neither the story, the sex, nor the acting deserves the attention this got in the adult video world. Told in flashbacks from an opium den, ex-cop Steven recalls the unsolved murder of a Greek antique dealer (Randy West, who's looking really trim in this video) married to Asia Carrera. With good nasty talk and rough sex, the best scene is between West and Carrera. This is a missed opportunity to equal the noirs of the '70s and '80s.

Explicitness: 8;   Sensuality: 4

Christine's Secret

SWEET COUNTRY LOVE

*Starring: Carol Cross, Taija Rae, Jake West, Chelsea Blake, Marta Ek-
berg, Joey Silvera, George Payne, Anthony Carino. Producer/director:
Candida Royalle. Femme, 1984. 72 minutes. (Couple's tape of the
month*—Penthouse; *winner of four Critics Awards: Best Picture, Cinematography, Editing, and Ladies' Choice.)*

Mysterious Christine (Carol Cross) arrives just after daybreak at
picturesque Love's Inn, a rambling New England farmhouse where the
spirit is far from puritan. After showing Christine to her room, the
owners snuggle in the quilts before starting their busy day. The daughter and the handyman romp in the barn. The newlywed guests scam-
per upstairs to celebrate their honeymoon. Melancholy Christine,
sensitive to the erotic atmosphere, settles into a Victorian bathtub to
make love to herself, though we see that a handsome stranger with really great abs watches her from afar while rubbing himself to climax.
Do they know each other? Will they get together? What *is* Christine's
secret?

This amatory slice of life is not burdened with a strong plot or distracting dialogue, so you, too, may be celebrating Eros before the tape
has finished. The warm sense of relationship between the frolicking
partners makes this a natural for couple viewing. Candida Royalle, a
former XXX-rated star, is one of the new breed of filmmakers dedicated
to making erotic films for women. She encourages her women stars to
choose the men who appear with them—many of whom are couples in
real life. *Christine's Secret* is one of her most successful efforts. *Most
memorable couple:* the owners of Love's Inn. *Most improbable but heavenly scene:* "swinging" on the swing.
Highly recommended.

Explicitness: 8;   Sensuality: 9   B,   M

Candida Royalle

Candida Royalle isn't the first woman to move from performing in erotic films to producing them, but when she announced her plan to make videos for women, everyone in the business told her she was crazy. While couples' movies have long been a recognized niche of the adult film audience, women's hostility to the genre was one of those truths that went unexamined.

Royalle felt convinced that women rejected adult videos because their needs and fantasies weren't addressed, so she raised money and made a video herself, on the proverbial shoestring. Femme (the first film and her company share the name) used a traditional format of six separate vignettes/loops, but these placed women as the center, not the object, of the action.

Next, she needed distribution, but the distributors wanted to buy the video outright for about what it cost her to make it. Determined to be a good businesswoman as well as an artist, she decided to distribute the videos, marketing them through a media campaign to reach an audience she knew existed. Other videos followed the first—Urban Heat (1985), Christine's Secret (1984), Three Daughters (1986), and Revelations (1993). Three Daughters was the first to tell a story, and it has been her most successful video to date. A Taste of Ambrosia (1987), Rites of Passion (1987), and Sensual Escape (1988) are her guest-director series, two-part videos of original stories, with each segment written and directed by a former actress, including Veronica Hart, Annie Sprinkle, Veronica Vera, and Gloria Leonard.

Royalle believes in a holistic view of life, "balancing the spiritual, psychological, and also sexual—when we shut down the sexual it takes away an important part of us. And it's easy to do that because in our culture men are encouraged to be sexual—woman to be polite."

Femme videos reflect her philosophy. She tries to show her women as whole, dimensional beings, even though the emphasis is, as the present terminology goes, sex positive. Keeping a woman's point of view means consensual sex, lots of foreplay, intercourse that reflects the stimulation women need to reach orgasm, attractive locations, long shots of the body that focus on facial expressions and emotional responsiveness, safe sex, and no outside come shots. Some concentrate on sensual situations with music backgrounds; others on stories told from a woman's perspective, daydreams of anonymous sex as well as relationships. This doesn't limit her video audience to women. Royalle gets letters from many men who say they welcome her softer approach and resent the industry's assumption that they want only raw, crude sex. Plus, they like feeling that they're getting inside information on what the women in their lives enjoy.

Royalle's videos have gained wide acceptance, and because her media campaign on their behalf worked so well she has become an international spokesperson, in demand for seminars and speeches. She is an invited member of the American Association of Sex Educators, Counselors and Therapists (AASECT) and has addressed diverse groups—from the Smithsonian Institution, the World Congress on Sexology, and the American Psychiatric Association to students at Princeton and Wellesley.

Her biggest problem was finding the time to run her business and make new videos, until her recent deal with PHE (see page 120), which now distributes her small catalog of films and provides financial backing for the new ones. She says that it's a relief to get back to the filmmaking and leave the business details to others. With new titles already in the planning stages, we can look forward to many more vids made with us in mind.

Christy's Comeback

DOCUCOMEDY

Starring: Christy Canyon, Jenteal, Asia Carrera, Shelby Stevens, Christal Rain, Dallas, Tony Tedeschi, T.T. Boy, Ian Daniels, Michael J. Cox, Steven St. Croix. Producer/director: Paul Thomas. Writer: A. J. Barber. Music: Buster Gonad. Vivid, 1995.

Christine Canyon returns to adult films, starring in a film about her return to adult films after a two-year retirement—erotic movies' version of a backstage docudrama. Christy sends up her own image— one minute acting the complete diva (after all, she's a famous star), a flicker of insecurity later locking herself in the dressing room to be coaxed out by the writer (he's the low man on the organizational totem pole and gets all the dirty jobs). There are some funny bits and it's good-natured enough, but Christy's screen persona left us lukewarm, though we applaud her large breasts with natural-looking droop as looking far sexier than the space-age boobies too often on view. Christy's willingness to be lured back to the silver screen from suburban housewifely bliss gains her some sympathy from our audience. This rates as a mild-mannered couples' film. **Recommended.**

Explicitness: 8; Sensuality: 6 A, 2W

Clair of the Moon

LESBIAN ROMANCE SET AT A WRITER'S CONFERENCE

Starring: Trisha Todd, Karen Trumbo, Faith McDevitt, Caren Graham, Sheila Dickinson. Producer: Pamela S. Kurie. Writer/director: Nicole Cann. Music: Michael Allen Harrison. Demi Monde Productions, Inc. Orion Pictures Home Video.

A high strung doctor/psychiatrist specializing in lesbian sexuality research clashes early and often with her writer's conference roommate—a straight, sexually assertive novelist. Before they resolve their differences, a whole lot of talking goes on. Some, with other members of the conference, ponder the literary life and works in progress. However, most of the conversation, philosophically, and psychologically revolves around lesbian sexuality, from the impossibility of communicating with men ("They speak a different language.") to the use of dildoes ("It's not about penises. It's about penetration."). The production looks polished—roughly equivalent to a made-for-television movie on the Lifetime network—but in their determination to convince as well as seduce, the filmmakers condescend to straight women and too often lose sight of the need to entertain. Finally, we are rewarded with a good erotic scene, so, if you are interested, persevere.

Simulated

Companion Aroused 2

MURDER ISN'T THE ONLY MYSTERY

Starring: Ashlyn Gere, Asia Carrera, Tera Heart, Sandi Beach, Dallas, Randy West, Steve Drake, Nick East, Guy Disilva, Paul Thomas, Evan Daniels. Producer/director: Paul Thomas. Writer: Paul Thomas. Music: G.G. Steele. Vivid/A Paul Thomas Film, 1994. 89 minutes.

Jerry (Randy West), a very rich guy whose wife has recently disappeared, has lost his grip along with his corporate job. Permanently befuddled, he wears a Macy's knit cap and plays checkers. A series of female "companions" service and amuse him in his "grief." The police are all over the place trying to solve the disappearance of his wife and getting no help either from Jerry, the most obvious suspect, or his current stunning companion Kylie (Asia Carrera).

When Jenny (Ashlyn Gere), who appears to be Kylie's replacement, arrives, sparks between these two ladies are instantly ignited, and the catty claws and snide remarks reveal their just-beneath-the-surface wild animal natures. Not as amusing as other cat fights we've seen, we found ourselves a little embarrassed watching these two women make fools of themselves over a brain-damaged guy. But let's not forget all that loot!

Adding to the aura of pathology surrounding these characters, Jenny shows a fascination with blood when she cuts Jerry's neck while shaving him. This scene becomes a full-blown S/M episode in which Jenny covers Jerry's head with a leather mask and drips the wax from a burning candle all over his thorax. He must be enjoying it since he doesn't even flinch.

In the meantime, through her police contacts, Kylie discovers that Jenny has a long history as a scam artist. Another murder is

committed before we find out the fate of Jerry's wife and at whose hands.
Recommended.

Explicitness: 8;   Sensuality: 7   B,   S/M

Contract for Service

LADIES WHO DON'T LUNCH

Starring: Summer Knight, Sharon Kane, Melanie Moore, Diva. Producer/writer/director: Ernest Greene. New Twist Productions/an Ernest Greene Picture. 1994.

An all-girl movie without penetration sex, Contract for Service is full of other forms of sexual excitement. This S/M video is played mostly with a sense of fun and good humor by ladies who supposedly might otherwise be lunching or shopping on Rodeo Drive. We saw, for the first time, a rubber bulb that is inserted into a woman's vagina and inflated as well as a lactation machine attached to each breast for stimulation. Boot licking, light whipping, bathing, and a variety of collars and straps are all used in a friendly, lighthearted attitude. The finale is worth the wait, and we think this video will make the insult "kiss my ass" sound like an invitation to pleasure.

What we didn't like about Contract for Service is the sound and music. The music is tiresome and the dialogue immaterial. You won't miss a thing by using the mute button on your VCR.
Recommended.

Simulated;   Sensuality: 7   B,   S,   S/M,   T,   2W

Corporate Assets

INSTITUTIONAL SLAVERY

Starring: Tish Ambrose, Eric Edward, R. Bolla, Rachel Ashley, Amber Lynn, Sheri St. Clair, Herschel Savage, Nick Random, Harry Reems, Jamie Gillis, Paul Thomas, Richard Parnes, Tamara Longley, Francois Papillon, William Marigold, Stephanie Bradley. Producers: Ed Leonard,

Thomas Paine. Director/writer: Thomas Paine. Music: DCG and lots of Mozart. Essex Video/Broad Appeal Film Works. 90 minutes.

White slavery is the only way to describe the situation Jill and three other women find themselves in. The corporation they work for, headed by the insidious and mean JW, rewards the achievements of his staff of men and women with sexual favors proffered by "in-house" workers who are also used to entertain JW's associates, including the kinky appetites of high-government officials like the secretary of state, whose quirk is a thing for wearing diapers. Described as living "like queens," the women have no personal expenses, and all their needs are taken care of by JW. In fact, they are JW's prisoners, and before long it's clear that each is looking for a way out. With the exception of a few occasions when cattiness reared its ugly head, we were touched by the way these women looked out for each other.

The narrative focus of the story is on Jill, who has broken JW's rules by corresponding with Winston (Eric Edward), a friend of her dead brother. The romance that develops between Jill and Winston becomes the catalyst that propels all the girls to get control of their own lives. Not without a sense of humor, *Corporate Assets* is a poignant erotic romance with a story to tell. What other X-rated videos might turn into a lark this video treats as a thoughtful exploration of how the desire for fiscal security can sometimes persuade women to surrender personal freedom.
Highly recommended.

Explicitness: 7;   Sensuality: 7   B,   2W

Corruption

NOIR FANTASY

Starring: Jamie Gillis, Kelly Nichols, Bobby Astyr, Tiffany Clark, Tish Ambrose, Alexis X, Samantha Fox, Sabrina Vale; introducing Tanya Lawson as the Girl in Blue and featuring Vanessa Del Rio as Erda. Producer/writer/director: Richard Mahler. Music: Bach, Mussorgsky, Albinoni, etc. VAC/Seven Crown/Richard Mahler Production, 1983. 76 minutes.

A noir morality tale set in a sleazy bar with various underground rooms where patrons can explore varieties of sexual experience, *Corruption* is represented as an allegorical tableau. Each of the rooms is monochromatically lit in a vivid color, creating a powerful erotic aesthetic. Allen (Jamie Gillis), whose favorite line is "Without honor business is useless," seems to have both business and personal associations with the people who populate the bar. He's pushed along from room to room experiencing various stages of sexual excitement, though he's never allowed satisfaction. Tanya Lawson, in the blue room, is stunningly beautiful—we couldn't tear our eyes away from her.

Bondage, necrophilia, and masturbation as art form are all part of this metaphysical trip. There is something strangely seductive about *Corruption* in spite of its lack of either character development or narrative coherence. Serious attention was paid to the quality of the music, which changes in style as Allen visits each of the rooms. *Corruption* also has one of the most affecting male orgasms we've ever seen, which contributes to making this classic video worthwhile entertainment.
Recommended.

Explicitness: 8;   Sensuality: 8   B,   S/M,   2W

Cousin Cousine

FRENCH ROMANTIC COMEDY FROM THE '70S

*Starring: Marie Christian Barrault, Victor Lanoux, Marie France Piser, Guy Marchand, Ginette Garcin, Syvil Maas. Director: Jean-Charles Tacchella. Pomereu/Gaumont, 1975. 95 minutes (**French with subtitles.**)*

Marie and Victor, cousins by marriage, become acquainted when their philandering mates disappear together during a family wedding. They start as friends and gradually become lost in a haze of love. The bedroom scenes, considered hot stuff in 1975, look pretty tame by today's standards, but that doesn't affect the amour. Fantasize a rainy country evening, fire in the fireplace, champagne in the ice bucket, and someone by your side in whom you want to encourage a subtly romantic mood. Not for all markets, but with the right guy it's a no-brainer. Besides, Victor Lanoux is dreamy. (This was remade as *Cousins*, starring Ted Danson. We think it sounds much sexier in French.)

Simulated

Crazy Love

WORK, SEX, AND MARRIAGE

Starring: Asia Carrera, Kylie Ireland (the shrink), Anna Malle, April, Rayveness, Joey Silvera, Jonathan Morgan. Producer: Paul Thomas. Director: Bud Lee. Writers: Barbera and Price. Vivid Films, 1995.

Joey Silvera plays the publisher of Ellis and Marie (Jonathan Morgan and Asia Carrera), a best-selling husband-and-wife team who are experiencing writers' block with their new book. Marie caught Ellis cheating with the teenage nymphet next door, and she refuses to write another word with him. Typical publisher Joey says, "Go to a marriage counselor or I'm canceling the advance." Before you can say "Money talks" they're sitting on Dr. Janine's (Kylie Ireland) sofa, telling their sad story. Consummate professional that she is, Janine advises Ellis to give Marie head right there (isn't she helpful) and, after one thing leads to another, the concerned doctor even strips and joins in to demonstrate how Marie should handle things the next time she catches Ellis having an extramarital fling.

Marie doesn't feel the score has been evened, so she pays a visit to Joey, this time for noneditorial service. Their pool-table tryst is interrupted by Joey's girlfriend, who then calls Dr. Janine (who happens to be Joey's ex-wife). It's remarkably silly stuff played by actors who display little heat no matter how intimately their bodies entwine. On the other hand, the silliness is equal opportunity, and Asia Carrera remains a treat to look at, so if nothing more thrilling turns up, at least this does not actively offend.

Explicitness: 8; Sensuality: 6   A,   2W

Crazy with the Heat 2

MOTHER/DAUGHTER CONFLICT

Starring: Ona Zee, Mike Horner, Roxanne Blaze, Lilli Xene, Marc Wallice.

A quickie movie whose minimal plot of mother/daughter conflict doesn't slow down the main event—long, long intercut sessions of couples coupling. We rented on a whim, expecting the usual industry practice of hooking a low-budget, totally unrelated video onto a successful and well-reviewed first effort—in this case *Crazy with the Heat 1* (a film we never found). So it was a welcome surprise when Ona Zee and Mike Horner got down to business in one of the better lovemaking assignations we have viewed. In our eyes, Mike has several big pluses. He looks like your attractive neighbor or the nice guy in the office down the hall, not a singles-bar stud. Given any material to work with, his acting is believable. And, most important, he seems engaged with women emotion-

Mike Horner 1

Mike Horner has appeared in a mind-boggling nine hundred explicit videos over the last fourteen years, so who better to satisfy our curiosity about how you make love to a woman with a camera and crew as invisible participants? He told us what we already had observed—sex in a video is not like sex in real life. "You have to open things up—the camera is the third person in the bed. Personally, you might whisper in someone's ear or touch them a particular way, but it wouldn't come across in a movie. Also, the director wants you to show a number of positions— woman on top, man on top, doggy style, reverse cowgirl, and so on—that look good for the camera. And he/she needs a certain amount of hard-core footage and another amount of soft-core footage for the cable cut [see the sidebar "Hard and Soft"]." If you still think Mike's job is a piece of cake, keep listening. "Then there is time pressure. These days many videos are shot in one day, which means shooting five full sex scenes plus twenty pages of dialogue in twelve hours!"

In spite of all the performance pressures, on film Horner comes across as a sensitive and caring lover. He says he brings what feels right to him to the sex, some from himself and some from the character he's trying to represent. "When I first started working I made a conscious decision to touch softly and to smile. Other people made fun of me [for smiling] but it comes

ally as well as physically, gives oral sex as if he enjoyed it, and uses not only his penis but his hands to pleasure his partner. For those who like good tushes and long hair on a man (we are *not* shallow, just appreciative), Marc Wallice turns in an enthusiastic performance with the ravishing Roxanne Blaze. Don't rush out to rent it, but if you come across it and value action over story line, give it a chance.

Explicitness: 8;   Sensuality: 8   SS

out of what I enjoy doing. When I move my hand across a woman's body, what will make a woman happy is what makes me happy."

Like most actors in this business, he sometimes gets asked to make convincing love to women with whom he has no natural chemistry, though these days he is likely to plead a previous engagement if he doesn't respond to his costar. "You can call on your imagination and fantasies, but obviously things go better if you are genuinely enthusiastic."

How do the women in his personal life handle his 9-to-5 job? Not very well. Horner says he knows it's difficult to wave goodbye-and-have-a-nice-day to your lover when his job description calls for him to have sex with beautiful women. But he also admits that he's emotionally immature in some areas. "You have to think of me as about the age of thirteen in my dealings with women. And besides that, when I'm not performing I'm shy." Given these circumstances, it's not surprising that he's never been married, though he has been involved in long-term relationships, two or three with others in the industry.

Horner began in the entertainment field as an operatic singer and a dancer. He's never been asked to use his dance skills, but after more than a decade in front of the camera he's finally getting a chance to sing in an upcoming video. Even actors as durable as Horner eventually leave performing, but as he gets older he'll be bringing his skills to the filmmaking aspect of his life. We're looking forward to a chance to watch him develop and grow. Go Mike.

Crazy with the Heat 3

MARITAL MELODRAMA

Starring: Asia Carrera, Celeste, Kylie Ireland, Kristina West, Sahara Sands, Nick East, Kyle Stone, Vince Voyeur. Producer/director: Fred Lincoln. Cal Vista, 1994. 80 minutes.

A couple wakes up after a long night and remembers that for some reason they got married. Each is determined to make the other leave the marriage, and how better to do that than to have sex with everyone except your legal partner. Even the presence of Asia Carrera, one of our favorite female stars, couldn't get us engrossed in this one.

Explicitness: 8.5;   Sensuality: 2   A,   C,   Couples

Curse of the Catwoman

EXPERIENCING OUR INNER FELINE

Starring: Selena Steele, Raquel Darian, Raven, Patricia Kennedy, Ashly Nicole, Zara Whites, Alexandral Quinn, Rocco Siffreddi, Marc Wallice, Jamie Gillis, T.T. Boy, Derek Lane, Randy Spears, Tom Byron. Producer: Louie T. Beagle. Director: John Leslie. Story/screenplay: John Leslie. Music: Bill Heid. VCA, 1991.

When the human Cats aren't prowling sex clubs and alleys in search of action, they live together in an uneasy truce, waiting for the fulfillment of "the prophecy" that will reveal the Queen of the Cats. Meanwhile, Raven rules as the Supreme Cat, with the wickedly well-built Rocco Siffreddi as her sometime mate. Into the house comes Selena Steele, Raven's improbable little sister, whom Raven tries unsuccessfully to declare off-limits to the male cats.

At the sex club they frequent, Selena hooks up with Marc Wallice and displays unexpected confidence when she tells him, "I'm not like anyone you ever met." She takes him home to prove it, but before their lovemaking is finished, Raven comes in, pulls Selena off Marc, and takes her place. Selena gets a my-name-is-trouble look in her eye, and you know the last hand hasn't been played in this game.

The way the Cat couples touch, whisper, and share looks speaks of genuine interaction, but here it's the women who swagger in control and the men who stand attentively at their sides, strong and supportive mates. Two of these tomcats, Siffreddi and Wallice, are among the more physically attractive men working in erotic films today. Given the right stories and opportunities, they might turn out performances on a level with the classics Eric Edwards, John Leslie, and Paul Thomas of the late '70s and early '80s. We should note that men who worry about organ size may find the Jamie Gillis-in-the-alley scene insensitive. At least one male reviewer called it a real turn-off.

John Leslie directs some very alluring sex scenes; beyond that he's playing his usual sly games with sex and power that are fascinating to watch and give resonance to an otherwise slight story. **Highly recommended.**

Explicitness: 8;   Sensuality: 8   A,   O,   2W

Cyrano

CLASSIC DRAMA PLAYED AS COMEDY

Starring: April Rayne, Angela Summers, Madison, Joey Murphy, Casey Williams, Steve Drake, Alexandria Quinn, Jamie Lee, Trinity Loren, Bionca, Peter Gale, Fred Simmons, Robin Hall, John Litmann, Easy Ryder. Producer/director/writer: Paul Norman. Pleasure, 1991. 65 minutes.

Paul Norman has done what many of you have probably wished you could do—write a happy ending to a sad story. As with Rostand's tale, Cyrano is handicapped by a strangely shaped proboscis, the use of which gives the concept of double penetration altogether new meaning. What an organ, and what fun to have two of them to play with!

As in the original, Cyrano is a romantic who has a way with words and a heart generous enough to help his friend Christian woo the lady Roxanne. Though experience warns us against making love stark naked in a barn with no place to lie except fresh hay, we couldn't help but applaud the relish with which the ladies of Roxanne's household enjoyed themselves in a big all-women orgy scene. Somewhere between a romance and a farce, Cyrano's costumes, locations, and generous amounts of swordplay and frolics in the hay (with Mozart's music)

60

make this video watchable and enjoyable. We particularly liked Norman's clever twist in giving Cyrano the happiness we know he deserves.
Recommended.

Explicitness: 7;   Sensuality: 6

 **The Dancers**

ROAD MOVIE

Starring: John Leslie, Georgina Spelvin, Richard Pacheco, Vanessa Del Rio, Joey Silvera, Kay Parker, Randy West, Mai Lin. Producer: Michele Ames. Director: Anthony Spinelli. Writer: Michael Ellis. Music: Chet and Jim Moore. B Film Presentation of a Cine-Star Production, 1982. 101 minutes.

Jackie's Dreams, an all-male dance troupe, travels the Podunk towns of America in a beat-up Cadillac. They make a meager living stripping in bars and clubs on Ladies' Only nights, kept going by Jackie's pep talks and the promise of that major gig he's sure is just around the corner. Among ourselves, we referred to them as "the Looker" Sebastian (Randy West), "the Intellectual" Jonathan (Richard Pacheco), "Mr. Bad the Jock" (Joey Silvera), and "Jackie the Operator" (John Leslie). Onstage they perform solo, shaking their boodies and struttin' their stuff for the appreciative ladies in the audience. And of course each finds a woman whose heart he steals.

All four are fully developed characters with stories to tell, and the dialogue is smart and quick-witted. Our personal favorite was Jonathan, an idealist who quotes John Dryden and T. S. Eliot and dreams of auditioning for a Chekhov play. His love scene with Georgina Spelvin is so emotionally and erotically charged it won Spelvin the Best Actress award at the sixth annual Erotic Film Festival.

Will any of Jackie's Dreams find happiness with the ladies who want to love them, or will they beat it for the freedom of the road? You won't know till the very end. This movie gave Pacheco, West, Leslie, and Silvera a chance to show a side of themselves not often seen in this genre.
Highly recommended.

Explicitness: 7;   Sensuality: 8

Debbie Does Dallas

COMEDY CLASSIC

Starring: Bambi Woods, Misty Winter, Pat Allure, Rikki O'Neal, Arcadia Lake, Paula Head, R. Bolla, Christie Ford, Robin Byrd, Eric Edwards, Jenny Cole, David Sutton, Herschel Savage, Jake Teague, Debbie Lewis, Kasey Rodgers, David Morris, Tony Mansfield, Pater Lerman, Ben Pierce, Georgette Sanders. Producer/director: Jim Clark. Writer: Maria Minestra. Caballero, 1978. 80 minutes.

A raunchy, good-natured porno classic (with '70s bodies to prove it) based on the popular "captain of the football team and cheerleader" fantasy. High school cheerleader Debbie has been accepted into the Texas Cowgirls, but her parents won't give her the money to get to Dallas. Her friends on the cheerleading squad decide to help raise the funds by taking odd jobs. Debbie discovers that working part-time for nerdy lecher Mr. Greenfeld (R. Bolla) in the sporting goods store doesn't pay very well, but showing Mr. Greenfeld her breasts does ("I'll give you ten dollars just to look. No touching."). A look leads to a squeeze, and these enterprising girls have a real cottage industry servicing the DOMs and, yes, DOWs around town.

Some of us felt this was more of a turn-on for men than women and didn't like the idea of allegedly pubescent girls selling their bodies for cash. Others felt it was a funny fantasy that gave a plausible, if not entirely admirable, reason for making it with all those Cro-Magnon Romeos—$$$. Make up your own mind, but if you decide to watch it, be warned—the production is tacky, the humor is earthy, and the consensual sex is graphic. And the bodies are real—hairy here and well rounded there; this film was made before tidy pubic hair was porn norm. *Best line:* Girls: "What's your secret, Annie? Your boyfriend looks really happy and we know you're still a virgin." Annie: "OK. Who's got a banana?" *Best moment:* Triumphant Mr. Greenfeld bursts out of the dressing room, suited up.

Explicitness: 9; Sensuality: 7   A,   M,   O,   S,   2W, 2W/M

Renting Videos

The number one question we are most often asked by women is, "Aren't you embarrassed to rent the videos?" "Indeed," we answer. "The ERA amendment did not pass, but we have the right to pick out a sexy movie." Even if we didn't want to watch one, we'd rent one right away just to make a statement of entitlement. Although, we must admit, sometimes we were embarrassed. The funny thing about that is, even in the low-down part of town, the male browsers were even more embarrassed. They usually vacated the adult section and pretended to be looking at something else until we left. If you are feeling hesitant, here are several ice-breaking ideas based on our experiences.

- Go in the morning, as soon as the store opens. The adult section gets crowded in the evening.
- Pretend you are renting several videos to show at a risqué wedding shower. Ask the clerk if he/she can make any rec-

Debbie Does Dallas 2

RAUNCHY SEQUEL TO RAUNCHY CLASSIC

Starring: R. Bolla, Bambi Woods, Lisa Cintrice, Ron Jeremy, Spike Adrian, Ashley Welles, Daniella, Jeanne Silver, Lisa Bee, Ron Hudd, Bobby Cohen, Bell Stevens. Producer/director: Jim Clarke. VCX, 1983. 80 minutes.

After all the energy Debbie and friends put into getting her to the Texas Cheerleaders tryouts, she's crushed to find out she's too young. So she hitchhikes to visit her aunt, who coincidentally runs a high-priced facility for working girls called The Ranch. The winsome Bambi

ommendations. This role playing is useful if you are one of those people who can't help making explanations to total strangers.

- Get dressed up in your job interview suit. A fedora or other hat with a wide brim is a helpful accessory. Look successful. Keep a pleasant, thoughtful expression.
- Or, dress as you would to go to a parent/teacher conference. Think good blazer, little-print dress, low-heeled shoes, and a canvas shoulder bag with the name of a museum or the public television station. Got the look? With this persona you can visit the grungy XXX-rated store next door to the bus station. The owner will be solicitous.
- Carry a notebook. Write in it. If anyone asks, tell them you're writing an article for Ms. magazine. (This approach also works for you men who want to rent but fear losing your hard-won, new sensitive-guy status.)

After the first few times, you'll find that nobody pays any attention to you, and you can relax and be yourself. By the way, the number one question we were asked by men is, "Weren't you turned on all the time?" We just smiled.

and the women of the ranch display cheerful camaraderie, but the feeling of sisterhood is a pale echo of the wit and spunk of the first film. Debbie seems melancholy to be in this dispiriting video, and who can blame her? The unevolved attitude displayed toward women puts this on the avoid-at-all-costs list. Debbie has many other sequels. Rent at your own risk.

Explicitness: 8;   Sensuality: 4   3W

64

Deep Inside ...(series)

GET TO KNOW YOUR FAVORITE STARS

As part of an ongoing series, each *Deep Inside* . . . video presents
a different female star of erotic videos. They answer questions, which
they first rephrase for the viewer so you don't have much sense of an
intrusive third party. "You want to know what my first adult movie
was. . . ." "My favorite partner or partners. . . ." "How I began acting in
movies. . . ." The answers are interspersed with four or five clips from
the star's favorite sex scenes. You may want to watch with a pencil and
paper nearby to jot down video titles.

Penis Size

*Penis size has been of concern to men forever and ever and ever.
No kidding.*

*Hostius Quadra, an ancient Roman with bisexual inclina-
tions, surrounded himself with magnifying mirrors to enhance
the size of his penis. Medieval Arabians considered penis size a
factor in a woman's ability to reach orgasm and conceive a
child. Queen Johanna I, a Neapolitan of the fourteenth century,
believed the proverb "Big nose, big hose." She was, alas, crush-
ingly disappointed in her husband's endowments.*

*Like other anatomical parts, penii come in various lengths,
thicknesses, and attitudes. Substantial size is, of course, advan-
tageous if you seek a career in adult moviemaking, which may
just be the only advantage. Getting wood (reaching and main-
taining erection), however, is far more important and will make
you a popular dude quicker than mere size.*

Those purported to be enormous are actually only a little

Deep Inside Annie Sprinkle

AUTOBIOGRAPHY

Starring: Annie Sprinkle, Heather Young, Ron Jeremy, Lisa Be, Sassy, Buddy Hatton and Bunnie Hatton, Judy Bilodeau, Ron Hudd, Mal O'Ree, Jake Teague, Ron Jeremy, Lee Star, Roger Ram, Sassy. Producer: Howard A. Howard. Director/writer: Annie Sprinkle. Video X Pix, 1982. 87 minutes.

Annie Sprinkle does things in her own inimitable way, and this *Deep Inside . . .* is not like the others in the series. She tells us she got a late start sexually but once she lost her virginity she made the ac-

bigger than the average. An erect penis on a 5'6" man will look bigger than the same penis on a 6' man. To fool the camera, various tricks of the trade are employed to make a penis look bigger than it is. Shaving or clipping public hair around the penis can give an enhanced appearance. Body builders, allegedly, have slightly bigger than average penises.

According to an Internet posting by Rob Heerdink (http.//www.E.R.Heerdink@far.ruu.nl) of the Department of Pharmacoepidemiology and Pharmacology at Utrecht University, researchers Hurray and Mernstein conducted a three-year study paid for by Dutch sponsors to investigate the correlation between race and penis size. Their research was conducted in Europe, Asia, Australia, and America. Their conclusion? American males claiming to be "superior whites" or "Aryans" had on average the smallest penises in the world. On the other end, it was found that the tribe of Batavarians, from northwestern Europe, were the record holders in penis size.

Our final word on penis size is the same as Juvenal's: "If you run out of luck it doesn't matter how long your penis is."

quaintance of half of Tucson. Then she faithfully acts out some of her sexual fantasies, such as attending an Annie Sprinkle film festival on New York's 42nd Street and sucking all the geezers in the audience. Luckily, CPR isn't needed, though the limber, big-breasted, totally obsessed Annie probably can do that, too. Formerly known as the Queen of Kink, these days she concentrates on photography, writing, directing erotic films, and political issues that are Jesse Helms's worst nightmare.

Explicitness: 8;   Sensuality: 4   A,   O(all-girl)

Deep Inside Nina Hartley

AUTOBIOGRAPHY

Starring: Nina Hartley, Britt Morgan, Marc Wallice, Eric Price, Mike Horner, Randy West, Peter North, Alex Jordan, Casey Williams. Producer/director: Wesley Emerson. VCA, 1993.

Nina Hartley, one of the busiest stars in erotic videos, shares how she got started, what her three-way marriage is like, why she thinks a penis can be too large, which vibrator she prefers, and other personal tidbits. She's so bright and well spoken that no matter how unusual some of her life choices are we find ourselves nodding and saying, "OK Nina, whatever." The video follows the series format, so five of her sex scenes from other videos are shown with her introductions and commentary. A good place to begin your viewing.

Explicitness: 9;   Sensuality: 6   A,   O,   2W,   2W/M

Deep Inside Ona Zee

AUTOBIOGRAPHY

Starring: Ona Zee, Mike Horner, Tom Byron, Frank James, Randy West, Tammy Reynolds, Sharon Kane, Shanna McCullough, D. Cashmere, John Martin, John Leslie, Cal Jammer. VCA, 1992.

Ona Zee started her career in mainstream television and movies and switched to the erotic side of the business later than most major stars. She says she's an exhibitionist and having sex with relative strangers in front of a camera turns her on. The video contains five scenes. She also talks about her marriage, her earliest sexual memories, and the crystal cock given to her by her shaman, but she isn't telling any big secrets. Ona and her husband, Frank, are entrepreneurs, and you can learn more about their relationship in their how-to videos *Learning the Ropes* (see "Instructional Videos and How-to Series").

Explicitness: 8.5; Sensuality: 6 A, O, 2W, 2W/M

Deep Inside Tiffany Minx

AUTOBIOGRAPHY

Starring: Tiffany Minx, Randy West, Chanel, Christina Appleighe, P.J. Sparxx, Jonathan Morgan. Producer/director: Wesley Emerson. VCA, 1993. 85 minutes.

Tiffany talks as if she wandered into the adult film business because she didn't have anything else to do one afternoon. When she was a child she wanted to be a ballerina, but these days her expressed ambitions include a three-way with Melanie Moore and Cody Adams. She says Melanie is the best female oral W/W she has found in the business, and she loves to take Cody's "great pop shot" in her face. The scenes she chooses to show us include a demonstration. Barely twenty-one, she has recently taken a break from her career to have her second child.

Explicitness: 9; Sensuality: 5 A, C

Deep Inside Tyffany Million

AUTOBIOGRAPHY

Starring: Tyffany Million, Mike Horner, Tim Lake, Kyle Houston, Bionca, Ritchie Razor, Wesley Emerson, Gerry Pike. Producer/director: Wesley Emerson. Music: Barry Boxx. VCA, 1995.

Tyffany answers questions about her first sexual experience, her teen years, her fantasies, and her present private life. At the time of this writing, that meant a bisexual marriage to male star Ritchie Razor and an unspecified woman. She comes across as a straightforward person who knows what she wants, and that includes size. Tyffany says, "Sorry boys, it matters." Her requirements for a man are a large cock

Linda Lovelace and Her Ordeal

> Deep Throat
> Don't row your boat
> Don't get your goat
> That's all she wrote
> Deep Throat
> —Lyrics of Deep Throat *theme song*

Linda Lovelace, aka Linda Marsciano, grew up wanting to be a nun. She ended up performing in one of the highest-grossing films of all time. Her husband and manager, Chuck Traynor, was paid $100 a day for her services—a total of $1,200 for the twelve-day shoot. Linda got nothing.

Finding herself, at twenty-one, living with her parents in their retirement community in Florida, Linda took the first easy exit she came upon, presented in the person of Chuck Traynor, owner of a dumpy bar in North Miami. He charmed Linda with nothing more than his Jaguar. By the time she found out that

and sweet breath, but for a woman she holds tougher standards, beginning with intellect. The scenes include one with Gerry Pike from *Sex 1994,* the Michael Ninn film. She swears it was a personal best—multiple orgasm, clenched teeth, red face, and all.

Explicitness: 8;   Sensuality: 7   T,   2W

he had a police record for assault and battery, was facing charges for drug (marijuana) smuggling, and had run a house of prostitution, she felt trapped. Traynor, effectively her jailer, forced her into prostitution at gunpoint and eventually into the 8-mm movie business. As she describes it, "Every day I either got raped, beaten, kicked, punched, smacked, choked, degraded, or yelled at. Sometimes I got all of the above. Strangely enough, what bothered me most was the endless verbal abuse."

The horror stories told by Linda in her book, Ordeal, which made her the darling of antipornography organizations, have been presented as evidence that women are coerced by the industry to perform in pornographic movies and are, furthermore, violated, abused, drugged, and so on. Even a cursory reading of Ordeal makes it clear that the horrors Lovelace endured were perpetrated by her husband/manager, at that time an outsider to the porn movie business. Clearly, neither Gerard Damiano, the producer of Deep Throat, nor his unsavory backers were eligible for the Citizen of the Year award. However, compared with the degrading and abusive treatment she suffered from Traynor, the filming of the movie was a pleasant experience for Lovelace. She also makes clear that her subsequent involvements in the pornography industry, including a stint at the Playboy mansion in Chicago, were entirely voluntary though never as successful as Deep Throat.

Deep Throat

RAUNCHY CLASSIC

Starring: Linda Lovelace, Harry Reems, Polly Sharp, Bill Harrison, William Love, Carol Connors, Bob Phillips. Producer: Lou Perry. Director: Gerard Damiano. Writer: Jerry Gerard. Arrow/AFV, 1972. 84 minutes.

Poor Linda can't have orgasms. She wants bombs, bells, and rockets; she gets mere tingles. Is she frigid? Was there perhaps a childhood trauma? Dr. Harry Reems to the rescue. His unorthodox examination discovers her clitoris in her throat. He also discovers that Linda has no gag reflex and satisfaction for all parties is guaranteed, except for one other dilemma—while Dr. Reems's erect penis measures close to twelve inches, the national U.S. erect average is six to seven inches. Linda needs at least nine for satisfaction. The doctor's dance card is full, what with his nurse and other prior commitments, and though he squeezes Linda into his schedule as any compassionate man would, he faces burnout. She must find an above-average-sized man of her very own.

Clearly this is a man's fantasy. Any woman knows that with a clit in your throat your first problem would be how not to make a spectacle of yourself at a business lunch. And your next problem would be how not to weigh four hundred pounds.

The movie was a monster crossover hit when it opened, and it marks the first time most Americans could go to a movie theater and see an erect penis, let alone close-ups of intercourse. For years it was one of the top ten grossing movies in the country—right up there with *Star Wars* and *E.T. Deep Throat* has an amiable tone, and there *was* that fantasy, but the production was crude (we have never seen a high-quality print), and there were other, funnier, sexier, better-looking erotic movies made about the same time. It all makes Linda Lovelace furious. On television and in print interviews connected with her book *Ordeal* she has said she made the movie under duress and in fear for her life. So once more it's up to us. Do we rent it and further enrich men who probably don't deserve it? You choose.

Explicitness: 7; Sensuality: 7

SEX À LA MODE

Starring: Zara Whites, Savannah, Amber Lynn, Racquel Darian, Viviana, Nina Alexander, Brad Gerig, Randy West, Jennifer Kingsley, Capri Danell, Marc Wallice, Brigitte Monroe, Peter North, Tera Heart, Blake West, Ashley Lauren, Casey Williams, Derrick Lane, Sandra Scream, Jeanna Fine, Zorena, Jon Dough, Mark Francis. Producers: Andrew Blake, Patti Rhodes. Director/writer: Andrew Blake. Music: Rock Hard. VCA, 1990. 82 minutes.

Zara is the owner of an erotic art gallery in Southern California. A greenish-blue plaster version of "Venus de Milo" was the only art we saw, though there are plenty of white gallery walls and sexy artists. We enjoyed the body-painting scene with Ashley Lauren and Tara Heart for its tactile effect, and the performance art piece on the staircase is positively inspiring. Platinum blonde Savannah, whose disfiguring auto accident and subsequent tragic suicide has been much written about and discussed, also stars here.

Desire has the hallmarks of all Andrew Blake productions: perfect people fabulously dressed in minimal yet luxurious settings. And like most Andrew Blake vids, the story is not the thing, so don't look for real narrative interest. Also, as usual is the irritating and redundant music. We recommend muting the sound. Then go ahead and revel in the visuals, alone or as background for a private party.
Recommended.

Explicitness: 7;   Sensuality: 6   2W

The Devil in Miss Jones (the original)

DEATH OF A VIRGIN

Starring: Georgina Spelvin (as Justine Jones), John Clemmens, Harry Reems, Clair Lumiere, Judith Hamilton, Erica Havens, Levi Richards. Director/writer: Gerald Damiano. VCA Pierre Productions, 1973. 68 minutes.

> "The first film to deal with serious subject matter. Georgina's performance is monumental in the annals of carnal cinema."
> Jim Holliday, author of *Only the Best*

Justine Jones led a blameless life until she put a bloody end to it. "Suicide," Mr. Abaca the heavenly bureaucrat tells her, "is the unforgivable biggie." Justine must go to hell. A good girl till the end, she barely argues with him but musters enough backbone to say that if another opportunity came her way she would lead a life of irredeemable lust. Compassionately, Mr. Abaca bends the rules. She will be sent to a teacher (Harry Reems) who can show her what's what in the lust department. By the time he's through with her, she'll deserve her fate.

Does she enjoy her lessons? Her gasps, pleas, and pained expressions illuminate the soul of a conflicted moralist. Good acting, but that doesn't make it a candidate for a simple evening of erotic stimulation, even when she moves beyond the ordinary to specialties such as grapes, bananas, a hose, silver paint, and a very big, live snake. Sin and its wages are a downer. On the other hand, if that turns you on, if you're curious about the range and history of adult videos, or if you want to fully appreciate the very funny sequel, by all means check out this celebrated classic. It's often recommended for lapsed Catholics.

Georgina Spelvin, when interviewed about the role, said that she didn't feel Justine was turned into a sex object for the gratification of men. In fact, it was the male penis that was turned into a sex object for Justine's gratification. She certainly never cared who was attached to it. Point of view is everything in these matters.

Explicitness: 9;   Sensuality: 6   A,   S/M,   2W

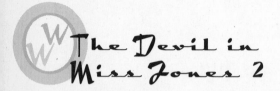

The Devil in Miss Jones 2

CLASSIC SEQUEL

Starring: Georgina Spelvin, Jack Wrangler, Joanna Storm, Anna Ventura, Jacqueline Lorians, R. Bolla, Samantha Fox, Michael Bruce, Bobby Astyr, Sharon Kane, Sharon Mitchell, George Payne, Ron Jeremy, Ashley Moore, Merle Michaels, Alan Adrian, Dena Ferrara, Joey Silvera, Kurt Mann, Fred Lincoln, Mark Ubelli, Adam DeHaven, Henri Pachard. Producer: James George. Director: Henri Pachard. Writers: Ellie Howard, Henri Pachard. Music: Barry Levitt. VCA, Nibo Films, 1983. 90 minutes.

The Justine Jones we meet in part 2 is a far cry from the tormented creature of *Devil* 1. Still played by Georgina Spelvin (the original Justine), she seems quite sanguine about life in hell except for one big annoyance—the residents may have all the sex they want, but orgasms are forbidden. (Strange rule in a place that looks like a penis theme park.) Justine's antics regularly cause a shattering blast of the orgasm alert and earn her a reprimand from the charming, world-weary Devil himself. He hasn't had an orgasm for 2,500 years. Why should anyone else have one? Before you can say "proactive sexuality," Justine shows him her moves. The Devil never has a chance. He not only comes in a not-to-be-missed scene, he makes a fatal promise in bed—Justine may return to earth.

In the gorgeously rounded body of Jacqueline Lorians, the delighted Justine settles into a life of eternal lust as the highest-paid call

girl in New York. But the now-obsessed Devil isn't through with her yet. This is one of our favorite videos to watch alone or as a couple— laugh-out-loud funny, sophisticated, well acted, and raunchy enough to remind you why you rented it in the first place. We liked the Devil, too.
Highly recommended.

Explicitness: 8;   Sensuality: 8   M,   T

The Devil in Miss Jones 4: The Final Outrage

SEQUEL

Starring: Lois Ayres, Erica Boyer, Krista A. Lang, Jack Baker, Tamara Langley, Kelli Richards, Kari Fox, Kristara Barrington, Patti Petite, Jack Baker, Paul Thomas, Marc Wallice, Tom Byron. Producers/directors: The Dark Brothers. VCA, 1987. 72 minutes that felt like a lifetime.

The reviewers said: Highest Rating *(Hustler)*, Highest Rating *(Adult Video News)*, Film of the Year *(Adam Film World)*. We say: ugly, stupid, mean, racist, and sexist.

Explicitness: 10;   Sensuality: 1   A,   O

The Devil in Miss Jones 5: The Inferno

SEQUEL BUT NOT EQUAL

Starring: Juli Ashton, Kelly O'Dell, Rowan Fairmount, Ariana, Serenity, Amanda Adams, Revecca Lord, Barbara Doll, Nikole Lace, Sindee Coxx, Serenity, Kelly O'Dell, Felecia, Vanessa Chase, Tammi Ann, Jeanna Fine, Dallas, Darcy McDaniels, Leslie Forbes, Mark Davis, Tom Byron, Joey Silvera, Luc Wylder, Marc Wallice, Jon Dough, T.T. Boy, Arti Choke, Nick East, Cal Jammer, Dave Hardman, Michael J. Cox, Hank Rose,

Dave Cummings, Rip Hymen (as the Devil). Producer/director: Gregory Dark. Music: Dino Ninn and Earl Ninn. Writer: Selwyn Harris. VCA/Dark Brothers, 1995. 92 minutes.

If the Dark brothers cut the very explicit sex out of this movie for cable release, they'd have a ten-minute short subject on the wit and wisdom of the Devil, featuring such gems as, "Miss Jones knew nothing about sex. She majored in women's studies at a top university," or, "To whom is a man being loyal when he forswears knowledge of all but one woman for the rest of his life? Nature? It's against nature." Well, he *is* the devil.

The filler between his aphorisms is uninspiring, no-holds-barred sex between (or among) strangers. We like the new Miss Jones (Juli Ashton), the supposed reason for the picture, but she's not enough inducement to watch it unless you're a fan of the Dark brothers' sexual slam-bang moviemaking. One note of interest is the debut appearance of "older man" actor Dave Cummings, a former U.S. Army lieutenant colonel who broke into erotic videos (sex roles, thank you very much) at the relatively advanced age of fifty-five.

Explicitness: 9; Sensuality: 4 A, DP, 2M/W, 5M/2W, O, T

Dinner Party

SEX ON THE MENU

Starring: Catalina, Celeste, Kaylan Nicole, Mark Davis, Steve Drake, Randy West, Debi Diamond, Misty Rain, Marc Wallice, Daisy, Asia Carrera, Gerry Pike, Yvonne, Kylie Ireland, Nick East, Juli Ashton, Tammy Parks, Sean Michaels, Vanessa Chase, Norma Jeane, Vince Voyeur, Diva, Jewel Night, Frank Towers. Producer/director/writer: Cameron Grant. Music: Let's Play Music. Ultimate Video, 1994. 90 minutes.

Dinner with Barbie and Ken and all their airbrushed, buffed, and soft-focused friends. Or, the sex games of the rich, beautiful, and vapid. In a movie styled and art directed in the manner of Andrew Blake, Randy West is the gracious dinner party host who suggestively coaxes his guests into revealing their most provocative fantasies. Over an elegantly set table the guests, one by one, expose their private reveries and secret wishes. Ending with a huge orgy scene for dessert, the flights of fancy range from various configurations of threesomes to games of doctor and dominance. One of the most titillating scenes puts a dainty woman in white shoes, stockings, and pearls with a big, muscular construction worker. That they happen to be total strangers serves to heighten the charge between them.

What's missing in this video, as with so many others, is a sense of relationship among the dinner guests. Too many of the sex scenes looked like people were on autopilot. There would have been exponential improvement in the heat put out by this video if the performers really looked at their partners. There's lots of foreplay in some of the vignettes, a redeeming quality, and many of the settings are straight out of *Travel and Leisure* locations. If beautiful people and settings ignite your fire and foreplay is what you crave, the *Dinner Party* is sure to please you.
Recommended.

Explicitness: 9;   Sensuality: 6   A,   B,   M,   O,   S,   T, 2W

Dirty Books

RUNNING A BOOK AND VIDEO STORE

Starring: Ashlyn Gere, Ona Zee, Tifanny Million, Kelly O'Dell, Mike Horner, Jonathan Morgan. Producer/director: Wesley Emerson. Writer: Martin Brimmer. VCA Platinum, 1992.

After paying all the bills of the bookstore she inherited from her father, Amanda (Ashlyn Gere) discovers that there's not a dollar left. If she doesn't act quickly she may lose the store altogether. Her ineffectual husband, Todd (Mike Horner), a struggling screenplay writer who hasn't managed to make a sale, is of no financial or emotional help. Their relationship has all the ingredients of a marriage coming apart: no money, no sex, no fun.

Against Todd's wishes, Amanda takes the advice of her accountant and "reengineers" the store, turning it into an emporium of sex books, toys, and videos, justifying her move by declaring that she's providing a public service. Indeed. Dare we say, sex sells. Before long, Amanda has effectively turned a fiscal sinkhole into a booming success. Tifanny Million, definitely not a raincoater, is the customer director Wesley Emerson chose to show shopping the toy section. We enthusiastically cheer his choice of a woman in this role. Her masturbation sequence behind the closed doors of the video preview room really delivers.

Pretty soon, Amanda is doing well enough to hire help and have a video signing. Famous porn star Vanessa Sonora (Ona Zee) not only signs videos but takes Todd in hand and, with gentle but firm encouragement, demonstration, and instruction helps him get over his prudishness and then offers him an opportunity to succeed in his writing career. Todd becomes a better lover and writer. Through the miracle of open-mindedness, a business and a marriage are saved.
Highly recommended.

Explicitness: 7;   Sensuality: 6   M,   T,   2W

The Dog Walker

SURREAL DRAMA

Starring: Christiana Angel, Isis Nile, Krysti Lynn, Lana Sands, Marva, Steven St. Croix, Joey Silvera, Jamie Gillis, Jon Dough, Tom Byron, Gerry Pike, Julian St. Joe, Alex Sanders, Jay Ashley, Jake Williams, David Pollmen, Sheldon Austin, Michael Anderson, Scott Walker, John Leslie. Producer/director: John Leslie. Evil Angel, 1994. 116 minutes.

Steven, a small-time crook, delivers a bag of diamonds to his crime boss and demands immediate payment. Big mistake. No sooner has Steven left the office through a back entrance then he's confronted by a sedan full of surly henchmen. As they viciously punch him, the elegant silhouette of a woman with a dog on a leash appears at the end of the alley. Steven collapses, and what follows are scenes from his life in a long, confused montage. Perplexed and bored, we wondered, "Is this the future?" The jumpy, surrealistic episodes include sex with women (including Steven's wife) who exist only to be hot and willing. After endless emotionless encounters, it's back to the alley, where our antihero Steven is in even bigger trouble than we knew. Again we see the silhouette of the woman with the dog. She has come for Steven. At this point you may want to recall that *dog* spelled backward is *God.* Deep.

John Leslie has transformed himself from one of the best actors in the business to one of adult films' leading producer-directors. This slick, expensive movie was much touted in 1994. We don't get it. By us, it's pretentious, not a turn-on, but if you like your sex rough, tough, and impersonal, it fills the need.

Explicitness: 9;   Sensuality: 6   A,   C,   O,   S,   2W

Don Juan DeMarco

THE YOUNG TEACH THE OLD

Starring: Marlon Brando, Johnny Depp, Faye Dunaway, Rachel Ticotin, Talisa Soto. Producers: Francis Ford Coppola, Fred Fuchs, Patrick Palmer. Director/writer: Jeremy Levin. Music: Michael Kamen. New Line Productions, 1995. 97 minutes. Rated PG-13.

"Every woman is a mystery to be solved," declares Don Juan (Johnny Depp). A sentiment we unequivocally agree with. Claiming, with no hint of guile, to have seduced and satisfied a thousand women, the Don is a most ardent and sincere movie hero who's in love with love. Alas, he's also delusional. Banished to a mental hospital, he's being treated by Dr. Jack Mickler (Marlon Brando, who's at his absolute best), a burned-out therapist eager for retirement who plays along with the Don's delusions. Depp's performance is brilliant. He never for an instant let's on that he doesn't believe every word he's saying. Jeremy Levin, previously a clinical psychiatrist, reveals the secret longings of our hearts and touchingly shares them with us. *Don Juan DeMarco* is his debut.

This romantic comedy for grown-ups will soften the edges of your cynicism. Don't be deceived by the PG-13 rating. There may be no nudity, but there's plenty of suggestive talk. The Don is no impostor. Believe him.

Simulated

Double Dare

(see entry under *Red Shoe Diaries*)

Dracula Exotic

TIME TRAVELING VAMPIRE

Starring: Jamie Gillis (as the Dark Prince), Samantha Fox, Vanessa Del Rio, Eric Edwards, Mark Dexter, Bobby Astyr, Gordon Duvall, Murray Bukofski. Producer/writer: K. Schwartz. Director: Warren Evans. Music: Leger Productions. Fat Boy Company/VCA, 1980. 98 minutes.

Mike Horner 2

Mike Horner says that these are difficult times for serious erotic filmmakers because of the low-budget to no-budget amateur competition. The flood of videos is increasing at an alarming rate: in 1993, 1,600 films; in 1994, 3,600; in 1995, 5,600.

Dreams of Desire, the second film Horner has written, directed, and produced, had a schedule of four and a half days and a relatively big budget for the industry—$50,000. Being in total control of the production enabled him to make the artistic decisions his way, not least of which was his choice of leading lady. Horner says that as he gets older he likes to be able to summon up some sense that at least for this moment he is the woman's lover. Since he was also acting the main male lead, he chose Melissa Hill, someone he liked both personally and sexually, for the female lead. Once she said "yes," he consulted her for people who were "on her list" to complete the casting.

"Everybody has a list of people in the business, from 'I'll leave my husband for him' to 'not in this lifetime.'" Melissa Hill liked Tom Byron, so he was hired as the other important male lead. Since Dreams was the first time Hill would do a scene

Jamie Gillis was born to play the role of antihero, so he's perfectly suited to portray middle Europe's Prince of Darkness—Leopold Michael Georgi Count Dracula. Besides being plasma starved, he's been in a foul mood since 1490, when he was denied his first love Surka (Samantha Fox), the gamekeeper's daughter. Her lowly rank put her out of bounds as a potential consort, and his princely ego could not accept her refusal to become his mistress, so he does the only thing his macho manners will allow—he rapes her, driving her to suicide. Five hundred remorse-filled years later he's still looking for his lost love. He finds her at last in her new incarnation, as an agent of the FIB (Federal Investigating Bureau) who is assigned to investigate him. The FIB, clever devils that they are, suspect the count of being a Russian spy.

with more than one man, Horner wanted to be certain she was as comfortable as possible. "She was nervous, and she had to feel in control. She can throw herself into sex but she is shy, not verbal, more of a girl next door." Horner sees the group scene as his star "first inundated by male desire, then becoming the ballerina princess and the goddess—elevated, heightened by the sex."

Tom Byron suggested Jill Kelly (who plays the other female lead) since they were eager to work with each other. Mike said he didn't have to direct their scene, just tell them what he wanted and stand back. Perhaps, he worried, they had taken the fantasy too far? We reassured him we didn't think so and that we particularly liked the continuation of the scene past the sexmaking to cuddling and conversation. The positive relationship between the two really comes through to the viewer.

To distribute this film, Horner made a deal with his friend Ona Zee, whose company, Ona Zee Productions, often concentrates on videos related to the interest in S/M she shares with her husband, Frank. In spite of some difference in emphasis, Mike likes her company and felt they would do a good job for him. He says five thousand copies would be considered an outstanding sale by industry standards (a number that seems amazingly low to us), but a few successful videos do many times that number. With the right breaks, Dreams of Desire could be one of them.

The espionage plot is all mixed up with the vampire story, which matters not a jot—where but in porn would you find Russian spies and vampires in the same movie? The campy ironic tone and the huge plastic fangs go a long way to defusing the potential for indignation in the raunchy and bizarre sex scenes, which involve not only rape but bloody beatings, Surka dressed up as Daddy's little sex toy, and the fabulous Vanessa Del Rio being raised from the dead. That's right, we're talking necrophelia here, done with high style. This hard to find vid has many fans in those who crave a vicarious walk on the wild side.
Recommended with caveat.

Explicitness: 7;   Sensuality: 8   3M/W,   O,   S/M

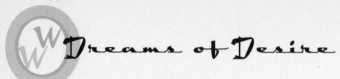

Dreams of Desire

IN DREAMS BEGIN REALITY . . .

Starring: Melissa Hill, Jill Kelly, Mike Horner, Kim Kataine, Brittany O'Connell, Sharon Kane, Brooke Waters, Tom Byron, Sindee Coxx. Producer/writer/director: Mike Horner. Music: Todd Bergendahl, Marc Churchull. Mike Horner Productions/Ona Zee Productions, 1995.

What do men want? Why do they stray? Mike (Mike Horner) strays because he wants sex (come on honey, he wants it now), and Melissa Hill has other things on her mind, thank you. When she sees him tumbling a big-breasted blonde in their bed she flees into a familiar erotic film format of dreamy fantasy sequences.

As producer and director as well as actor, Mike Horner manages to put a great new shine on this material. The masturbation sequence with Melissa watching Tom Byron while the camera watches both of them especially pleased us because it's filmed so that you can see her, and through a window see what she's watching—full-length body shots that involve us with expressions and reactions instead of the more usual tight close-ups of the respective crotches. In another scene, Melissa lets a desperate Jill Kelly into her room, and the two women talk about the problems of men in relationships, so their lovemaking evolves as a natural response to their frustrations. And Jill Kelly's encounter with Tom Byron may be the hottest in the whole video. It's hard to choose a favorite among so many good candidates, and that's the way we like it. *Most unusual moment:* Melissa Hill on a glass table lit from beneath.

Highly recommended.

Explicitness: 8;   Sensuality: 8

Easy

MELODRAMA

Starring: Jesie St. James, Dewey Alexander, Deseree Clearbanch, Ronald Davis, Laurien Dominique, Don Howard, Georgina Spelvin, George Spelvin, Grant Stockton, Johnny Wilson, Jack Wright. Producer: Sam Norvell. Director: Anthony Spinelli. Writer: Original screenplay by Jack Livingston. Music: John Duvalli. Cal Vista International/Skylark Productions, 1978. 85 minutes.

If you find yourself having daydreams of, as they say, "being taken against your will," the story of the beautiful and athletic Kate Harrison (Jesie St. James's first leading role) will give you significant new fantasy material. Looking for love after a divorce, she has the bad luck of being raped three times in the course of this video—the first time by a student (male) and the second by a friend of his, also male. She doesn't seem to fight these aggressors very hard, giving in to the old stereotype as she becomes a willing participant. The third rape, erotically the best scene in the video, takes place after she's left her teaching job and moved to another town. Having found what she thinks to be true love in Victor (Jack Wright), Kate is caught off guard when Georgina Spelvin gets into her house and announces that Victor is hers and proceeds to violently and aggressively rape Kate, who puts up a losing fight. After a fair amount of thrashing about, what began as a brutal encounter turns into the most scorching sequence.

A good story, with above-average acting, especially in the spirited performance of St. James, whose face and body the camera does well to linger on. The various outdoor settings in northern California and inspired music combine with some hot sex scenes for a rousingly good video.

We had many discussions about the inclusion of this video. To some, the first rape scene was reason enough to excise it. For others, the high quality of the writing and performances combined with true-to-life plot (including a scene in which Kate has an encounter with a blind man who considers himself the best lover in America) made all the difference. It's up to you.

Explicitness: 6;   Sensuality: 7   2W

Ecstasy

IRONIC LOOK AT MARITAL SEX

Starring: John Leslie, Shana McCullough, Chanel, Katie Thomas, Tom Byron, Barry Blake. Producer/director: Anthony Spinelli. Writer: Michael Ellis. Plum Productions, 1986. 81 minutes.

Barney (John Leslie) and his wife (Shana McCullough) are having trouble in bed. He can't get excited; she calls him a wimp. He asks her to talk dirty to him, then he says she's doing it all wrong. He wants a woman who's innocent, who's never sucked a cock, maybe never even seen one. She wants a real man who will take her, make her feel loved. Instead of hiking off to a marriage counselor with these problems, the bickering

Rape

We don't think a woman exists who has ever found rape (non-consensual sex) acceptable in any way in real life. But we do know more than one who finds it a turn on in her fantasies.

Among the videos reviewed in this book you will find some in which rape scenes are included. In a few of the videos (Roommates and Anna Obsessed) the rapes are violent and unwelcome assaults and are appropriately treated as such. In others, it's clear that the woman, in the safety of her own mind, is having fantasies of being forcibly taken. The fantasies women have of being taken against their will and made love to are primarily of the "swept away" variety reminiscent of John Wayne and Maureen O'Hara movies, which in their nonexplicit form used to be Hollywood staples. In them, Prince Charming, represented as whomever she wants him to be, makes the right moves and sweeps the pretty maiden off her feet. She wants him, she loves him. He will no doubt marry her and be a fine father to their children. She doesn't have to worry about being a bad girl, she is not powerless to stop him, nor is she in danger

twosome decide to share their fantasies. (If they had viewed one of the "How-to" series that begin on page 233, they would have approached the idea more cautiously.) He starts off with a Rabelasian tale about an innocent French maid he seduces, then she tells about an ardent lover who performs discreetly hot anal sex. Between stories, they continue to quarrel until at last he gets angry enough to perform to his satisfaction, if not to hers.

We thought two of the fantasies were way above average—the seduction of the maid (also played by Shana McCullough) and a job interview between John Leslie and a blonde Valkyrie at least 6'2" in her vampy high heels. Much of the feeling of involvement in these scenes comes from the John Leslie sex talk, a seemingly spontaneous sotto voce conversation he keeps up with his partner ("Do you want me to

of being hurt. Such fantasies are not a suppressed wish to be raped. An indication that we may be experiencing a paradigm shift in our culture is Nancy Friday's report in her most recent book on women's fantasies, in which she notes a decrease in rape fantasies and an increase in dominatrix scenarios.

In yet a third category, the sexual encounter begins with the woman resisting what appears to be an unwelcome advance and ends with her fully participating and apparently enjoying herself. This third category is strictly a male fantasy. In his mind, she really wants it and is just being a tease by resisting. The man feels he has a right to do as he wishes. And, more to the point, she will become responsive and it will be OK. Fortunately, women, and many men, have come a long way from the days when women who said "no" were thought to have meant "yes" but were too shy to say so.

We included these videos because we found them in stores that carefully select their inventory with women customers in mind. Their inclusion in this book in no way condones the behavior they represent. We have been mindful to describe the action so that readers can avoid what they don't want to watch.

Scenes depicting women being raped are now regularly excised from existing videos, and the adult industry, with rare exceptions, no longer includes them in large part because actresses like Nina Hartley will not perform in them and producers like Jane Hamilton and Candida Royalle will not make them.

squeeze it?" "Arch your back just like that, just like that"). It's the tone that makes it work, the soft voice, purring, teasing, or urgent. That tone and the words create an intimate connection that bodies joined together don't always convey. We refer to it as the Patented John Leslie Sex Murmur. You'll hear it in many of his movies, but it's one of the effects that makes this **Recommended.**

Explicitness: 8;   Sensuality: 7   A

Ecstasy Girls

BOYS MEET GIRLS

Starring: Jamie Gillis, Georgina Spelvin, Serena, Leslie Bovee, Laurien Domenique, Desiree Cousteau, Nancy Suiter, Stacy Evans, John Leslie, Paul Thomas, Frank Hollowell, Turk Lyon, Con Cover, Robert Bullock, Chiquita Johnson, J. Reynold. Producer: Harry Lime. Director: Robert McCallum. Writers: Bill Barron, Harry Lime. Music: Ronnie Romanovitch. Caballero Control, 1979. 97 minutes.

Jerry (Jamie Gillis) wants to be an actor but makes ends meet as a hired "escort" for women stars. He's offered a chance to earn some "real money" by the scheming producer J.C. It seems J.C.'s childless, blue-nosed billionaire brother is dying and J.C. has a nasty little plan to ensure that their sister and her four daughters are disinherited. (He wants all the money, not just one-sixth.) To accomplish this, Jerry is supposed to seduce all five women and film the hot action as verifiable proof to show their sure-to-be-outraged relative.

Jerry hires two other aspiring filmmakers (John Leslie and Paul Thomas) to help him since it's tough to score and hold a camera at the same time. He personally takes on Nancy, the nasty twin, in a rowdy leather scene that probably will be cut under the new laws (look for an older rental copy), while John Leslie makes the team with the sporty daughter in an original all-time use of a hammock. So it goes, from light S/M to romantic violins in the spring rain, including Jamie Gillis's very touching change of attitude with "older woman" Georgina Spelvin. At last, their mission accomplished, will our boys let their consciences or ambitions be their guide?

Jamie Gillis, brunette and often bearded, has a bad-boy edge. He looks like the person you were involved with just before the doctor finally gave you a prescription for Prozac. When he plays the hero, it's a hero whose ethics are up for negotiation. His ability to act and deliver on carnal cue was one of the many reasons the late '70s and early '80s are called the golden age of erotic films. *Best scene:* Hard to choose, but we'll go with romance and a sudden spring shower.
Highly recommended.

Explicitness: 7;   Sensuality: 9   A,   S/M,   T

Emmannelle

SOFT CORE SERIES

(French, dubbed into uninspired English. *Sometimes spelled* Emanuelle *on the video box.)*

A popular soft-core series that spanned decades, these handsome, if humorless, movies are shot in exotic locales and feature chic, well-dressed men and women. Sylvia Kristel, the original Emmanuelle, has clean-cut good looks, a modest demeanor, and a slim body, surprisingly full breasted and sensuous. Her only visible occupation is to have affairs. After Sylvia retired, several other Emmanuelles followed her. Laura Gemser, a small-boned, dark-skinned beauty with long, straight black hair, appears in the largest number of films and plays a more sophisticated, less innocent heroine.

The nudity is frank (for the women, not the men), and the sex is simulated, though often close to the real thing except for the taboo penis and insertion. The backgrounds and fashions remain fresh; the attitude toward women is old-fashioned, especially in the earlier videos. In the later films, Emmanuelle always has an occupation, shifting from model to journalist to movie star on the whim of the plot. Many women had their first erotic movie experience with Emmanuelle, since the films' beauty and expensive production gained them a racy respectability.

Simulated (all in the series)

Emmannelle

Starring: Sylvia Kristel, Marika Greene, Jeanne Colletin, Christine Bolsson, Alain Cuny, Daniel Barky. Producer/director: Just Jaeckin. Columbia International, 1974.

Jean, a French diplomat posted to Bangkok, believes his young wife, Emmanuelle, should become more sexually sophisticated, have affairs. After her first disastrous experiment, he sends her to be tutored by Mario, a man who, though still in his world-weary looking seventies, still reigns as the sexual arbiter of their amoral circle. The decadent experiences Mario arranges with nameless, interchangeable Thai men succeed in separating Emmanuelle from all feeling about sex except the physical. The philosophical thoughts on sex and sexuality offered by Jean sound weird and dated, like rereading the '70s Playboy philos-

ophy in the '90s, when even Papa Hugh Hefner, the most famous
swinger of them all, is monogamously married and a doting father. The
backgrounds are great, however, including a too-brief visit to one of
Bangkok's famous sex clubs. The rest may be of interest only to those
on a more personal sentimental journey.

Good-bye Emmanuelle

*Starring: Sylvia Kristel (the original Emmanuelle), Umberto Orsino, Jean
Paul Bouvier. Director: Francois Letterier. 92 minutes.*

Emmanuelle and her husband, Jean, have moved their open marriage to the Seychelle Islands, presented here as an outpost of comfortable white colonial life supported by a polite black service class.
There, Emmanuelle pursues a French film director scouting a location.
The rules of the marriage let her do as she wishes, but Jean senses
danger and becomes jealous when the director tries to take Emmanuelle to Paris. He's right to worry. The pupil has learned the
lessons he taught her too well. Worth renting for the glorious Sey-
chelles scenery and island architecture.

Emmanuelle 4

*Starring: Sylvia Kristel, Mia Nygren, Deborah Power, Sophie Berger,
Patrick Bauchau (as Marc), Gerard Dimiglio, Sonia Martin, Christian
Marquant. Director: Francis Giacobetti. Screenplay: Francis Leroi, Iris
Letans. Production of a Francis Giacobetti Film, 1984. 81 minutes.
Rated R.*

Emmanuelle, here briefly called Sylvia, "lives for love" and must
escape feelings for Marc so strong they threaten her freedom. She
eludes him in Hollywood and impulsively decides to change her body
and face with the help of a distinguished Brazilian plastic surgeon. The
bandages come off and behold! Sylvia Kristel is Mia Nygren. Don't you
love beauty makeovers? "I had a new body and had to develop a soul
to go with it." Soul developing requires erotic adventures in dangerous
and exotic locations all over Brazil. At one of many parties, she sees
Marc in search of Sylvia. Will he recognize her in spite of surgery? Will
the reborn Sylvia, once more named Emmanuelle, resist her old love?

Emmanuelle in Egypt

Starring: Laura Gemser (as Emmanuelle), Annie Belle, Al Cliver, Susan Scott, Theodore Chialpin. Director: Brunello Rondi. 1977. 86 minutes.

Emmanuelle, now a model, pays a visit to a beautiful older woman and her nubile daughter who live in Egypt, where they can pursue their unorthodox sexual tastes. Emmanuelle is in the company of her boyfriend, a photographer named Carlo, who shows his power over her by shouting abuse and photographing her lying next to dead animals. The only bright spot in this enigmatic tale of decadence is that no one ever says "childhood trauma" or "low self-esteem." It's curiously refreshing to meet the filmmaker's assumption that bad behavior needs no explanation.

The real heroine of the movie is not Emmanuelle but an androgynous nymph named Pia, whose clear-sighted voice of reason breaks the spell that mysteriously binds them and helps Emmanuelle liberate herself from the creepy Carlos. Not, however, before a goat has been graphically killed and his blood drunk by the crazed model. Toxic.

Emmanuelle the Queen

(also called *Emmanuelle Queen of Sados*)

Starring: Laura Gemser, Gabriele Livia Russo, Harris Stevens, Nadia Neri, Vagelis Vartan, Gordon Mitchell, Pantelis Agelopou. Director/writer: Ilias Milonakos. Music: Giovanni Ullo. Andromeda Films, Athens and Othellos Films, Cypress, 1982.

Emmanuelle (Laura Gemser), is briefly married to a rich brute who beats and abuses her, aided by his devoted staff. As good luck would have it, her lover Mario is a killer-for-hire nicknamed "the Rose." So the abusive husband has an "accident" and Emmanuelle finds herself the guardian of her rich fifteen-year-old stepdaughter, Livia, and in control of the estate. Then it's her turn to even old scores.

European countries have different work rules than the United States, and while we don't know her actual age, the girl who plays Livia (including several nude scenes and a rape) has the barely formed breasts and baby fat of a young girl. Really inappropriate. **Not recommended.**

Emmanuelle in America

Starring: Laura Gemser, Gabrielle Tanti, Roger Browne, Lars Boch, Paeoli Senatore. Producer/director: Joe D'Amato. VidAmerica, 1978. 86 minutes.

Emmanuelle (Laura Gemser) is a photojournalist, sometimes working under the name of Laura Rogers. She goes undercover with her tiny camera, exposing a man with a sexual harem who deals drugs to pay for his expensive tastes, a spa where rich older women discreetly arrange to have their kinky needs met, and a Washington insider who plays torture films of Third World political prisoners to heat up his bedroom action. When the newspaper won't publish these last photographs, Emmanuelle and her understanding boyfriend, Phil, take off for an extended vacation on a tropical island inhabited by lovable "natives" with quaint mating rites. A puzzling mishmash of a plot, but some OK scenes (if they just hadn't spoiled it with the tropical island interlude where attitudes are right out of an old Jungle Jim movie).

Emmanuelle 5

Starring: Monique Gabrielle, Charles Foster, C. Hardester, Dana Burns Westberg, Bryan Shaner, Yaseen Khan. New Horizons. 1987.

A blonde Emmanuelle (Monique Gabrielle), premiers her scandalous new movie and cheerfully flaunts her sexuality to reporters and cameramen. One of her admiring fans, Prince Rajid, insists she must be an honored visitor to his island country when the movie opens there. Boyish zillionaire Charles Foster, the preppy fellow who saved her from a mob of sex-crazed men in Cannes, cautions her that the prince is definitely not nice. Phil, the faithful photographer, tells her Rajid makes Darth Vadar look like Mother Teresa. All the advice only fuels her determination not to let any man tell her what to do. As she assures everyone, "I never met a man I couldn't handle."

You won't need a crystal ball to guess what's in store for our intrepid heroine, but the sight of Emmanuelle with an assault rifle fighting her way off the island makes for a change from orgies and gives this episode a uniquely American flavor.

Emmanuelle 6

Starring: Nathalie Uher, Jean Rene Gossart, Tamira Thomass Ober-mueller, Melissa Ilena D'Arcy. Producers: A. S. P., Georges Korda Gustavo Rodriguz as Tony Harrison, Hassan Guerrara, Dagmar Berger, Tamira, Rania Raja, Edda Kopke. Director: Bruno Zincone. Writer: Jean Rollin. Music: Olivier Day. 1988.

A blondish, curly haired Emmanuelle (Nathalie Uher), visits a house in the French countryside, which the man who greets her says is her house. She suffers from amnesia and doesn't know she is a rich and fabulous sexual icon. Gradually, the memories come back of an Amazon cruise with other models and a trunk full of valuable jewels, of men who lusted after her, men she lusted after, and a drug lord who, when he couldn't own her, tried to sell her to the highest bidder. So much for the benefits of foreign travel.

Her house is staffed by a number of ambiguous people whose function is to help her regain her memory and then "have memory restored to your body as it has been restored to your mind so you can once more be the sensual Emmanuelle the world loves."

Endlessly

ROMANCE AT THE BEACH

Starring: Nikki Dial, Alex Jordan, Tiffany Minx, Nicole London, Crystal Wilder, Marc Wallice, Jonathan Morgan, Terry Thomas, Rob Savage, Rasha Ramona. Director: Paul Thomas. Vivid, 1993. 75 minutes.

Skip the first two-thirds of the big orgiastic party scene at a beach house. It's raunchy and unnecessarily loud. Just another tedious orgy, it didn't hold our interest. The last third (cue it up to the hot tub scene) is an altogether different story. Marc Wallice, of the gorgeous flowing hair, seems to be the owner of the beach house, and instead of boogying with his guests he's walking on the beach where he comes upon the beautiful Nikki Dial. They spend the night just walking and talking, enjoying the evening and the sound of the surf while scenes from the wild party are intercut.

Back at the house early in the morning, now empty of the revelers, Nikki and Marc, having gotten to know each other a little better, make some of the most romantic, passionate, erotic love we've seen. Moving from the hot tub to the living room then the bathroom and so on through

the house, they engage in ardent, inspired sex in nearly every possible way, with the camera capturing every nuance of feeling and excitement. What makes this work is the real affection these performers show for each other. They look soulfully into each other's eyes; their sexual attraction is palpable and infectious. The last third of *Endlessly*, in our opinion, should be sprung free to stand alone, liberated from the rest of the mindless, boring debauchery.
Highly recommended.

Explicitness: 7;   Sensuality: 9 (scene described)   A,   SS (one scene)

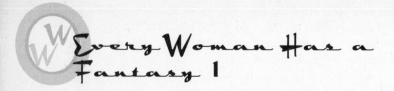

Every Woman Has a Fantasy 1

DELICIOUSLY UNCONVENTIONAL MARRIAGE

Starring: Rachel Ashley, John Leslie, Kristara Barrington, Shantell Day, Lisa George, Erica Boyer, Martina Nation, Robert Byrne, Francois Dumas, Blake Palmer. Producer: Sandra Winters. Director: Edwin Brown. Writers: Sandra Winters, Edwin Brown. Music: D'Artagnan. VCA/Winters/Lucas, 1984. 90 minutes.

John Leslie becomes enthralled by his wife's bedtime recounting of her women's group's shared sexual fantasies. First he wants a secret tape recording; next he spies on the group from a coat closet. Unsatisfied with these results, he nags until she takes him along, all tootsied up in hat, wig, and full make-up as "Jennifer," her out-of-town cousin. Charming curiosity is the way he plays it, so you can ignore the issues of sisterhood and breach of loyalty. The women in the group won't be the only ones who get taken unawares in this encounter.

Part of the fun lies in the sense of genuine relationship between Leslie and Rachel Ashley, as a woman more than able to hold her own with an unconventional husband. Some of the sex is male centered, but we give our highest approval to the first scene between Rachel and John and Rachel's phone sex encounter with Robert Byrne. The clothes and hair, conventional for the early '80s, bothered one of our more fashion conscious WW—most of us didn't mind at all. A great couples movie.
Highly recommended.

Explicitness: 7;   Sensuality: 9   M,   2W/M

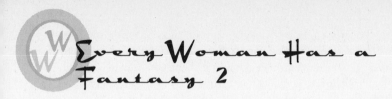

Every Woman Has a Fantasy 2

COMEDIC SEQUEL

Starring: Lois Ayers, John Leslie, Nina Hartley, Paul Thomas, Keli Richards, Karl Foxx, Troy Tanier, Misha Garr. Producer: Sandra Winters. Director: Edwin Durrell. VCA/An Edwin Durrell Film, 1986. 80 minutes.

Lois Ayers (replacing Rachel Ashley as the wife of John Leslie) arrives for a relaxing massage before a television appearance to promote her new book on fantasy. Instead of a masseuse, she finds a masseur, who reassures her with a limp flip of the wrist that he isn't into women. What a liar he turns out to be. Next we see her on television with the host and hostess of an adult cable show. As she describes the fantasy in her new book, we see it acted out by Nina Hartley et al., including a great lingerie modeling scene for fashion fans.

Then it's off to home and waiting husband John Leslie—but first the limousine driver has something not to be missed up his sleeve. In older rental videos, "the lady and the driver" limo fantasy is an outrageously sexy encounter that even those who usually don't like S/M games found tantalizing. Recently purchased copies have been trimmed. Too bad. If you can find an older copy, grab it.

This is not quite a sequel to the first one, and while we think number 1, starring the womanly Rachel Ashley, is one of the all-time best, we also **Highly recommend** 2 for both couples and solo viewing.

Explicitness: 7;   Sensuality: 8   B,   O

Every Woman Has a Fantasy 3

AND SO DOES EVERY HUSBAND

Starring: Julie Ashton, Steve Drake, Peter North, Felicia, Misty Rain, Adam Wilde, Vince Voyeur, Kia, Vanessa Chase, Amber Woods, Alec Metro, Jake Steed, Jon Dough, Candy Conners, T.T. Boy, Steve St. Croix, Melissa Hill, Jordan St. James, Gerry Pike, Ron Jeremy, Dave Cummings,

Rebecca Wild, Ariana, Tom Byron, Michael J. Cox, Krista Maze, Luscious Phillips. Pamela Santini, Sunny Day, Jack Hoffman, Adam Ant, Mack Blue. Producer: Antonion Passolini. Director: Edwin Durrell. Writers: Edwin Durrell, Oola Blume. Music: Dino Ninn. VCA Platinum, 1995.

Julie Ashton, who stars in the third video of this very successful series, is one of the most beautiful stars we've seen. For those who wonder what sort of person gets into this line of work, Julie majored in history and Spanish at Colorado State University and taught seventh- and eighth-grade Spanish (she's a certified teacher) before deciding to dance full-time, a career choice that led to making her adult movie debut in May 1994.

Every Woman Has a Fantasy 3 follows the fantasy format of the first two films, but it is not in any way a sequel. Here Alex (Ashton) and Tom (Steve Drake) have everything a young couple could wish for except a really exciting sex life. Too timid to communicate, each thinks the other isn't really interested much in sex. He has the nerve to tell her that women don't have fantasies like men, and she doesn't know how to broach the subject of what turns her on with him. To make up for what they don't get from each other, she spends her idle hours at the pool and beauty parlor dreaming up a wild assortment of mini-orgies while he visits a fantasy booth during his lunch hour to watch women masturbate and couples make love behind one-way glass.

Can this marriage be saved? The rest of the narrative revolves around how Tom and Alex, pursuing sexual fulfillment in their own individual ways, discover each other's secret lives and lose their ho-hum love life for fireworks. One Wise Woman we know who logs a lot of time at the gym preferred this to the first two vids in the series both for the sensational quality of the bodies and the freewheeling, hard-edged sex. *Best scene:* It's a tie between an orgy at the beauty parlor that could transform future haircut experiences and the great bed talk when Alex finally shares her fantasy with Tom. **Highly recommended,** especially for couples who'd like to polish their communication skills.

Explicitness: 8;   Sensuality: 7   2M/W,   O,   S/M,   T,   2W, 2W/M,   3W

Exposed

LIAR, LIAR, PANTS ON FIRE

Starring: John Leslie, Sharon Kane, George Spelvin (aka Anthony Spinelli), Kitty Shayne, Lysa Thatcher, Jon Martin, Lynn Lucas, Kelly Stuart, John Seeman, Susan Nero, Blari Harris, David Morris, Jody Miller. Producer: Wesley Emerson. Director: Jeffrey Fairbanks. Screenplay: Randy Cole. VCA, 1979. 86 minutes.

Max, a producer in trouble, needs his latest adult movie finished on schedule so he can pay a debt before some heavy guys break his legs. Alas, his film's arrogant director bullies the sensitive male star, who walks out. The movie is in the toilet . . . unless Max can persuade his old friend Willie Gordon (John Leslie) to come out of retirement for a week and make one last picture.

Willie used to be one of America's biggest male porn stars. Now, happily married to a wife he adores, Willie contentedly runs a photography business and mows his suburban lawn. Wife Annie doesn't know anything about his past, and he intends to keep it that way, even if that means letting himself get blackmailed into a lusty rough sex scene with a predatory neighbor and turning down Max's offer of $1,500 a day to star in *Cheerleaders in Bondage*.

This beguiling, sexy movie has a few flaws in the plausibility department, but for that matter so do most Hollywood romantic comedies. It makes our all-time top classics list, not least because couples actually say "I love you" during intercourse. What a novel concept. *Best scene:* Willie and Annie tenderly make love. Mighty fine.
Highly recommended.

Explicitness: 7;   Sensuality: 9   2W/M,

Extasy

ROMANTIC LEATHER DRAMA

Starring: Tifanny Million, Sarah-Jane Hamilton, Frank Towers, Steve Drake, Tom Byron, Mike Horner, Christina Angel, Gerry Pike, Will Jarvis, Davis Hardman, Kelli J. Klass, Winter Layne, Felonia, Richard Cranium, Dick Nasty, Claudio, Cherri Wellz, Gina Rome, Arnold Schwartznepecker, Rees Johnston, Warren Scott, Dalny Marga, Breanna

Malloy, Mo Rivers, Hank Rose. *Producer: Hector Castenada. Director/writer: Robert McCallum. Music: Wally Rathbone. Western Visuals Gold, 1995. 103 minutes.*

Everybody has a secret. Marissa's (Tifanny Million) is a dark and dangerous sexual past unknown to her upright lawyer husband, Wyatt. When she gets caught stealing an expensive bracelet that she could have afforded to buy, she calls on an old partner-in-sex Sarah-Jane Hamilton to help her out of the jam. Sarah-Jane, who works in a sex club, predicts that, happy marriage or not, Marissa will get into even bigger trouble if she doesn't acknowledge her real nature. She can run, but she can't hide from who she is.

Marissa tries, she really does, because she loves her husband and they have a satisfying sexual relationship. But one night when Wyatt has to work late she puts on her black leather duds and goes down to Sarah-Jane's club to have just one little submissive fling (not safe sex either). Compulsives know that one is never enough, whether it's a forbidden brownie or a fling on the dark side. Marissa takes more risks and is recognized in her leather regalia by a lawyer (Mike Horner) in her husband's firm. He snitches without a moment's hesitation and even gives Wyatt a ticket of admission to the club. Will Wyatt use it? Will Tifanny be there? Can tragedy be averted?

The industry standard is seven sex scenes per video. This movie manages eight, with sex way above average, whether it's showing the loving relationship of a married couple or the thrill of anonymous encounters (we fast-forward the scene where Tifanny squeezes milk out of her breasts, an act we hear has earth mother appeal for some men). Those huge plastic bosoms look like flotation devices, so it's a tribute to Tifanny that we find her scenes erotic anyway. **Highly recommended.**

Explicitness: 7; Sensuality: 7   C,   Lactation,   O,   S/M

OVER THE TOP COMIC FANTASY

Starring: Annette Haven, John Leslie, Sharon Adams, Seymour Fritz, Norman Hazzard, Edward Hazzard, Ingrid Jennings, Georgie Little, Andrea Parducci, Bench Parsley, Manny Street, Pepe Peru, Joe Sherman, Wilmot Waurer; with Chris Anderson, Becke Bitter, Kandi Barbour, Mary Darling, Gerlading Gold, Kassy, Rhonda Jo Petty, Laura Smith, Piper

Milk Duds™

The backlash against fake tits is here, and that's the best news we've had since we began researching WW. It will be a pleasure to look forward to more real bosoms on female talent. As far as we're concerned, fake tits are the real disgrace of the porn business

Why, you may well ask, would women choose to trade in a pair of perky, touchable, squeezeable darlings for a faux pair of plastic pop-ups that bring torpedoes to mind and approximate a halved melon? Firm, we get. But plastic? The answer from ladies who've succumbed is that, in the first place, that's what men demand, or at least that's what the industry thinks they demand. In the second place, it's just too hard to resist pressure from producers and directors who frequently foot the medical bills for implants and can withhold work if they don't like the bulk of your breasts.

The backlash is coming from more than one front. Jim Holliday now has a feature called Real TIckeTs, about stars with their original parts; Alex Jordan's production company insists on using real-breasted women only. Hallelujah, and let the mammary madness stop! Elsewhere (see the review of Voyeur 2) we've mentioned our suspicion that John Leslie is a natural-bosom man. We have no documentation to back up this pronouncement. It's just a hunch.

Here is a partial list of those souls with courageous individuality who have bravely resisted the point of the knife (for a more complete list look for the "Natural Bosom Alliance" on the Internet): Brandy Alexander, Roxanne Blaze, Christy Canyon, Nikki Dial, Debbie Diamond, Jade East, Samantha Fox, Shauna Grant, Veronica Hart, Annette Haven, Sioban Hunter, Sharon Kane, Traci Lords, Ginger Lynn, Sharon Mitchell, Tiffany Mynx, Isis Nile, Annie Sprinkle, Georgina Spelvin, Tiffany Storm.

Smith, Niki Stevens, Seka, Ray Welles. *Producers: David Frazier, Svet-lana. Director: Svetlana. Writer: David I. Frazier. Music: Ivan Claude Lewless. Gemini Film Production/Collectors Video, 1980. 80 minutes.*

F, should you be wondering as we did, is for *fantasy.* Or maybe it's not.

John Leslie, who refers to himself as the "Cannonball Express," feels henpecked and frustrated. One morning, in the middle of a fight with his wife, he storms out of the house. Leslie is a taxi driver whose vehicle has seen better days. Driving along a bucolic country road he's suddenly surprised when the voice of "dream girl" comes over the radio of his cab. She's full of dirty talk, and Cannonball, forgetting all about his marital woes, begins to perk up. In no time his cab dies in the middle of the road, forcing him to get out and fiddle under the hood in a guy kind of way. Alas, dream girl has disappeared when he returns to his seat. The fun in this film really begins when he goes to a nearby house to use the phone.

He first finds himself in a room decorated to thrill the heart of every ten-year-old girl occupied with gorgeous, life-sized dolls everywhere. Being a guy who just cannot help himself, he peeks under their skirts and discovers they look anatomically correct and, oh my, even better, they feel anatomically correct. One of the dolls manages to squeak, "Wind us up. Wind us up." In no time they have all come miraculously to life.

The decor in this high-spirited wet-dream factory is fantastical, each room more extravagant than the last. The other characters are as varied as a Chicago gangster, the Golden Girl, Cave Woman, and the Princess. Leslie visits them one by one, enjoying the exotic offering of each, heeding the philosophy offered by this rhyme:

> Run so fast, run so slow
> The clock of fate on the go
> We live our lives from chime to chime
> But escape we must from time to time.

The writing is so clever you will want to watch it again to get all the jokes. *F* has a huge cast and must have been made with an equally large budget. Our only complaint is the print we watched. The color was a little washed-out and grayish. Other than that, *F* is a real winner.
Highly recommended.

Explicitness: 7;   Sensuality: 6   M,   O,   2W

Fabulous 40's

WOMEN IN THEIR PRIME LOOKING GOOD

Starring: Jolina Mitchell, Jerilyn Walter, Claudia Gallian, Jacqui Landrum, Lillian Muller, Carol Cook, Susan Brink, Jan Steele, Roxanne Miller, Patricia Marquise and her daughter, and Victoria. Playboy.

Through luck of the genetic draw and vigilant care, these women, all in their forties, have maintained faces and bodies that Playboy graciously publishes dressed in scanty attire. They pose, talk about themselves, and play peek-a-boo with their clothes. Their jobs range from business executive to writer and construction worker. Jacqui Landrum (forty-nine) dances with her husband and partner of twenty-five years. Patricia Marquise, a travel executive, poses with her daughter, who is a Playboy model. Some of the women seem more comfortable than others, but overall this is more of an inspiration than a turn-on. It might make a motivational present for a friend facing the landmark birthday.

No sex, not even simulated.

Fanny Hill

THE ENGLISH CLASSIC VIA SWEDEN

*Starring: Diana Kjaer, Hans Ernbach, Keve Hjelm, Oscar Ljung, Tina Hedstrom, Gio Petre, Mona Seilitz, Astrid Bye. Producer: Tore Sjoberg for Minerva. 1968. Rated R. (**Swedish with subtitles.**)*

At one time, this modern-dress dramatization of the famous Victorian erotic novel *Fanny Hill* was considered hot stuff, mostly because of the videos Fanny sees when she innocently applies for a job in an upscale "massage parlour," as well as her subsequent unfettered love life. These days, it seems sweet, slow, and more dated than a historical version would have been.

Simulated

Fantasex

BOY TRYING TO BECOME A MAN

Starring: Terri Hall, Jeffrey Hurst, Jennifer Jordan, Roger Caine, Melody Gerdon, Michael Jeffries, Juliet Graham, Lyndee Mitchell, Ward Summers, Mark Ubell, Benton Gardner, Roland Reals. Directors/writers: Howard Winters, Robert Norman. Producer: Bud Green. 1976. 80 minutes.

Fantasy, in the tradition of Thurber's *Walter Mitty,* is the story line of *Fantasex.* Instead of a nagging wife, Bernie Lipschitz (Roger Caine), a quintessential nerd, is saddled with a mean, selfish mother from hell who won't let him grow up. She pesters him with directives like "Drink your milk" and "Don't play with yourself." Poor Bernie, no one else is playing with it either.

He and Miss Jane Laverne (Jennifer Jordan) are luckless souls working for a brutish, uncivilized porn publisher. Bernie uses the stories he works on as a resource for his fantasies, which involve more than the usual "in out." We particularly enjoyed his dreams of matricide reminiscent of Richard Widmark's 1947 thriller *Kiss of Death.* We wish the opening scene, a poker game for the beer and pretzels crowd in which Bernie plays Big Bart, had come later in the movie. It was so mean-spirited and ugly we almost didn't watch the rest of what turned out to be a very endearingly funny, though melancholy, film.

The reality of Bernie's life is dismal, ugly, and lonely. By contrast, his fantasies are exceptionally sweet, especially the picnic in the park and the wedding fantasy with his co-worker Jane. Each eyes the other as a love object. Will Bernie ever get the nerve to ask Jane for a date? *Fantasex* closes with the aphorism "We pass this way but once. Silence is fool's gold." If you're lonely, learn a lesson from Bernie and Jane. **Recommended.**

Explicitness: 7;   Sensuality: 8

Fantasy Booth

EXHIBITIONIST'S DELIGHT

Starring: Ona Zee, Donna Dollar, Beverly Glen, Melanie Moore, Sahara Sands, Jenna Wells, Heaven Lea, Tifanny Million, Tiffany Minx, Tammi Ann, Ted Craig, Jonathan Morgan, Mike Horner, Cody Adams, Lance Manyon, Ritchie Razor, Bobby Neuwave, Jason Rowe, Shimon Peress, Bigus Dickus, Tony Collins. Producer: Frank Zee. Director: Ona Zee. Ona Zee Productions, 1993. 82 minutes.

Fantasy booths are peep shows usually in the back of XXX-rated arcades where women perform in padded boxes with one- or two-way windows. Customers pay to have the window shade raised while women act out fantasies "just for them." (Madonna used a fabulous version of these in videos.) Ona Zee, over forty but going strong, fantasizes about her customer as he is fantasizing about her, and eventually their fantasy replaces reality. Next into the booth comes the star Donna Dollar (Tifanny Million), who, as a grand finale, squeezes milk out of her breasts. We remind you, not for the last time, about the fast-forward button on your VCR. *Best line:* shouted by Donna, who walks backstage and sees what her boyfriend/manager is doing: "How can you sleep with her? She doesn't even have a fan club." If the explicit and cheesy repel you, don't even think about this one, but on the positive side it has a welcome sense of humor, suggests an intriguing fantasy to play out at home, and provides the curious with a glimpse into an aspect of the business most will never experience first-hand.

Explicitness: 9; Sensuality: 7 A, C, Lactation

Fantasy Dancer

DATE DREAMS

Producer/director: Linda Vista. Writer: Lucy Waze. Lavender Blue Productions, 1988.

A man and a woman go to a strip club. Apparently it's their first date—she has the hunted look of a polite person who can't wait for the evening to be over. A beautiful, slim black woman dances onstage. Woman number one leaves her date, goes onstage, and makes love to

Shave and a Haircut

There is more than one way to tell the date of an often undated adult film. Classic videos from the late '60s and '70s clearly demonstrated the reason for the evolution of the slang term bush. Since, up to a point, fullness or lushness was considered desirable, we assume the need for an unobstructed close-up, as well as a move to the thong as the undergarment of choice, accounted for the fad of complete shaving that began in the late '70s and early '80s. This plucked-chicken effect is not flattering to most women, and even fans of explicitness finally realized it. By the late '80s and early '90s the total shave had given way to a kind of topiary effect for both sexes. For women, pubic hair can be clipped short, confined to a narrow tree lawn or mohawk of hair down the center of the mound, or left as a decorative tuft at the top.

We asked Nina Hartley about shaving, and she said that it probably started as a necessity because so many of the women also work as dancers in very scanty costumes. And now they like the effect of shaving because they are proud of their genitals and want to show them off. That's a positive point of view we hadn't considered.

What we had noticed is that men have been given an equal opportunity to get tidied up. No longer are the hairy backs and shaggy balls of an earlier generation welcome, though long hair to the shoulders and tasteful chest hair is still acceptable. The muscular new man is neatly groomed in his nether parts, to look both cleaner and larger. These days, complete shaving is almost always limited to the fetish films for those who enjoy watching the process take place. Go figure.

the dancer for a long time. The ending is perfunctory. Fairly primitive effort.

Explicitness: 6;   Sensuality: 6   T,   2W

Felicia

FRENCH DOMESTIC MELODRAMA

Starring: Rebecca Brooke, Beatrice Harnois, Jean Roche, Roland Charbaux, Nicole Daudet, Ray Prevet, Mariene Myller, Eva Kriss. Producer: Max Pecas. Director: Roger Michel. Writer: Max Pecas. 1976. 99 minutes. **(French with English dubbed.)**

Felicia is the house guest from hell. The bad seed all grown-up and, if not murderous, definitely noxious. An adolescent sent to Deauville (the film is set in France) to spend a few weeks with friends of her mother, Felicia is dripping with attitude and before long she complicates the lives of Paul (Jean Roche) and Gabrielle (Rebecca Brooke), an otherwise happily married couple. Behind her surly attitude and innocent look, Felicia's latent sexuality seeps out as she effectively manipulates and eventually overwhelms Paul and Gabrielle. She spies, tattles, and eventually manages to seduce them.

We had a split decision on this film. To some, Felicia's behavior seemed severely disturbed, making Paul and Gabrielle's sexual response to her appear inappropriate. To others, Felicia was an adolescent with raging, out-of-control hormones, a condition she was likely to grow out of. A few also interpreted Paul and Gabrielle's use of fantasy as a way of spicing up their marriage. Felicia's age was an issue to all of us. She is supposed to be eighteen years old but looked more like sixteen.

With one of the best developed stories we've seen, *Felicia* feels like a real film with sex of various kinds as a major element, especially the exceptional first segment. We would have preferred a subtitled version.
Recommended with caveat.

Explicitness: 7;   Sensuality: 7   S,   2W,   2W/M

The Felines

INFIDELITY A LA FRANCAIS

Starring: George Guerret, Nathalie Zeiger, Janine Reynaud, Pauline Lar-rieu, Jacques Insermi. Producer: Rene Levey-Balensi. Director: Daniel Daert. Music: Vladimir Cosma. 1975. 75 minutes.

Maude (Janine Reynaud) and Oliver (Jacques Insermi) are a very rich fiftyish couple living in Paris. Oliver, balding and full bellied, breeds horses, using them as an excuse to visit his mistress, Claire (Pauline Larrieu). Sensing that Claire would like to replace her, Maude is astute enough to know that tears, accusations, and arguments will only drive Oliver away. Accepting as fact her husband's auxiliary interest, she resourcefully manages to take and keep control of the situation she finds herself in.

While watching American erotic films at the home of a friend, Maude finds the perfect bait in the very young (can this girl be eighteen? we think not) Florence (Nathalie Zeiger). A streetwalker who's purported to have slept with everyone in Paris, Florence puts on a good semblance of innocence and purity. Determined to get even and not mad, Maude makes Florence an offer she cannot refuse: she can live with her and Oliver in their spectacular house and have access to piles of money. To answer Florence's question of what she must do in return, Maude says only, "Oliver is a charming man, isn't he?" The French have such enlightened attitudes regarding sex, don't they?

We loved the scenes of Paris and the French countryside, which are beautifully shot. The episode with a pair of Oliver's horses took us by surprise. It was refreshing to see middle-aged bodies unbuffed by weightlifting and the stairmaster having a go. Maude's clever manipulation of her husband affords a lesson in one-upwomanship to every two-timed wife.

Explicitness: 6;   Sensuality: 6

Femme

WOMEN ON THE MARCH

Starring: Tish Ambrose, Michael Knight, Sharon Kane, Klaus Multia, Carol Cross, George Payne, Rhonda Jo Petty, Jerry Butler, David Israel-Sandler. Producer/writer: Candida Royalle. Director: Lauren Niemi. Saga Films ab/Lunarex Ltd./Femme Prod.

Here are vignettes made specifically with women's fantasies in mind: rock star and fan, TV idol and viewer, gallery viewer with two men, home cosmetics saleslady and customer, and maid in a dressing room. Our favorite is Rhonda Jo Petty as the business-suited cosmetics saleswoman with Sharon Kane as her mesmerized customer. Very cool. The conversation is minimal to none—these women get right down to business, though, since this movie is made by a woman for women, they do it with a twist. There's a lot of foreplay, the camera doesn't linger on the genitals in gynecological detail, and for a welcome change there are no external come shots. The sex is naturalistic, not the acrobatic display of positions favored by most erotic videos, which tend to be shot for camera angles, realism be damned.

This is the first movie produced and directed by Candida Royalle, and her company shares the name, Femme. They were still learning their stuff on this video, but for anyone interested in women and erotica it's **Recommended.**

Explicitness: 7;   Sensuality: 7   2W

Firestorm

ROMANTIC MELODRAMA

Starring: Victoria Jackson, Eric Edwards, Kay Parker, John Leslie, Sharon Mitchell, Sharon Kain, Rikki Harte, Sean Elliot, Michael Brice, George Payne, Veronica Hart, Kurt Mann, Adam DeHaven, Allison Royce, Ward Summers, Bran Arnold, Lilah Glass, Joanna Storm. Producer/director: Cecil Howard. Writer: Anne Randall. Music: Peter Lewis, Dave Ogrin. Comand Video/A Cecil Howard Film, 1983. 104 minutes. (**Shot on film.**)

The very rich, bitchy, and morally challenged Mrs. Magda Balcourt (Kay Parker) has invited hack writer Kenneth Cushing (Eric Edwards) to move into her mansion to write her life story. Estranged from her philandering husband, Lee (John Leslie), whose bedroom is on the other end of the house from hers, Mrs. Balcourt's real agenda is to seduce Ken as an act of revenge. Also part of the household is Magda and Lee's young daughter, Claire. She tragically lost her sight on her sixteenth birthday when she caught her fiancé and her mother flagrante delicto. Jealous, controlling, competitive, ruthless Magda goes into a rage when she discovers that Ken and Claire have fallen in love. The lovers at first escape, but the heartless Magda is determined to have her way and manages to shatter Claire's chance for happiness.

Complex and unpredictable, *Firestorm* tells a fully developed story of revenge and malice. The sex isn't routine, and we were grateful that the camera didn't focus its unblinking eye on genitalia. Outstanding performances by a stellar cast, excellent character development by writer Anne Randall, and a budget that allowed for a variety of settings and good production values raise *Firestorm* above the ranks of just a sex video. **Recommended.** (See the review of *Firestorm 2*. A third sequel has been made, but unfortunately it seems to be out of circulation and we haven't had the opportunity to review it.)

Explicitness: 7;   Sensuality: 6   M/2W

Firestorm 2

FATHER DOESN'T KNOW A THING

Starring: John Leslie, Rene Summers, Eric Edwards, Ali Moore, Rhonda Jo Petty, Michael Gaunt, Paul Thomas, Sharon Kane, Ron Jeremy, Tiffany Clark, Sonia Hio, Joanna Storm, Rikki Hart, Tish Ambrose. Producer/director: Cecil Howard. Comand Video, 1987.

Firestorm 2 doesn't make much sense without *Firestorm*, so we recommend that you begin with the first in this series of three videos. The action has moved to New York City, where Ken (played by Eric Edwards again) is broke, having squandered his ill-gotten gain in record time. Claire (Rene Summers, who was at one time, and may still be, married to Eric Edwards) has disappeared, and dear old Dad Lee (John Leslie), has just been sprung from the slammer with the help of some unsavory Arab oil sheiks to whom he is now indebted. Lee, whose fortune Claire inherited after her mother's death, hires a private eye recommended to him by cellmate Johnny the Biscuit to find Claire. You might guess that his quest isn't simply paternal.

In spite of time spent behind bars, Lee hasn't lost his touch with the ladies, financial problems and all. Sex, money, sex, family values, and sex all contribute to moving the story along to an inconclusive finish. As hard as we looked, we couldn't lay our hands on *Firestorm 3,* though we believe it's out there someplace. We want to know what happens next—which earns a **Recommended** for this complicated tale of intrigue.

Explicitness: 7;   Sensuality: 6   2W

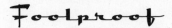

HARD-BOILED PRIVATE DICK

Starring: Brittany O'Connell, Leena, Randy West, Sahara Sands, Tony Tedeschi, Deborah Wells, Kitty Yung, Sierra, Peter North, Steve Drake, E. Z. Ryder. Producer: R. C. White. Director: Stuart Canterbury. Music: G. G. Steel. Writer: Nigel Crinch Gibbons. VCA Platinum/Angel International Films, 1994.

Meet private eye Tony Tedeschi in a moody story about a violent man (Randy West) who is convinced his wife is a two-timer and hires Tony to get the goods on her. Tony finds no supporting evidence and tells the man his wife is true blue, expecting him to pleased. Wrong. It's up to Tony to find proof of her guilt or *he* is in trouble. So the pliable Tony, rationalizing the wife would be better off without her creepy husband, sets about his assignment. Meanwhile . . . The plot provides plenty of surprises. What it lacks is a sense of connection between any of the unlikable characters. There's no one to care about, no one to root for, and the sex lacks heat or passion. The video is recommended for couples on several lists, possibly because the wife gets her innings, but we yawned our way through it.

Explicitness: 8;   Sensuality: 6   A,   2W

Forever Young

FUTURISTIC DRAMA

Starring: Asia Carrera (top billing), Nick East, Hypatia Lee, Tina Tyler, Easy Ryder, Brooke Waters, Valeria, Grey Waters, Marc Wallice. Producer: Paul Thomas. Director: Austin Ellison. Writers: Austin Ellison, Will Green. Vivid, 1994. 80 minutes.

We couldn't decide if this was a spoof of *The Picture of Dorian Grey* or a testimonial for rolfing. As hard as we tried, we found it difficult to follow the plot twists and turns of this video. The very rich and successful Easy Ryder has no joy in his life and cannot abide the thought of his aging body and declining sexual appetite. A mere $12 million, chicken feed to a corporate raider, will get him an experimental procedure involving the breaking of his bones and a new body. The procedure turns him into the attractive and virile Nick East, who has plenty of opportunity but little enthusiasm for sex. With the exception of a highly erotic tub scene, Asia Carrera's performance as the new love interest lacks her usual seductiveness. Throughout the video Nick has dreams of his old and new self tied together trying to free themselves of each other, until in the final shot when he's able to jettison his old body. At last he's ready to face his new life.

Explicitness: 9;   Sensuality: 5 (except for the tub scene which we rate 8)   A,   M,   O

Foxtrot

STARTING THE NEW YEAR RIGHT

Starring: Marlene Willoughby, Samantha Fox, Veronica Hart, Vanessa Del Rio, Merle Michaels, Sharon Mitchell, Tiffany Clark, Linda Vale, Sandra Hillman, Marissa Constantine, Bobby Astyr, Jake Teague, Richard Bolla, Ron Jeremy, David Morris. Producer/director: Cecil Howard. Writer: Ann Randall. Original music: Peter Lewis. Command Video, 1982. 92 minutes.

How about some good clean sex on your washing machine to take advantage of the vibrating spin cycle? This is just one of a number of unusual tricks in *Foxtrot*.

It's New Year's Eve in the inarguably most decadent cities in America—New York, Beverly Hills, and San Francisco—and everyone is getting ready for the big celebration. The Hollywood producer, who seems to be taking his cues from the youthful Roman Polanski, manages to spend the entire day in bed amusing himself with a variety of women who come to minister to his assorted appetites while his entire household is getting ready for the big bash. In San Francisco, a returning sailor (Ron Jeremy) discovers that the "good" girl he's idealized has an unexpected surprise for him. And in New York the young woman treats the married voyeur across the street to an indiscreet display of her endowments and appetites.

One of the appeals of *Foxtrot* is the variety of ages represented by the characters—from a young college student to a man past middle age. Those who have pushed the envelope of sixty will be inspired. And the sex talk is original and playful.
Recommended.

Explicitness: 9; Sensuality: 6 A, M, 2M/W, O, 2W, 2W/M

The Goddaughter, Part 1

SPOILED GIRL JOINS FAMILY BUSINESS TO SAVE DADDY

Starring: Cameo, Joey Silvera, Randy West, Mark Wallice, Nick Knight, Alicyn Sterling, Summer Knight, Stacey Nichols, Dominique Simone, Taylor Wane, Leanna Foxxx, Jacqueline, Ron Jeremy, Mickey Ray, Fred Lincoln (as Don Genardi). Producer: Jerry Dawson. Director: Fred Lincoln. Writer: Patti Rhodes. Music: Jimmy Mack. AFV, 1994.

Italian Don Genardi's daughter Theresa (Cameo) keeps fooling around with the wrong guys, and after Guiseppe (Joey Silvera) blows one of them away the Don sends both Guiseppe and Theresa to America to keep them out of trouble. The spoiled Theresa is so angry with Guiseppe that she spends most of her time trying to annoy him, even when it involves putting herself in danger. Meanwhile, the Don knows that his olive oil company is in trouble, and he warns Guiseppe that American tough guy Victor del Vecchio (Randy West) is trying to take over by setting him up. Not coincidentally, Victor happens to be Theresa's new flame. The plot, production values, and acting are above average; there's some violence, unusual for these videos though hardly noteworthy by network TV standards. If you don't have the time or interest for both, then we suggest you skip directly to part 2; part 1 leaves you hanging in the middle of a story.

Explicitness: 7;   Sensuality: 7   A,   3M/W,   2W

The Goddaughter, Part 2

THE SAGA CONTINUES

Starring: Cameo, Joey Silvera, Dominique, Derex Lane, Devonshire, Randy West, Taylor Wayne, Steve Drake, Michy Ray, Ron Jeremy, Fred Lincoln. Producer: Jerry Dawson. Director: Fred Lincoln. Writer: Patti Rhodes. AFV, 1994. 80 minutes.

Part 2 opens with Theresa back in Italy telling her father she has to return to America. She walks in on Victor del Vecchio (Randy West) as he's showing off for his poker buddies by making it with a call girl. Theresa is cool. She tells Victor that boys will be boys and he should get himself tested before he expects to spend any time in her bed. Then she plants a bug in his car. She and Guiseppe (Joey Silvera) have a common goal at last—to turn the tables on Victor and save Don Genardi's olive oil business.

The box promises that these movies were shot on location in Rome, and probably two scenes were, both of which coincidentally feature the director, Fred Lincoln, playing Don Genardi. At least some of the scenes under the credits are of Florence, not Rome. Other than that, most of the action happens in the United States or indoors on sets. We wouldn't pick on the filmmakers for their mild deception if they hadn't advertised something they didn't deliver. If you're going to rent only one, make it part 2, since it begins with enough background information to follow the plot. *Best scene:* Randy West gets his, in more ways than one, from a female assassin with a wicked sense of humor. (Clearly we have a double standard operating here, since if the scene had happened the other way around we would have raised the roof about violence. We'll try to be better.)

Overall, this is an expensively mounted production, and while we felt cutting it to fit into one video would be an improvement, it's still **Recommended.**

Explicitness: 7;   Sensuality: 7   A,   3M/W,   2W

Goin' Down Slow

IT'S THE THOUGHT THAT COUNTS

Starring: Shanna McCullough, Ona Zee, Robert Bullock, Joey Silvera, John Leslie, Kathleen Jentry, Alicia Monet, Megan Leigh, Richard Pacheco, Peter North, Tom Byron. Producer/director/writer: John Leslie. Music: Bill Heid. VCA, 1988. 85 minutes.

A woman, played by Ona Zee, masturbates while peering through the blinds at her neighbor's lovemaking. She knows the man isn't the neighbor's husband. Should she tell? And more important, if she does tell, can she seduce this man herself? Such a difficult dilemma deserves the best advice, and she decides to write to none other than Madame Rona, an Agony Aunt at a magazine. When Madame Rona—who happens to be Robert Bullock, not a woman—gets the letter, he laughs at the snoopy Ona, not realizing that his wife, Shanna, is the neighbor being watched. His involvement with his secretary and dissatisfaction with his career blinds him to his wife's activities. Soon enough, light dawns, but his wife defiantly refuses to tell him anything. A tragedy is set in motion, though tragedy implies we care what happens to any of these narcissistic characters.

There is relatively little sex here, and what we do see doesn't make us want to see more. At least one scene (our guess is marital rape) was cut from the version we viewed. The redeeming quality is the great bluesy score, way above average for these movies.

Explicitness: 7; Sensuality: 6 M

The Grafenberg Spot

ANTIC "HOW TO" SPOOF

Starring: Ginger Lynn, Harry Reams, Annette Haven, Amber Lynn, Traci Lords, Nina Hartley, John Holmes, Lili Marlene, Rick Savage, Rita Erotica, Thor Southern. Producer/director: Mitchell Brothers. 1985. 79 minutes.

Ginger Lynn has a little problem. At times of great excitement, spurts of liquid gush from her vagina. Unfortunately, the love of her

Kegel Exercises

You probably already know where your pc muscles are, even if you don't know what they are. If you don't, you can locate them by squeezing while you are urinating. When you stop and start your pee you've got your pc's. Now take that movement out of the bathroom and do the exercise recommended by Dr. Kegel (and named after him, lucky fellow). Squeeze, relax. Squeeze, relax. That's all there is to it. You want to do about one hundred repetitions every day of your life. Do them in groups of ten, in time to your favorite song, whatever makes it easy. Fitting them into your exercise regime shouldn't be much of a problem since you can invisibly improve your sex life while you're running a board meeting, driving a carpool full of Little Leaguers, or watching a video. No one will know what you're doing, and if your activity puts an enigmatic smile on your face, it will only add to your charm.

These muscles are useful for giving the big hello to a penis during intercourse and toning up your vagina after childbirth. And if that isn't enough reason to rev up your exercises, consider the news that well-exercised pc muscles can keep you out of those waterproof panties for seniors that June Allyson pushes on late-night television. Are we motivated or what?

life, Harry Reams, finds it disconcerting to have pee in his face during oral sex. He cannot woo such a wet woman.

Ginger seeks advice from doctor and sex specialist Annette Haven, who explains that it isn't pee at all, it's the magic of female ejaculation. In support of this she graphically demonstrates how to find and what to do with the G-, or Grafenberg, spot, which causes such extraordinary orgasms. (The explanation differs somewhat from the one you'll hear in *The Magic of Female Ejaculation,* in the section "Instructional Videos," but the method of stimulation is essentially the same.)

Three things we found especially welcome about the video are a sense of humor instead of another earnest demonstration, a glimpse of the amazing John Holmes doing his fourteen-inch thing in Ginger's fantasy, and the opportunity for women to give men a "facial" for a change. Quite a turn-on, isn't it fellows? Lest you feel challenged by the deluge these women produce, the Mitchell brothers included some sly outtakes at the end that clue you in to yet another use for the Kegel exercise.

Recommended.

Explicitness: 7;   Sensuality: 7   W/2M

Great Sexpectations

CUPID STRIKES AGAIN

Starring: Kelly Nichols, Eric Edwards, Honey Wilder, R. Bolla, Chelsea Blake, Joanna Storm, Rene Summers, Tanya Lawson, George Payne, Jerry Butler, Silver Star, Dick Howard, John Leslie. Producer: David Stone. Writer/director: Henry Pachard. Music: Ian Shaw. VCA, 1984. 85 minutes.

Though billed as a sequel to *Sexcapades,* you don't have to have seen that movie to enjoy this one. The only link between the two is a lighthearted point of view and Harry Crocker (played by the preppy-looking Eric Edwards), for a brief glorious moment a legit director but now unhappily returned to his roots in erotic films to make much needed dollars.

R. Bolla, our favorite diamond in the rough, plays a producer with a script for Harry. Honey Wilder is Bolla's wife, Charger, whose job is auditioning prospective male stars in front of her husband. He pragmatically says that any actor who can keep an erection with Charger while he watches them won't have problems getting wood on camera.

The movie being made has a large cast and a crew that includes

"fluffers," whose oral attentions to the male performers guarantee wood on cue. Harry marinates himself with vodka and closely directs every scene until his beautiful and notoriously strong-minded star Marilyn Camp (Kelly Nichols) tells him that she and John Leslie, "the Big Drill," will improvise their lovemaking. It's superb, which leaves Harry more upset and confused than ever. Could he be falling in love with his star? Not quite as sprightly as *Sexcapades,* and the script reflects Harry's ambivalence about the business, but for us relationships always carry the day.
Highly recommended.

Explicitness: 8;   Sensuality: 7   A,   2W

Heaven's Touch

AN ANGEL'S WORK IS NEVER DONE

Starring: Sharon Kane, Kelly Nichols, Joanna Storm, Michael Knight, Gayle Sterling, Ron Jeremy. Producer/director: Warren Evans. Caballero, 1983.

Shy, handsome Henry Artinger (Michael Knight) doesn't drink, smoke, or gamble, so his oafish office supervisor decides his vice must be women. In a spirit of fraternity-house mischief he spreads the word that "Mr. Artinger has ten inches. It's always the quiet ones." Three pretty office workers waylay Mr. A in the Xerox copy room, determined to check his measurements for themselves. He's showing them a fine time when he suddenly pulls a John Garfield. Henry is on his way to heaven.

Unfortunately, a mistake has been made. Henry wasn't scheduled to die for many years, and at his insistence ("Do the words *you're not being a very good sport* mean anything to you?") a new body will be found. Until then, his spirit must be parked in a temporary accommodation—coincidentally the body of the owner of Armstrong Industries, the very company where Henry worked as an accountant.

The body is available because Barry Armstrong's wife (Sharon Kane) and her lover (Ron Jeremy) have just succeeded in killing him with kindness. It seems that Barry had a weak heart, and the two schemers did him in with a surfeit of exciting sex. With Henry residing in Barry's body, however, they don't know they succeeded, and they escalate their efforts. If all this sounds vaguely familiar, you probably saw *Here Comes Mr. Jordan* or the 1978 remake, *Heaven Can Wait.*

Michael Knight is good-looking in an early Christopher Reeve way, but he certainly wasn't cast for his acting ability. On the other hand, acting may not be the primary consideration here—we give high marks to his fling with Joanna Storm and the hot and heavy scene with Sharon Kane. A more than satisfactory diversion. **Recommended.**

Explicitness: 7;   Sensuality: 7   O,   3W/M

Hidden Obsession

ANDREW BLAKE AT HIS BEST

Starring: Janine Lindemulder, Heather Hart, Julia Ann, Francesca Le, P.J. Sparxx, Kym Wilde, Peter North, Randy West, Celeste, Woody Long, Tracy West, Steve Drake, Paula Price, Diedre Holland, John Dough, Melanie Moore, Neck E, Sheila Stone, Marissa Malibu, Sunset Thomas, Dominique Simon, Laurel Canyon, Bruce Gates, John Lee. Producer/director: Andrew Blake. Ultimate Video, 1992. 90 minutes.

Moonlighting for a friend of her agent as an erotic story writer, fashion magazine writer, and sometime Penthouse Pet Janine Lindemulder cooks up twelve sometimes-sparkling, sometimes-unzipped and wild erotic stories of varying lengths and degrees of success. A dildo formed of ice, shaving, strap-ons, whips, and light spanking are among the toys and techniques employed toward achieving sexual ecstasy.

The third story wins the prize for ingenuity and the eighth for a high sensuous charge, and the last includes a multiracial couple. The sights and sounds are quintessential Andrew Blake, though the intercutting distracts the viewers from the erotic charge. A little extended focus on one scene and fewer stories would have made this a more effective video, but as it is, it offers plenty of variety and top-of-the-line bodies and clothes. There's food for fantasies here; better with a partner so you can create your own heat. For that purpose, **Highly recommended.**

Explicitness: 7;   Sensuality: 6 (except for stories 3 and 8, which we rate 8)   B,   M,   O,   S (light),   T,   2W

History of the Blue Movie

FILM HISTORY 101

Produced and directed by Alex de Renzy. A Screening Room Production. California Video Distributors, 1970.

In case you're wondering, the oldest erotic video available is *A Free Ride*, made in 1915. The first customers were rich people and expensive brothels, since in the '20s in Paris a ticket to one of these short films could cost as much as $20 (that's over $100 in today's money). These and other facts link film clips from dozens of old movies, including "keyhole portraits" from the '20s and '30s stag parties, animated cartoons, and famous strippers from the '50s preening and posing. As the decades progress toward the freedom of the "sexual revolution" of the '60s, you'll also notice the changing fashions in female nudes and nudity (or lack thereof) and an almost sociological demonstration of the shifts in our public attitudes toward sex. Erotic? No. Entertaining? Absolutely.

Explicitness: 7

Honey

ITALIAN DRAMATIC FANTASY

Starring: Clio Goldsmith, Catherine Spaak, Fernando Rey, Susan Scott, Donatella Damiani, Lino Troisi, Adriana Russo, Pino Pennese, Francisca Fernandez, Lucy Merenda. Producer: Toni Di Carlo. Director: Gianfranco Angelucci. Story: Gianfranco Angelucci, Liliana Betti. Screenplay: Enrique U. Herrera. Music: Riz Ortolani. Vestron Video/Vogue Film, 1981. 89 minutes. **(Italian and Spanish coproduction, dubbed in English.)**

The industry most frequently explored in adult videos is the so-called sex industry itself. The second most frequently explored seems to be book publishing. In *Honey,* a beautiful, elegantly dressed woman bursts in on a publisher and demands at gunpoint that he read her manuscript out loud. Now! (Many would-be writers have had this fantasy.) It's the story of Annie's (Clio Goldsmith) adventures, sexual and

Ziplow's Law

In his 1977 Film Maker's Guide to Pornography, *Stephen Ziplow provided the seven-ingredient recipe he considered de rigueur for an adult movie. It's ironic that an industry that's supposed to be devoted to breaking rules sticks to them so fervently. All these practices were regularly included in the 8-mm loops. What changed with the advent of "narrative" pornography is that the 70-plus-minute length gave filmmakers the opportunity to include them all.*

1. Masturbation: by women, with or without toys. These almost always employ in-your-face close-ups of genitalia.
2. Straight sex: or the old "in-out." Positions included are missionary, woman on top, doggy, side to side, and so on.
3. Lesbianism: or g/g for shorthand. Ziplow doesn't say much about this ingredient. We assume it's included in the service of male fantasy.
4. Oral Sex: both fellatio and cunnilingus.
5. Menage a trois: a threesome, most frequently interpreted as two women and one man, frequently subsequent to the g/g. Occasionally, one woman is used to service two men, although the two men barely acknowledge each other's presence.
6. Orgies: a lot of cavorting naked bodies. Because these scenes are expensive (everyone has to be paid, after all), they're frequently not included.
7. Anal sex: controversial to women and in the age of AIDS.

otherwise, in a darkly lit and moody Italian *pensionne* in what looked to us like Milan. Annie is in no rush to leave the *pensionne* in search of the hidden treasures of Italy. Instead she interacts with the others—guests and staff—who include the patronne; her sister, the peeping maid; a dance student and her teacher; a yogi, and a female cleric determined to help Clio overcome the flesh through humiliation.

Moods shift from the erotic to the sensuous to the sadomasochistic as the unexpected ending results in uncorked champagne and everyone's satisfaction. **Recommended.**

Simulated

Hot Dallas Nights

LONE STAR LOONIES

Starring: Hillary Summers, Raven Turner, Tara Flynn, Alexander Kingsford, R. J. Reynolds, Slim Grady, Turk Lyon, Greer Shapiro (as Miss Millie). Producers: Julian Dynski, Vivian O'Dell. Director: Tony Kendrick. Writers: Robert Oakwood, Tony Kendrick. Music: Leonard Conjurski; orchestrated by B. J. White. VCX/Miracle Films Release, 1983.

In 1982, when this spoof was made, the sexy soapy TV show *Dallas* topped the ratings. All the familiar South Fork figures appear in new guises, as two generations of the Brewing family—incredibly rich, totally dysfunctional, and inexplicably living under one roof. Instead of oil, this family has a fertilizer business and plots to corner the local manure supply. Enough said about that.

We fancied the cute cowpoke Duke, who, interrupted in his trysts, makes do with a chicken (off camera) until the last reel. The whole movie strikes that broad note, but it's good-natured fun, the women come out of it OK, and we preferred this ending to that of the original—the two sisters-in-law (with double-headed dildo) move into the same room, a twist that never made it into the doings at South Fork. The last word is Mama's: "Well I don't know what's going on up there but somebody's stolen all our bananas." If you aren't old enough to remember the prototype, you'll probably find this inexplicably silly stuff. **Recommended for nostalgic laughs.**

Explicitness: 8;   Sensuality: 6   S/M,   T,   2W

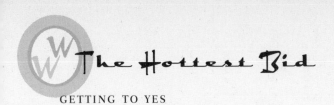
The Hottest Bid

GETTING TO YES

Starring: Gwen Somers, Dennis Mathews, Lenore Andriel, Tracy Miller, Belinda Farrell. Director: Debrah Shames. Producer: Lynn Larkin (for Dumar Enterprises). Writer: Udana Power. Music: Maria Muldaur. Sexuality consultant: Lonnie Barbach.

> "A romantic plunge into eroticism . . . a sensual delight" *Patti Britton Ph.D., couples' therapist;* "Turns up the heat, but delivers humor and heart as well" *Donald Liebenson, film credit*

Jessica and Marty, two lawyers who work in the same office, are on their way to a black-tie charity auction at which women will bid for dates with eligible men. Marty makes his best friend, Jessica, promise she'll bid up to $300 for him. She does, but allows the sweetly aggressive Angelique to win while she, wounded in love relationships, bids $550 for a walk and picnic with an appealing dog who goes for the highest bid of the evening. A lighthearted look at sex and love in the '90s—including tantric sex, massage, and the classic line "We've got to get you out of these wet clothes."

When Jessica's whining grates on your last nerve, you can concentrate on the scenic San Francisco backgrounds—Mt. Tamalpais, the Fairmont Hotel, Muir Woods—and the sight of shy, slightly passive Marty in the grips of the determined Angelique. Director Debrah Shames excels at romantic situations, fantasy, and foreplay and leaves the actual sex somewhat to the viewers' imaginations, which makes this a good choice for newcomers to the erotic video scene. Mature viewers take note: Maria Muldaur ("Midnight at the Oasis," etc.) has done the sound track, which puts this, like all Shames's films, way above average musically speaking. *Fashion alert*: Women who feel too thigh challenged to get into sexy underwear, check out the bustier-floating panel skirt worn in the mountaintop fantasy. Look and learn. **Highly recommended.**

Simulated

House of Dreams

HARD-EDGED BLAKE

Starring: Ashlyn Gere, Jeanna Fine, Raven, Veronica Dol, Saber, Randy West, Danielle Rogers, Sebastian, Valerie Stone, Nicole Wild, Randy Spears, Kristen, Rocco Sifreddi, (introducing) Zara Whites. Director: Andrew Blake. Caballero Home Video, 1990. 80 minutes.

Zara Whites, a slim-legged, pouty-lipped *Vogue* confection, sleeps in a white-walled *Architectural Digest* beach house and has an out-of-body *Playboy* dream with mysterious strangers. There's no dialogue, just music, and Blake's detached balletic couplings have a way of turning kinky S/M toys such as ball gags into pretty props.

It's no accident that we think of glossy magazines when we see an Andrew Blake film, since he was a painter and photographer before he created the eight erotic features that have enormously influenced contemporary adult movies. He makes sex as tantalizingly irresistible as one of those perfect dinner tables in *Gourmet*—you know yours will never look quite that good but you'll want to give it a try.

Suzie Bright, one of our favorite writers on women's sexuality, watched this video during an interview with Blake and asked him about it and others of his films. He said that he makes the men as faceless as possible because he prefers looking at women. He sees the men as "props, furniture." This may account for our split opinion on Blake. His movies look good, offer a tease, but some of us prefer more sweat and story. You'll never know until you watch for yourself. If you've yet to sample a Blake, you'll find a complete list in the "Index of Videos by Category." Many writers pick this as the top Blake. Our vote for the two best are *Hidden Obsession* and *Sensual Exposure*. Maybe it depends on which one you see first.
Recommended.

Explicitness: 8;   Sensuality: 7   B,   M,   3W

The Hunger

PARK AVENUE VAMPIRES

Starring: Catherine Deneuve, Susan Sarandon, David Bowie, Cliff de Young. Producer: Richard Shepherd. Director: Tony Scott. Writers: Ivan Davis, Michael Thomas, from a novel by Whitley Strieber. Music: Michael Rubini, Denny Jaeger. MGM-UA, 1983. 99 minutes.

Take note the next time your honey sends the oysters back and orders barely cooked steak. You may have a nascent vampire on your hands. Cool, flashy, and atmospheric, *The Hunger* is a vampire movie wrapped in a pseudoscience concept about tampering with the human biological clock. Miriam and John (Catherine Deneuve and David Bowie) are centuries-old vampires haunting their Manhattan neighborhood for victims, shoving their skeletons into the basement furnace after draining them dry. When John's clock runs out, Sarah Roberts (Susan Sarandon) becomes Miriam's unwitting sexual and gustatory victim. Miriam's seduction of Sarah in a toothsome lesbian scene is what made *The Hunger* a modern gothic classic. We would have thought that by now vampires would know enough to hang out in blood banks or maybe form a twelve-step group to get over their addiction, but then we wouldn't have this tony remake of *Dracula*.

Highly stylized production design (which makes great use of a sparsely but elegantly furnished apartment lit in a smoky blue), great clothes by Milena Canonero, not to mention the brilliant make-up job on Bowie, have all contributed to making *The Hunger* a perennial favorite.

Simulated

Immortal Desire

NEW-AGE DRIVEL

Starring: Sarah Jane Hamilton, Gerald Pike, Debi Diamond, Brad Armstrong, Angela Baron, Dyanna Lauren, Colt Steele, Celeste, Serenity, Lady Paree (as the Voodoo princess), P.J. Sparxx, Serenity Wilde, Diva Sasha Savage, Paree, Tony Tedeschi, Alex Sanders, Lana Sands, Tony Marito. Producer: Jonathan Moore. Director: Philip Christian. Music: Saint. A Philip Christian Film, in association with Vivid Images, 1993. 85 minutes.

Joyous Sex Between Consenting Adults

Established in 1970 by Phil Harvey, a graduate (in Slavic studies) of Exeter and Harvard who did a stint in the Peace Corps in Pakistan, PHE is the premier provider of adult videos through mail order. It started as a mail-order source for condoms, a very advanced outlook twenty-six years ago, when acting responsibly regarding birth control, not to mention venereal disease, was considered the obligation of women. Being young and a touch rebellious, Harvey found himself breaking the laws of municipalities, like the entire state of Utah, where community standards did not support condom sales. Committed to promoting what Bernie Oakley, director of new business development calls "joyous sex between consenting adults," their product lines now include, besides videos, toys, books, and aids of various kinds. The business is now owned by about fifteen stockholders, all of whom are long-time employees.

A full-service source, PHE publishes various catalogs for its diverse markets. Adam and Eve specializes in tapes, toys, books, and condoms. For you World Wide Web surfers, Adam and Eve can be reached online at http://www.aeonline.com. PHE also has two video clubs (Video Mail and Video Gold Club), as well as two newsletters (Private Lives answers questions from cus-

If you're not old enough to have missed the psychedelic images of the '60s and '70s, *Immortal Desire* will take you on a trip to the dark side of Voodoo, psychedelics with hallucinogenic nightmares and magic potions. In their quest for immortality, Sarah Jane Hamilton and Gerald Pike make a deal with Voodoo princess Lady Paree. Things don't work out as planned, and the pair is fated to a perpetual search for true love, taking them from 1692 Salem to Verdun during World

tomers, and *Sex Over 40* gives info on just that). *For more information on how to get PHE's various catalogs, see the listing in the mail-order section at the back of the book.*

Each tape considered for inclusion in one of PHE's catalogs is vetted first in an internal review process, and those that pass are sent to independent sex therapists, whose OK PHE must have before adding a video to their inventory. The role of therapists is to check for prurient interest (pedophilia, incest, rape, violence, etc.) and to determine if videos have any value. House of Dreams, for instance, cannot be sold in its original form. One of the actresses has a red ball gag in her mouth, making it impossible for her to say "Stop." Raunch is not one of the aspects the therapists consider. Frequently, PHE will excise the offending portion of videos to meet their standards or to make them cable-ready for Adam and Eve channels.

Headquartered in the heart of Jesse Helms country near Chapel Hill, North Carolina, because that's where Mr. Harvey happened to go to graduate school, PHE employs three hundred people, is open twenty-four hours a day, and ships over twenty million catalogs a year. Their internal demographic research reveals that their customer is educated, white-collar worker, married, twenty-five to forty-five years old, and 80 percent straight male.

In addition to supplying videos through the mail, PHE will sometimes fund productions, as they have done in the case of Dinner Party *and* My Surrender, *both of which you'll find reviewed in this book.*

War I to contemporary Los Angeles. The story, though, is even less relevant than in most erotic videos. It's the shifting time periods, exotic costumes, and all the talk about sorcery and potions that make it work. *Immortal Desire* could be just what you're looking for to spice up your next Halloween party.

Explicitness: 7;   Sensuality: 7

In Love

TWENTY YEAR CHASE

Starring: Kelly Nichols, Jerry Butler, Jack Wrangler, Tish Ambrose, Joanna Storm, Samantha Fox, Michael Knight, Susan Nero, Beth Allison Broderick, Will Pendelton. Producer/director: Chuck Vincent. Writer: Henry Pachard. Music: Ian Shaw. VCA, 1983. 83 minutes.

A big-budget saga of love found and lost that covers the span of twenty years, *In Love* tries hard to be a great erotic movie but doesn't quite make it for us. Andy (Jerry Butler) meets Jill (Kelly Nichols) while on a business trip to Florida. He's married, she's not, and after a weekend of high romantic assignations, Andy leaves for home without Jill. He says he wants to come back for her; she says No, definitely not. That's what happens in 1962. Their brief encounter becomes a twenty-year obsession in which Andy's rise and fall and rise in his business life, the collapse of his marriage, and his yearning for Jill is chronicled—in between affairs with other ladies here and there. Jill's adventures in communes as a hippie and success as a famous writer is counterpoint to Andy's story. Every once in a while he catches a glimpse of Jill but never seems to quite catch her. All the major cultural upheavals between 1962 and 1983 are incorporated into the scenario, and while *In Love* is a noble attempt to make an erotic movie look and act like a feature release, it fails on several counts, not the least of which are tedious writing and unsympathetic characters.

Explicitness: 6; Sensuality: 6 O

In the Realm of the Senses

CLASSIC MASTERPIECE

Starring: Tatsuya Fuji, Elko Matsuda. Producer: Anatole Dauman. Director/writer: Nogise Oshima. Oshima Productions (Tokyo), Argos Films (Paris), distributed by Fox/Lorber Home Video. Banned at the 1976 New York Film Festival.

A young woman, formerly a prostitute, enters a respectable household as a servant. Soon she and the master of the house are engaged in a seduction that quickly turns into passionate obsession. Set in

Tokyo in 1936 and based on real events, the film is ravishing—elegant, well acted, and thought provoking. Not only are the actors exquisite and the lighting and settings beautifully rendered, but the explicit lovemaking is photographed so artfully that even the close-ups of genitals look like paintings.

We recommend it, in fact we urge you to see it, though possibly not as prelude to a loving evening. The erotic strangulation technique employed is extremely dangerous, and the bloody ending left the squeamish among us reaching for the fast-forward button.
Highly recommended.

Explicitness: 7;   Sensuality: 8   A,   T,   3W

Insatiable

STYLISH SEDUCTRESS

Starring: Marilyn Chambers, Jesie St. James, Serena, John Leslie, Robert Pennard, David Morris, Richard Pacheco, Mike Ranger, Joan Turner; special guest star, John C. Holmes. Producer/director: Godfrey Daniels. Writer: Daniel Short. Music producer/arranger: Don G. Sciarrota, Dennis C. Nickols. Songs sung by Marilyn Chambers, Katch Phillips, Wendy Yergin, Chris Sciarrotta. Caballero, 1980. 80 minutes.

After her appearance in *Behind the Green Door* and the revelation that she modeled for the photograph of the young mother on the Ivory Snow box, Marilyn Chambers became an instant legend in erotic videos. Her movie persona reflected the personal one she revealed in interviews, a woman whose sexual desires were insatiable and sometimes masochistic, who didn't lose control so much as briefly give it up for her own gratification.

Here she plays Sondra Chase, a world-famous model, movie star, and sexual adventuress. The accidental death of both parents left her very rich, and a little lonely. Since she can't find a man to keep up with her sexuality, she tries to fill the void with work. Her friend and agent Flo (Jesie St. James) has a movie offer for her, discussions about which more or less make up the rest of the film.

This minimal plot is a thread on which to hang a series of sexual encounters, including a fling with a motorist in trouble; another with the planned movie's supporting actress; a fantasy that features the uncircumcised Mr. 14 inches, John C. Holmes; and the memory of her first experience, a quasi rape by the young gardener on her family's estate. This last scene has caused controversy about *Insatiable* since it was made. Sondra says, "No, no, no," and the gardener says, "You know you want it," and carries on. It's against everything we believe, so why didn't we mind it here? First because the girl is played by the clearly mid-thirtyish Ms. Chambers, who lets us see her younger self's desire for the boy in the way her body says, "Yes." Second because she's narrating and enjoying the memory. A few people we know put their fingers firmly on the fast-forward button for this scene, and others won't watch the video at all, in protest. That last choice means missing the romantic moonlit encounter between John Leslie and Flo, one of our personal all-time favorites.

The backgrounds are tastefully top drawer, and Chambers's slim, almost bony, body and natural look convey an intelligent woman who chooses not to be bound by conventional sexuality. **_Highly recommended with caveat._**

Explicitness: 7;   Sensuality: 8   3M/W,   2W

Inside Out

SERIES FROM PLAYBOY ENTERTAINMENT GROUP

"Where the Twilight Zone meets the erogenous zone . . ." Each tape in this series contains between eight and ten episodes, related by their point of view and overall presentation. If you watch the Playboy channel you may have seen some of them or ones like them—they are used as fillers between movies.

The episodes begin with a pertinent quote—from sources as diverse as Max Jacob, Pliny the Elder, and Lewis Carroll—and end with a kind of O. Henry twist. They are adult entertainment, but sex, while definitely present in the stories, is more of a motivating force than a turn-on. The writing is often both witty and literate, and both sexes for the most part have normal, not bunny, bodies. The sex is simulated. Worth renting for the amusement, especially number 4.

Simulated (all in series)

Inside Out 2: Eight Tales of the Unexpected

Producer: Alan Poul. Directors: Nicholas Brandt, Nigel Dick, Martin Donovan, Linda Hassan, Paul Rachmann, Tony Randel, Yuri Sivo, John Wentworth. Writers: Peter Atkins, Tony Randel, Kenneth Deifik, Harry

Kondoleon, Temple Mathews, Dirk Shafer, Steve Vickery, Joe Frank, David Rapkin. Playboy Enterprises/Propaganda Films. 90 minutes.

This volume is the least interesting of the ones we viewed, though it has some good moments. Check out the mock biography of a fifty-inch chunk o'love who looks like the Venus of Willendorf but, being a modern sort of Venus, calls one of her huge breasts Fame and the other Fortune. We also liked the shaggy dog story about a farmer, his daughter, and a traveling salesmen. Generally the wit is pessimistic—what fools these mortals be.

Inside Out 3

Writers: Bernard Rose, Kenneth Deifeck, David Lawson, Joe Frank, David Rapkin, Temple Matthews, Ken Rudman, Stuart Cave, Bernath, Mitchel Stone. Directors: Charles McDougall, Bernard Rose, John Wentworth, Joe Rachman, Martin Donovan, Alexander Payne, Stuart Cave, David Bernath.

The tone of this video is also pessimistic, and the humor is often cutting. That's OK while you're watching, but it leaves a gloomy aura, as if you had spent ninety minutes listening to Peggy Lee sing "Is That All There Is?" Best episodes include one about women roommates who hear on the news that an atomic bomb will hit their town in ten minutes. How will they spend those last precious moments? Sex? Or ice cream? It's a hard call. Our other absolute favorite was Olympic star Greg Louganis playing a romantic and protective pet fish.

Inside Out 4: Erotic Tales of the Unexpected

Producer: Alan Poul. Writers: Barbara Allyn, Beverly Levitt, Alison Adler, Rand Ravich, Tim Evans, Larry Golin, Joe Frank, Richard Heft, Mark Romanck. Directors: John Wentworth, Charles McDougall, Charles Mc-Douglas, Antoine Fuqua, Paul Rachman, Richard Shepherd, Adam Friendman, Nigel Dick. 1992. Unrated.

The best of the collections so far, this video has ten short stories—half with a strong element of romantic fantasy, the other half laugh-out-loud funny. We liked them all, but single out for special mention "Jilted Lover," written and acted by Joe Frank. He plays a jealous fellow whose ex-lover's new beau epitomizes the romantic, attentive, sensitive, impetuous man of most women's dreams. Joe finds him disgusting. "My Cyberian Rhapsody" is a little sci-fi strangeness that features a sassy Asian-American clerk who deserves a video of her own. Very satisfying and likely to leave you in a happy, playful mood. **Recommended.**

The Italian Stallion

ROCKY'S ROOTS

Starring: Sylvester Stallone, Nicholas Warren, Frank Micelli, Henrietta Hom, Jodi Van Prang, Barbara Storm. Producer/director: Morton Lewis. Wonderful World of Video, 1970.

Star watchers' alert: Sylvester Stallone made an adult movie before he got his big break in *Rocky.* You catch glimpses of his unaroused penis and see simulated sex. Now for the mysteries. The movie was made in 1970. This version is dated 1978 and introduced by a woman who seems to have acquired ownership of the copyright. What happened during the intervening eight years? Why is it the single worst-quality print we have ever seen? And is there any reason to watch this unless you have a thing for hippies or rate as a total Sylvester Stallone groupie? Well, it's inspirational to see how far he's traveled in the subsequent decades.

Simulated

Jealous Lovers

NO FRILLS

Starring: Kascha, Francois Papillion, Marc Wallice, Bionca, Carol Cummings, Scarlet Windsor, Don Fernando, Tom Byron, Tina Gordon. Producer: Paul Del Mar. Director: Norm L. Pera. CDI Home Video, 1989.

A sleeps with B, who sleeps with C while A makes it with D. No group sex, no anal, one lesbian scene, nothing kinkier than a vibrator and a set of beads. Mostly blondish, youngish, healthy-looking California neighbors enthusiastically doing the wild thing.

There are no frills. People get naked before they say hello. The backgrounds look like the cameraman rented the production company his place to make a little extra money. Still, the adults are consenting, and everyone involved seems to have a fine, athletic time. This probably is more a guy turn-on than a girl turn-on. If your man likes to watch erotic videos, and you don't suffer from body anxiety, watch it together. Then you can both get turned on.

Explicitness: 8; Sensuality: 5   A,   T,   2W

John Wayne Bobbitt Uncut

AUTOBIOGRAPHICAL FARCE

Starring: Veronica Brazil, Crystal Gold, Jasmine Aloha, Tiffany Lords, and the one and only John Wayne Bobbitt. Director: Ron Jeremy (who also appears in a small part). Screenplay: Boom Boom Anderson. Producer: Mark Carriere. 1994.

"Ever since this whole thing happened all anybody wants to see is my penis. Now you can." We've all heard more on the subject of John Wayne Bobbitt's poor, mangled penis than we ever wanted to know, but the most basic questions remained unanswered—how does it look? does it work? can he use it? Now, thanks to JWB's entrepreneurial spirit, you can see for yourselves. America is a wonderful country.

In case you don't want to rent the video and watch John Wayne earn his six-figure fee, we watched it for you. The most famous penis in the world is of modest size by XXX-rated video standards, and in tight close-ups, a scar and a bump are visible. In this supposed reenactment of the "accident" and his life since then, we meet the hitherto unsung heroine of his story—a busty nurse who proved to him that he didn't have to wait two years to find out if feeling would return to his organ. As his physical therapist, she has special access to her patient and puts it to good use. Following their encounter we see him demonstrating his recovery again and again with shapely, willing women who all look like Las Vegas Barbie (though rumor has it that shots of prostaglandin were necessary before little John rose to the occasions). We can't say the video is erotic, but it did satisfy our ever-prurient curiosity while providing a few startled laughs. This effort has a sequel called *Frankenpenis* that uses footage from the actual operation. We say we've heard quite enough from you, John Wayne Bobbitt.

Explicitness: 8.5;   Sensuality: 3   A,   C,   M,   O,   2W/M

Jungle Heat

SAFARI ADVENTURE

Starring: Rosa Carcciolo, Rocco Siffreddi, Nikita Gross, Attila Schulter, Swetta Silvestru, Cyntya Raffael, Zaltan Kabbay, Tae. Director: Joe Damato. Writer: George Hudson. Music: Peter Mountain. Ultimo Euro Film, 1995. (**Dubbed in English.**)

Set in an African jungle and intercut with stock shots of wild African animals, *Jungle Heat*'s adventurers are on safari in search of a lost city. It's the same lost city an explorer was looking for twenty years earlier when he, his wife, and young son disappeared. (Starting to sound familiar?) While most of the safari group are off on their search, Jane (Rosa Carcciolo) takes a walk alone in the jungle in spite of having heard the eerily scary call of Ape Man, the guardian of the lost city. She gets trapped, falls on her head, and passes out. Rosa Carcciolo is a lovely brunette and has a sophisticated look not often found in this genre. Before you can say "Tarzan of the Jungle" out comes Rocco Siffredi, his hair flowing and his handsome loins wrapped in a cloth. Finding Jane flat on her back, he looks under her skirt sniffing and tasting her—hmm, smells and tastes good.

Off he carts her and gently strips off her safari outfit. When she comes to they compare body parts. No, she doesn't have one of those. Where is it? he wonders. After taking inventory they exchange names and he makes her the appropriate jungle wear—a nice garment of animal skins, for which she gives him a kiss and grabs hold of his penis. Frightened—Oh my God, he wonders, she's not going to eat it, is she? when she pops it into her mouth. Hmm, feels different, but good. And of course, they do the wild thing.

The rest of the movie takes place back in civilization with the Ape Man being introduced to genteel living English style and the various pleasures of the flesh with other women in the household. Alas, he's not at home in this environment, and he and Jane decide that it's best if he goes back to the jungle. Will she join him? We smell a sequel.

With paradisal settings (both jungle and civilization), sex that's part hijinks and part just good fun, *Jungle Heat* is special. **Recommended.**

Explicitness: 8.5;   Sensuality: 8   A

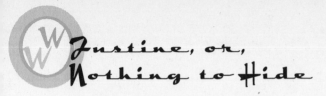

Justine, or, Nothing to Hide

FATHER/SON/GIRLFRIEND TRIANGLE

Starring: Roxanne Blaze, Mike Horner, Tianna, Nick East, Lacy Rose, Dyanna Lauren, Alex Sanders, Brad Armstrong. Producer/director: Paul Thomas. Writer: Raven Touchstone. Cal Vista, 1993. 101 minutes.

Nick East wants commitment from his lover, Roxanne Blaze, though she evades all his relationship questions with noncommittal answers. He has to take a business trip, leaving her on her own, but he calls his father and asks him to look after her if she needs help. Meanwhile, Nick's father, played by Mike Horner, is having a problem of his own—in spite of his date Tianna's energetic efforts, he can't manage to sustain an erection. Next day he sheepishly goes to a sex shop looking for a cock ring "for my brother." Guess who works there as part of a graduate research project for her college professor? She and Mike strike sparks, and a sexual cat-and-mouse game ensues. She's attracted to him, doesn't want to cheat on her boyfriend, and gives him a false name. Any town is a small town when a man has a mission, and Mike manages to find her. The erotic dance begins, with neither of them aware of the other's real identity.

Once Roxanne does find out that Mike is her boyfriend's father, she is torn. He attracts her in a way his son never has. She can see no good will come from this triangle, but she can't see how to end it—and besides, she wants a little more time. For his part, Mike suspects nothing, is crazy about the woman, and finds the kinky sexual games they play both exciting and frightening.

The women in this movie are *unbelievably* sexually aggressive and pull out vibrators at a moment's notice, but they also are vulnerable. An interesting facet of the story is the style of the woman who appeals to Mike compared with the one who doesn't, since there are some similarities in their approach to sex. Playing hard to get no longer means what it did in Grandmother's day, but elusiveness is still irresistible. **Highly recommended.**

Explicitness: 8;   Sensuality: 8   A,   B,   M,   O,   S,   SS (one scene),   T

Hard and Soft

If you watch Justine: Nothing to Hide *on pay cable, you will see a hot movie, but at certain critical times the camera will cut away from the main action to something suggestive—for example, the back of Roxanne Blaze's head or her fist opening and closing. You're watching the soft, or cable, cut. Guess what's happening in the explicit version.*

Most adult filmmakers who hope to sell more than a few thousand copies of their tape make two versions—one explicit, the other with certain critical cuts for a softer X-rated version. The goal is to get distribution in the many lucrative markets for erotic movies that want it hot but not too hot. For example, on cable channels such as Playboy and AdultVision, the rules are: genitals may show, but not penetration; men may have their

The Last Seduction

SEDUCTION WITH A HARD EDGE

Starring: Linda Fiorentino, Peter Berg, J. Y. Walsh, Bill Nunn, Bill Pullman. Producer: Jonathan Shestack. Director: John Dah. Writer: Steve Barancik. October Films, 1994. 110 minutes.

Bridget Gregory (Linda Fiorentino) will not be pushed around. When her husband, Clay (Bill Pullman), gives her a hard time, she absconds their ill-gained drug money and splits for a small town in upstate New York. He chases after her, but she puts into motion a plan using her brains and sexuality, which turns out to be a deadly combination for anyone getting in her way. She seduces Mike (Peter Berg), one of the schmos at a local bar who can't quite believe his good fortune in having such a sophisticated woman's attention. Combining nonchalant malevolence with an icy sexuality, Bridget

faces in women's pubes, but no visible cunnilingus; and no full erections. In parts of the United States, "community standards" dictate that the cable cut is the version for sale or rent, and the Playboy Catalog also usually sells the cable version of explicit films. Most film distributors leave it up to individual movie rental stores to know which version they can sell or rent without getting hassled, but since local law enforcement agencies often go after the distributor, some of them have ZIP codes redlined in their computer. If you live in a conservative area, you may get the cable cut whether you order it or not, and if you live in Utah, legally prudent distributors won't sell you anything.

When you rent a movie as part of your evening's entertainment in a hotel, the cut you see depends on the locality where you're staying; but adult movies make up a lucrative 60 percent of the hotels' movie rental business, and in big cities those movies usually are explicit. (If you're traveling on business you might want to make arrangements at the desk so your taste in movies doesn't get spelled out on your itemized bill.)

uses Mike to outmanipulate everyone. If your taste in movies includes noir, you're in for plenty of dark humor and sex in *The Last Seduction*.

Simulated

Last Tango in Paris

ARCHETYPAL EROTICA

Starring: Marlon Brando, Maria Schneider, Jean Pierre Leaud, Darling Legitimus, Catherine Sola, Mauro Marchetti, Dan Diament. Producer/director: Bernardo Bertolucci. Writers: Bernardo Bertolucci,

Franco Arcalli. Les Artistes Associes/PEA/United Artists, 1973. 129 minutes. **(Available in both X- and R-rated versions.)**

After his wife's suicide, Marlon Brando plunges into an impulsive relationship with a young French girl. What begins with a chance encounter and a no-questions-asked affair turns serious and then tragic. If you're passionate about film, a fan of Brando and/or Bertolucci, or simply curious to know what caused all the uproar and butter jokes when it was released, then of course you should watch this—in fact, it was for movies like this one, not sporting events, that the wide-screen TV was invented. Please also note that while it has extremely erotic moments it seemed to us to provoke more conversation than lust. Choose accordingly.

Simulated

Latex

HIGH-TECH FUTURE SHOCK

Starring: D. Michael Ninn, Sunset Thomas, Jon Dough, Julie Ashton, Tifanny Million, Jeanna Fine, Lacy Rose, Barbara Doll, Jordan Lee, Tasha Blades, Emerald Estrada, Cal Jammer, Tom Byron, Colt Steele, Brick Majors, Ritchie Razor, Vince Voyeur, Veronica Hart, Kelly Nichols, Mike Horner. Producers: Jane Hamilton, Michael Ninn. Director: Michael Ninn. Writer: Antonio Passolini. Music: Dino Ninn. Special effects: Michael Lancaster, Abe Forman. VCA Platinum, 1995. 120 minutes.

A visually stunning video, *Latex* was hailed as a masterpiece by the adult industry. Apart from being a totally hard-edged and sharp saturnalia, it is an apologia for the freedom of sexual self-expression.

The consequences of hiding our sexuality under the skin (latex) is inevitable madness and insanity. A glossy, highly produced 1995 *AVN* Best Picture Award winner, *Latex* is a tour de force employing sometimes indecipherable but nevertheless powerful visual images done no doubt with the aid of some powerful computers and sophisticated software. (Cal Jammer, whose suicide is the focal point of a *New Yorker* article on the adult industry by Susan Faludi, is in the cast.)

Attention is lavished on costumes, makeup, and art direction, all saturated with coolness. The sex looks like a lot of hard work for not much fun. With characters resembling androids, the filmmakers warning of a dehumanized future would have been better served with a more subtly intelligent approach. Incorporating images reminiscent of highly polished music video productions, Latex pushes hard against the boundaries of what polite society might consider proper and displays a coarseness that goes far beyond what you might expect to see on MTV.

Veronica Hart/Jane Hamilton, who has left performing to become a director at VCA, has a nonsexual role as a doctor in *Latex*. We must say, she looks terrific, and we wouldn't mind at all if she went back to doing sexual roles.

Explicitness: 9; Sensuality: 4 A, C, M, S, T, 2W

Le Parfume de Mathilde

FRENCH COUNTRY FANTASY

Starring: Draghixa, Julia Chanel, Christophe Clark, Maeva, Elodie, Simona Valli, Elisabeth Stone, Eric Weiss, Richard Langin, David Perry, Thomas Smith, Manon, Kathy. Director: Marc Dorcel. Writer: Jean Rollin. Music: Marc Dorcel. Vivid/arc Dorcel Presentation, 1994.

Jeremy, the Lord of the Manor, was deceived and humiliated by his more sexually experienced first wife, Mathilde, who freely shared her charms with everyone, including the household help. About to marry the orphan Agnes, a young virgin fresh from behind the walls of a French convent, Jeremy has resolved to avenge himself on her for Mathilde's crimes. The unsuspecting, innocent, naive Agnes is conveyed to the arranged marriage by her adopted parents, who, after dropping hints about what will be expected of her, have the chauffeur of their Rolls Royce stop on one of those gorgeous French country roads and show her a few moves by way of preparation.

And so begin Agnes's many humiliations. Coerced into wearing her see-through wedding dress and carrying her Louis Vuitton suitcase, she's dropped at the entrance of Jeremy's estate and off she goes down the dirt road to meet her groom. The ultimate insult will be her public deflowering in the presence of the wedding guests, all of whom look as if, given half an opportunity, they might ravish her themselves. Flinching and whimpering, she submits to the insults and learns the lessons of vice and lechery Jeremy instructs her in. We had a sharp split of opinions on this. Some of us felt she should have found a mad-dog lawyer to sue everyone involved, beginning with her guardians and the nuns, while others saw themselves in the ingenue role. Many of us would have been happy to surrender our virginity to Lord Jeremy, while others would have told him to introduce his spoiled-brat self to Miss Rosy Palm.

Why didn't Mathilde just walk out? Does she believe in Jeremy's inherent goodness, or did the nuns teach her secret lessons? Whichever, Agnes not only survives the abuse but prevails in the end. We commend the use of characters well past their thirties, charmed that the French have a more matter-of-fact attitude about age than North Americans. The country settings, indoors and out, are luxurious and irresistible.

Explicitness: 8;   Sensuality: 8   A,   B,   M,   O,   S (light)

Legal Tender

PORN VICE

Starring: Jerry Butler, Victoria Paris, Tracey Adams, Aja, Buck Adams, Al Brown, Peter North. Producer/director/writer: Buck Adams. Music: Barry Box. VCA, 1989. 100 minutes.

If you miss the guy talk of *Miami Vice,* this one's for you. Everyone is looking for Eddie (Jerry Butler), who has just been released from the pen and is known to be planning a big score of some sort in which he'll get even with some "old friends," who happen to be the cops who put him away. *Legal Tender* is full of big-budget Las Vegas and LA location shots, blasting guns, chases in fancy cars, helicopters, and plenty of sex. Much of the sexing is way above average and filmed with both full-body shots and facial close-ups, so we can see the reactions as well as the action. We wish as much attention had been paid to dialogue and character motivation. A few more clues to Buck's character and crimes were in order. For instance, after seeing a prostitute, Eddie breaks down and cries. Where did this emotional outburst come from? Nothing we saw gives an indication. At 100 minutes in length, we thought a more entertaining story could have been developed with less boring results, unless you or your partner are addicted to TV-style shoot-em-ups and get off on murder and mayhem and car chases.

Legal Tender is one of the few movies Jerry Butler made after the publication of *Raw Talent,* the autobiography in which he trashes nearly everyone he ever worked with.

Explicitness: 8;   Sensuality: 4

Like Water for Chocolate

ESSENCE OF SOUL IN THE RECIPE

*Starring: Lumi Cavazos, Marco Leonardi, Regina Torne, Mario Ivan, Ada Carrasco, Yareli Arizmendi, Claudette Maille, Pilar Aranda. Producer/director: Alfonso Arau. Writer: Laura Esquivel. Music: Leo Brower. Miramax, 1993. 113 minutes. (**Spanish with English subtitles.**)*

Food and passion. Is there a more enchanting combination? Add to this alchemical magic a setting in colonial Mexico in 1910, the year of the Mexican Revolution. Tita's (Lumi Cavazos) formidable, dictatorial mother, Mama Elena (Regina Torne) decreed at Tita's birth that her youngest daughter would never marry but would devote herself to caring for Mama in her old age. Years later she forces Tita's lover, Pedro (Marco Leonardi), to marry Rosario (Yareli Arizmendi), one of Tita's older sisters. "You cannot exchange tacos for enchilada," says Nacha (Ada Carrasco), the household's cook and Tita's champion. Pedro, whose gaze Tita describes as "exactly how raw dough must feel when it comes in contact with boiling oil," acquiesces to the marriage in order to be near Tita. Her apparent resignation to the role of spinster isn't what it seems. Subsuming her lust into cooking lavish meals, Tita's desires permeate the food she prepares, affecting in fantastically unexpected and high-spirited ways those who eat it, causing them to be overcome with their longings.

Like Water for Chocolate will make you laugh, cry, and hunger for love and food.

Simulated

The Lover

LITERARY DRAMA

Starring: Jane March, Tony Leung; with Frederique Meininger, Arnaud Giovanietti, Melvil Poupaud, Lisa Faulkner, Xiem Mang. Narrated by Jeanne Moreau. Producer: Claude Berri. Director: Jean-Jacques Annaud. Based on a novel by Marguerite Duras. (We viewed the widely available unrated version with 12 minutes added from the European version that were cut in the original U.S. release.) MGM/UA, 1992. 103 minutes. **(In French with English subtitles.)**

A French schoolgirl meets a rich older Asian as she returns, unchaperoned, to a religious boarding school. Set against the hot, dusty background of Indochina in 1929, a place and time where their love is unthinkable, the two begin an affair in turn passionate, obsessive, and cruel. He tells her that now that she is not a virgin he never would be permitted to marry her. She tells him that she couldn't love a China Man.

The relationship becomes more remarkable when you consider that the tough, vulnerable fifteen-and-a-half-year-old child/woman went on to become the distinguished French writer Marguerite Duras. The languid, marvelously produced film, based on her best-selling autobiographical novel, transports you at its own dreamy pace. Jeanne Moreau narrates the story, and we admit we succumbed completely. Even if the film itself weren't beautiful and erotic, we'd rent it again just to listen to her voice.

Simulated

Lovers: An Intimate Portrait, 1— Sidney and Ray

DOCUMENTARY

Starring: Candida Royalle, Sydney Rae, Tasha Voux. Producers/directors: N.E. Chambers, R.C. Horsch. Introduced by Candida Royalle. Femme Productions, 1993. 70 minutes.

Before you can get your dander up about the sexual games Sidney and Ray enjoy in this candid unscripted interview/documentary, Candida Royalle offers five minutes of attitude adjustment on the difference between actually forcing someone to do something against his/her will *(we don't do that)* and the sexual fantasies a couple can act out to keep boredom from the bedroom *(good idea)*. Together for four years, the couple is not married. He is in his forties, with hair thinning on his head but luxuriant on his muscular body. She is in her twenties, slim, and well toned for a real person with a day job. Sex in the comfort of their bedroom turns them on, but so does sex on the dance floor of a crowded club. She likes to tie him up and tease him with her body, withholding sex until she grants it as a favor. Pretending that sex is out of the question when she really wants him to fight her into submission is another favorite game. This last scene is one of those instances where her voice-over makes the game guilt free by letting us know she enjoys what's happening.

We see them act out all but the dance floor stuff, and more besides, chatting in voice-over about their preferences. The production has the rawness of a low-budget documentary, which some found a downer and others felt added to the voyeuristic rush.
Recommended.

Explicitness: 7;   Sensuality: 7   B,   S,   S/M,   T,   2W/M

Lovers: An Intimate Portrait, 2— Jennifer and Steve

DOCUMENTARY

Producer: N.E. Chambers. Director/writer: R.C. Horsch. Music: I B Neimand. Introduced by Candida Royalle. Femme Productions.

Steve (thirty-two) and Jennifer (twenty-four) are a "real" couple, but they're not exactly the folks next door. Jennifer tells us she graduated from a seven-sisters college, has a master's degree in art history, and dances in topless and bottomless bars because she loves to dance (and strip). Steve makes films (unspecified) and appears comfortable with Jennifer's proclaimed desire to have every man in the world want her. In bed Jennifer says, "I like to be degraded." Steve ties her up, she says "No" when she means "Yes," and he "pushes her boundaries." Afterwards, by his own troubled admission, what he did and what he felt capable of doing frightens him.

The documentary uses simple backgrounds, for the most part red sheets and red walls whose reflected color softens the harsh cinema verité look of *Lovers 1.* Some of the sex is hot, and yet we came away more worried about the couple than turned-on. We think what two consenting adults do is their business, but we hope they'll check out Ona and Frank Zee's videos *Learning the Ropes* (see page 245) so some mutual boundaries are set on the games before someone really gets hurt.
Recommended.

Explicitness: 7;   Sensuality: 7   A,   S/M

Lust on the Orient Express

SOPHISTICATED SLEUTHING

Starring: Gina Carrera, Pat Manning, Tracey Adams, Kelli Richards, Paul Thomas, Jamie Gillis, John Leslie, Francois Papillion, Eric Edwards. Producer/director: Tim McDonald. Caballero, 1986.

John Leslie plays a mystery writer who tries to get his creative juices flowing by taking a trip with his wife and muse, Gina Carrera. Their first night on the Orient Express a man drops dead in their compartment, knife in his back. Among the passengers/suspects are fading film star Eric Edwards, the eccentric lady Pat Manning, and mysterious Arab Jamie Gillis with harem. The harem turns out to be a very important key to a missing diamond. Lots of high-gloss production makes it fun to watch. Think Nick and Nora Charles unzipped. **Recommended.**

Explicitness: 7;   Sensuality: 7   O,   M,   3W

Mad Love

GHOSTS ON A RAMPAGE

Starring: Kendall Marx, Aja, Brandi Wini, Rene Morgan, Jon Martin, F. M. Bradley, Damian Cashmere, Tony Montana, Rick Lee, Jon Dough, James Dalton, Richard Pacheco, with Walter Eletric (as Ben Davis). Producer: Louie T. Beagle. Director: John Leslie. Writers: Richard Pacheco, John Leslie. Music: Bill Heid. Evil Angel, VCA, 1989.

An old man and a leather-clad young woman sit at opposite ends of a table in an elaborately decorated Victorian house. She lets in two passersby and encourages them to have sport sex with her on the dining room table as the man watches. Cut to a young husband (Jon Martin) being shown around the same house. He and his wife (Kendal Marx) are moving to San Francisco, where they'll house sit for a few months until they find a place of their own. Uh oh. When things sound too good to be true, check under the beds, or in this case between the sheets, which are riotously overflowing with the sleazy

ghosts of previous occupants. At first it's sexy, but all too soon things take a dark turn. *Best scene:* Jon and Kendal celebrate their upcoming move.
Recommended.

Explicitness: 8;   Sensuality: 6   M,   2M/W,   O,   2W, 2W/M

Makin' It

CAREER GUIDANCE

Starring: Mina, Kaitlyn Ashley, Debi Diamond, Tricia Yen, Isis Nile, Marc Wallice, Sean Michaels, Ed Powers, Wayne Wright, Jim South, Steve Austin. Director: Toni English. Vivid, 1994. 75 minutes.

Are you looking for a career change that requires little experience and practically no training? Would a role as a performer in erotic videos interest you? The subject of erotic videos comes up as two young men are boasting about how many women each can handle at one time. One of them bets the other that he can get a gig as a performer. A call to Vivid (coincidentally the name of the company that made this video) refers them to World Modeling (818-986-4316—if you care to take note). Wayne Wright makes an appointment with adult film agent Jim South, who explains how it all works, including the requirement for an AIDS test. Mina is Wright's shy female counterpart, who, although not ready to perform sex on video, does want to pose nude for magazines.

The sex isn't extraordinary, but the studio and backstage scenes gave us a peep into this universe. Gone are the catered lunches, limousines, and posh dressing rooms of the not-so-distant past. These days, if you're female, you'll in all likelihood have to provide your own lingerie and probably have to do your own hair and makeup. If your star is rising you'll be able to choose who you will and won't perform with. If you're a guy, your main job is to get wood—regularly, reliably, and on demand. Performing in adult videos is no get-rich-quick scheme. With competition from amateurs who with their home video cameras supply thousands of hours of erotica at virtually no cost, stars no longer make up to $5,000 a day. Expect to be paid something between $200 and $800 a day once you're established. Top performers may make about $1,500 a day. With many videos being cranked out in fewer than five work days (sometimes in no more than one very long

The Spice of Life

For every pot, there's a lid. And for every way people get turned on, a video exists to make it quick and painless. The more extreme examples are not to be found in WW, but we thought you'd want to know what you're missing. If you're serious about exploring an option, you can find a large selection of specialty films listed in the Adult Video News *annual, available in adult bookstores.*

amateur—folks at home crank up the video camera on Saturday night and sell the results. The largest growth area of the business.

anal—back-door sex with penis or toys. Lately, anal sex seems to be the most popular focus of adult videos, usually photographed with the eroticism of a chainsaw movie. Videos exist that show nothing else.

Asian—videos made in Asian countries and exported to the United States for fans of Asian women. Asian women also appear in U.S. mainstream tapes, though we've never seen an identifiably Asian man.

bestiality—lock up your poodle, your horse, your sheep. Illegal to show in U.S. adult videos.

black—many videos have biracial casts, but all-black tapes (e.g., *Sherlock Homie*) are available. Check out *AVN* for further guidance.

bondage—from playful silk stockings (*Three Daughters*) to elaborately wrapped ropes and rituals (*Tokyo Decadence*). Serious bondage is a separate genre, but it often overlaps with S/M.

cat fighting—two or more women scratching, biting, rolling around; almost always part of the women-in-prison genre.

chubbies—some men are turned on by women over three hundred pounds—sweet bundles o'love. We viewed a few, but the films tend to be cheaply made, harshly lit loops. There's a business opportunity here for a filmmaker with a soft-focus lens and a pink light.

cross-dressing—practiced by men and women but is more noticeable in men, since these days most women wear trousers. Not the same as transvestites, cross-dressers usually are heterosexuals who fetishize clothing.

defecation—pooping on another as fetish, not metaphor. Not legally available in U.S. videos.

fetish—an object invested with sexual feeling, such as a woman's high-heeled shoe or panties. Videos exist for many fetishes.

foot fetish—shoe sniffing, foot licking, toe sucking. Traditional statistics state that 52 percent of American men fantasize about having sex with a woman wearing high-heeled shoes.

golden shower/water games—peeing on another. No longer found in U.S. mainstream adult videos.

micturation—same as a gold shower.

pony girl training—woman pulling light cart and/or pretending to be a horse with elaborate bridle, saddle, and reins (see a brief example in the Andrew Blake movie *Sensual Exposure*).

rubber—from aprons to elaborate latex suits that in their extreme mode look like the Creature from the Black Lagoon.

S/M—includes subspecialties, such as genital clamps, hanging, hot wax, imprisoning, paddling, pegging, tying up, whipping. Most of these are more or less self-descriptive, except for hot wax, which is what Madonna did to Willem Defoe with a candle in *Body of Evidence*, and pegging, examples of which can be viewed in the erotic photographs of Robert Mapplethorpe as well as in *Skin*. In the United States it is illegal to show S/M and penetration in the same scene.

> **shaving**—the process of shaving the (usually female) pubic area. There are whole videos devoted to this practice.
>
> **spanking**—sometimes playful, sometimes not so playful, but involves a hand, not a paddle or whip (see *Justine*, or, *Nothing to Hide*).
>
> **tickling**—two or more women tickle each other. A kinder, gentler form of cat fighting.

day), it's easy to understand why so many successful stars earn their real income dancing. Don't quit your day job if you decide to take the plunge.

Explicitness: 8;   Sensuality: 5

The Man Who Loves Women

AUTOBIOGRAPHICAL SLICE OF LIFE

Starring: Tara Monroe, Lana Sands, Janet Jackme, Ariel Day, Wednesday, Peter North, Tom Byron, Sean Michaels. Producers/directors: Thomas Stone, Sean Michaels. Music: Dr. Sammy Shears. VCA, 1994.

Sean Michaels, winner of the 1993 Woodsman of the Year award from XRCO, is one of a handful of crossover African-American adult video performers. We've enjoyed other sparkling performances from Michaels but found the premise and performance of this one a touch crude.

We're on a trip down mammary lane in which Michaels is allegedly being followed by a camera crew making a documentary of his life. His first stop, after a series of quick-cut snippets, is at a boutique where he helps a woman try on dresses for a party. Being a generous dude, he pays for the dress and invites her to coffee at an outdoor spot where very little of what they say to each other could be heard over the sound of street noise. That's one way of saving money on a writer! She lets him lick her toes in public, and accepts his proposition when he gets around to it. What a girl will do for a new frock! The rest of the video is more of the same, with a veritable rainbow coalition of women begging him for what he's got.

Explicitness: 6;   Sensuality: 3   A,   2W

A Man with a Maid
(see *Naughty Victorians*)

The Masseuse: She'll Rub You Right

LESSONS IN LOVE

Starring: Randy Spears, Hypatia Lee, Viper, Danielle Rogers, Porsche Lynn. Producer/director: Paul Thomas. Writer: Mack Haggard. Vivid, 1990. 90 minutes.

Jim (Randy Spears) is a twenty-eight-year-old all-American male with a gorgeous body and still a virgin. Go figure. What's a guy to do? His solution is to go to a masseuse, to whom he confesses his embarrassing condition. He's lucky to find the raven-haired and warm-hearted Barbara (Hypatia Lee) to take him in hand (and other places). Breaking all the rules of the parlor, she does as he asks, giving his piston a workout, including a sudsy shave (not on his face). He manages to get a date with her outside the massage parlor, and through several encounters she relieves him of his virginity, teaching him the many arts of love, including instruction on cunnilingus. (Every woman should share Barbara's tips with her man.) All the while, she keeps control of the situation. Jim gets too attached to Barbara, and she fends him off with a ruse that doesn't hurt or embarrass him, giving the movie a surprise last twist that will make you smile. **Highly recommended.**

Explicitness: 8;   Sensuality: 7   B

Masseuse 2

MASSAGE PARLOR MELODRAMA

Starring: Ashlyn Gere, Leena, Christina West, Steven St. Croix, Randy West, Steve Drake, Tony Tedeschi, Annette Chang, Candy Marie Saint, Asia Carrera, David Schroeder, David Epstein, Paul Baumgartner, (introducing) Carl Radford. Producer/director: Paul Thomas. Writer: Neil Wexler. Vivid, 1994. 85 minutes.

Women workers at walk-in massage parlors exist on the low end of the sex business food chain. Ashlyn Gere plays a seasoned pro, whose ready-for-anything façade conceals the romantic hope that a rich man she met in the park (Steve Drake) will marry her. Between customers she reads books on the history of erotica, looking for some way to define herself and her job other than society's stigmatized labels. Asia Carrera plays a relative newcomer to the scene, still drawing the line at oral sex. She accidentally runs into her ex-husband, now in a twelve-step program for alcohol abuse, and finds herself unwillingly attracted to him.

The drama has an engrossing story with characters you care about and two amazing and one tender sex scene that proved again that it isn't the content but the way it's played that counts. Ashlyn Gere, first with cross-dressing customer Carl Radford and then with an abusive husband (Randy West) and his passive wife, centers her strong sexuality in a way that uses her character's hostile, aggressive attitude for maximum turn-on. Her reaction to Randy West defused our potential indignation, but this is not a sweetness-and-light feature—in spite of Asia's elegant seduction of her ex. Depending on your state of mind and the nature of your relationship, this might be one to view alone or with a woman friend before watching it with a mate.
Highly recommended.

Explicitness: 9;   Sensuality: 8   A,   S,   T,   2W/M

Memoirs of a Chambermaid

THE REALLY GOOD OLD DAYS

Starring: Krista Lane, Shanna McCullough, Rene Summers, Ona Zee, Brandon, Nick Random, Robert Bullock, Wayne Stevens. Producer/director: Eric Edwards. Arrow, 1987.

Krista Lane, a writer in search of material, rents an old, furnished Victorian house. Once there, she starts poking around and finds a diary of Molly (Shanna McCullough), a turn-of-the-century chambermaid who was in love with the son of the house. Krista starts writing about it, but soon she's doing more than writing as the people come alive to her. She is Molly, and the son (Brandon) is making love to her. Very compelling love it is and much better than anything that's happening to her in her own time. Gradually she's pulled more and more into the nineteenth century as she merges with the diarist. Is the writer's erotic imagination at work, or is Krista really entering another time and space? Swooningly romantic and niftily costumed, this is a delicious way to spend an evening. **Highly recommended.**

Explicitness: 7; Sensuality: 7 A, M, S/M, 2W, 2W/M

Midnight Heat

NOIR THRILLER

Starring: Jamie Gillis, Joey Carson, Sharon Mitchell, Tish Ambrose, Sue Nero, Michael Bruce, D.D. Burke, Howard Filene, Fred Rain, (introducing) Cheri Champagne. Producer: Robert Michaels. Director/writer Richard Mahler. Music: Andrew James. VCA, 1983. 77 minutes.

As a desolate, low-level hit man, Jamie Gillis' performance shines in *Midnight Heat*—in and out of bed. Shot at slightly slower motion than usual on what looks like a rainy November day in New York's Bowery, the film opens with an office scene in which Allen (Gillis) walks into the office, is acknowledged by the gentleman at the desk, and calmly shoots him point blank. Stopping off at his apartment after a visit to a prostitute, he and his wife (Sharon Mitchell) make love in an intimate and moving way with plenty of foreplay. Their moment of closeness magnifies her loneliness, and she announces that she's leaving him, declaring, "You are a cold, remote man. You never let anyone get close to you."

We next see him in a seedy Bowery hotel, staring out the window at nothing particular. He's on the run and reflective about the condition of his life. Perhaps in search of consolation for his soul, he thumbs through a copy of the *Gideon Bible*. What he finds and uses is the number of an escort service. Instead of the one he ordered, two women show up; he asks one of them to leave, asking the other, Diane (Cheri Champagne), to stay. In a philosophical mood, they muse about the writings of Nietzsche and the meaning of T.S. Eliot's poem *The Hollow Men*, quoting lines by heart. To the question of what it is women really want, Diane says, "More than a quick fuck, a gold chain, and flowers on her birthday."

A relentlessly dark movie, this film is for the true fans of noir. An unpredictable plot, exceptionally well written and acted and with good music, *Midnight Heat* is an original. About a modern man caught up in his own fantasy of living on the edge and the motto "The more dangerous something is the more we forget about everything else." It's a thoughtful film consumed by a gloominess and ennui that will leave you huddling closer to your mate, grateful for the warmth and safety of your cave.
Highly recommended.

Explicitness: 6;   Sensuality: 8

Mirage I

THE LITERARY LIFE

Starring: Ashlyn Gere, Mike Horner, Nina Hartley, Greg Rome, Eric Edwards, Peter North, Taylor Wane, T.T. Boy, Marc Wallice, Alice Springs. Producer/director/writer: Eric Edwards. VCA, 1991. 90 minutes.

Publishing executive Jennifer Randal (Ashlyn Gere) comes driving up a lonely dirt track and parks beside a trailer. Shyly she scuffs her feet in the desert sand and confides to the famous reclusive author Kyle Collins (Eric Edwards) that she, too, wanted to be a writer. Some meanie told her she lacked imagination, so she settled for an editorial job. He looks bored—no doubt he's heard it all before from pretty women in tight cutoffs—but he offers her the guest room when it gets late.

During the night a prospector enters her room. (Men don't have to be handsome to be convincing objects of lust, but this one needed more help from the costume department than Old MacDonald's overalls, one size too tight.) He feebly announces that he is her worst nightmare, and Ashlyn, who could eat him for lunch on a slow day, takes carnal control of the situation. Next morning she realizes it was all a strange dream, but when she picks up a page from Kyle Collins's new manuscript, *Mirage,* her dream is described. What is going on?

The movie proceeds at a rather erratic, stagily acted pace until Nina Hartley and Mike Horner enter Ashlyn's fantasies in a romantic al fresco scene. After that, things pick up significantly. Ashlyn and Mike have an excellent scene—and the movie ends with a delicious little twist.

Except for Ashlyn's initial costume of cutoffs and cropped top (later explained by the unusual nature of the author/editor relationship) her clothes were quite believable for someone working in an office. We particularly liked the midnight-blue dress she wears in a party scene. However, she, Nina Hartley, and Taylor Wane all appear unusually peaked. We prefer natural-looking makeup and hair, but as every woman knows sometimes the natural look is the end result of a lot of time, effort, and flattering lights. Perhaps the tired faces (mentioned in the script) are meant to indicate intellectual effort, the result of nights spent reading. On the other hand, Eric Edwards (in a nonsex role) had a fascinating, dissipated aura, and we noticed that Mike Horner seldom looked better than he does here coming in from a rainy night.

Recommended.

Explicitness: 8;   Sensuality: 7   A,   M,   2M/W,   2W, 2W/M

Mirage 2

NIGHTMARE OF PUBLISHING

Starring: Ashlyn Gere, Trixy Tyler, Britt Morgan, K.C. Williams, Tom Byron, Mike Horner, Randy West, Nina Hartley, Tom Thomas. Producer/director/writer: Eric Edwards. Music: Julian Keen. VCA/Platinum, 1991. 80 minutes.

You'll find it impossible to understand part 2 without having seen part 1. Eric Edwards knows how to put romance into his videos, and *Mirage 2* is no exception. Jennifer (Ashlyn Gere of the overinflated tits) has taken over Drake Publishing. Having revealed herself to be the author of Drake's best-selling books, she is now the head honchette. Her secretary, Shayna (Britt Morgan), has ambitions of her own and isn't happy when Jennifer describes Shayna's manuscript as "nothing that blows my dress up." A remark Shayna will not forget or forgive.

Canan Brennan (Mike Horner), who lives in what looks like a deserted Old West town, is the new author Jennifer is cultivating. She sends Shayna there to work out some publishing details with him. Shayna takes along her boyfriend, Jason Gimball (Tom Thomas). On the train ride, they put their time to good use by moving from foreplay in their seats to a full-blown wonderful time in the train's tiny bathroom. Thomas is a creative and original lover. He endeared himself to us when he wiped Shayna's backside with a paper towel after they finished their delicious lovemaking. Unfortunately, budgets being what they are, the train wasn't moving and they don't experience that back-and-forth jostle you would expect to encounter when you slip into the bathroom of a moving locomotive.

While Shayna negotiates with the up-and-coming Canan, Tom tours the ghost town, running into Molly (Nina Hartley) at the bar, where they do it with gusto and full-throttle enjoyment as only Hartley can portray. She's having such a great time you want to cheer her on with a "Do it again Nina!" And she looks delicious in her barmaid costume. While all this is going on, Jennifer continues to have those spooky, disturbing nightmares that plagued her in *Mirage 1*. The unexpected ending comes just when she feels like she's going to lose it.

Recommended.

Explicitness: 6;   Sensuality: 8   M,   2W/M

My Surrender

TAKING A CHANCE ON LOVE

Starring: Jeanna Fine, Alex Sanders, Nici Sterling, Wilde Oscar, Jill Kelly, Mark Davis, Gina Rome, Claudio. Music: James Mack and Candida Royalle. Writer/producer/director: Candida Royalle. PHE/Femme Productions, 1996.

April Hunter (Jeanna Fine) is a very private filmmaker, whose speciality is making erotic videos for partners who want a permanent record of themselves as they play out their favorite sexual scenarios. We see her working with three couples' and their fantasies: the naughty schoolgirl, the lady pornographer, and the recent widow. After the filming, the fulfilled couples are closer than ever, but April's only continuing relationship is with her video equipment. That's just fine with her, until architect Alex Sanders lays persistent siege to her imagination and heart.

Jeanna Fine, with her husky voice and cropped hair, projects both brains and vulnerable sex appeal (although her breasts look inflated to the point of pain), and she and Alex Sanders make a convincing couple. Their courtship will appeal, especially in the fantasy sequence, despite occasional lapses into therapeutic jargon. If you find yourself wondering why April can't go out with the man once or twice before getting into all that relationship talk, fast forward to the action. You're probably over-thinking the situation.

Those who hoped that Royalle's arrangement with PHE meant a return to the big budget look of *Christine's Secret* and *Three Daughters* may be a little disappointed. The backgrounds are studio minimal. They are, however, expertly lit, and careful attention was paid to details that make all the difference to our satisfaction. This means, among other things, sleek costuming, artful underwear, impeccably groomed performers, and polished props. *Best scene:* Couple number three makes passionate love in front of a coffin. We loved them so much we rewound and watched it again.
Highly recommended.

Explicitness: 7;   Sensuality: 8   A,   S/M

Naked Came the Stranger

MEDIA COUPLE IN MIDLIFE CRISIS

Starring: Levi Richards, Darby Lloyd Rains, Mary Stuart, Alan Marlow, Helen Madigan, Christine Hutton, Kevin Andre, Ronda Fuller, David Savage, Steve Anthony, Marc Stevens. Producer/director: Henry Paris. Writer: Penelope Ashe. 1975. 80 minutes.

A group of writers at *Newsday* looked at the steamy novels topping the best-seller list and decided they could do as well or better.

Each wrote a chapter or two of a book they titled *Naked Came the Stranger,* which eventually was published under the pseudonym Penelope Ashe. The book did become a best-seller. Not that it was particularly good as sexy novels go, but the story behind the novel was a public relations dream. As happens to most best-sellers, a movie was made, but with two differences. First, the movie was sexier and more amusing than the book; second, unlike most movies based on novels, the camera didn't discreetly pan away when the action got down and dirty.

The protagonists, Billy and Gilly, are popular husband-and-wife radio talk show hosts. She has discovered her husband playing extracurricular "love bunny" games with the show's script girl, Phyllis, and after following them and listening outside the door while they make love, she figures that anything he can do she can do better. She'll show him! Eventually she does, though not without stumbling into a number of embarrassing and hilarious potholes along the road to renewed true love. *Favorite line:* "A woman should never be jealous of what her husband does before 7 o'clock."

The sets and clothes are conspicuously dated, but otherwise it's a heavenly romp of sex and laughs. If you can find it, grab it.
Highly recommended.

Explicitness: 6; Sensuality: 8 S, 2W

Naughty Victorians (aka A Man with a Maid)

CLASSIC PERIOD PIECE

Starring: Susan Sloan, Beerbohn Tree, Jennifer Jordan, Angel Barrett, Heather Austin, Raymond Court-Thomas. Producer: John Butterworth. Director/writer: Robert S. Kinger. Based on the Victorian erotic novel A Man with a Maid. Music: Sir Arthur Sullivan. VCA, 1983. 82 minutes.

Alice (Susan Sloane), dutifully returning the books of her ex-fiancé Jack (Beerbohn Tree), takes shelter in his house from a sudden violent rainstorm. Her fear of thunder is pathetic, but Jack promises she won't be able to hear it in his "snuggery." Quite a resplendent room it turns out to be, with hidden features Jack gleefully demonstrates as he takes forcible revenge on Alice for breaking their engagement. "You played with my heart. And now I will play with your body." Aha. Once the first shock of violation is over, Alice joins in the sport, even introducing several other unsuspecting women to Jack's hideaway.

This handsome production makes witty use of Sullivan's music (no lyrics), and showcases wondrously wrought Victorian costumes and backgrounds. Unfortunately, truly great underwear isn't always enough. Jack takes Alice's maidenhood in one thrust and refuses to satisfy her on the grounds that he isn't interested now that she's not a virgin. In not-so-Victorian language, he rapes all four women, no matter that their cries for mercy turn to cries of pleasure. His shabby behavior gets an overdue comeuppance (not part of the original novel), but by then we've also been treated to some forced mother/teenage daughter incest that left us feeling queasy. We found the attitudes far from erotic. The only thing this video put us in the mood for was a domination scene in which we held the whip.

Explicitness: 9;   Sensuality: 4   A,   B,   T,   3W,   2W/M

The Nicole Stanton Story, Part 1: The Rise

GLITZY MELODRAMA

Starring: Eve Allen, John Leslie, Randy West, Joey Silvera, Megan Leigh, Nina Hartley, Kendall Marx, William Otis, Jon Martin, Rene Morgan, Scott Irish, (special guest appearance) Annette Haven (as Violet Masterson), Peter North, Jade East. Producer: Henry Pachard. Director: Alex de Renzy. Writer: Neil Wexler. Caballero, 1989. 82 minutes.

Shameless hussy Nicole Stanton (Eve Allen), beguiles John Leslie into marrying her for money—his money for her. They go from introduction to nuptial vows in record time in spite of his daughter's and future son-in-law's efforts to thwart the greedy Nicole. The stars in Leslie's eyes are so blinding that he doesn't even notice her gauche manners at the dining room table, where food isn't the only thing eaten with relish. Not satisfied with becoming a lady who lunches in Beverly Hills, Nicole manages to shift her husband's assets from his name to hers, proving that how you use what's between your ears can be more profitable than how you use what's between your legs.

Leslie's performance of a man in love is charming and convincing, and Allen's performance of a bitch without conscience is worthy of Hollywood. With some very comical moments, especially in the subplot involving Leslie's bratty daughter, *The Nicole Stanton Story* is about money, sex, power, money, and betrayal. **Recommended.**

Explicitness: 6;   Sensuality: 7 (one scene)   M,   O

The Nicole Stanton Story, Part 2

BAD GIRL MAKES GOOD

Starring: John Leslie, Eve Allen, Megan Leigh, Rocco Siffreddi, Nina Hartley, Randy West, Peter North, Kendall Marx, Jade East, Scott Irish, Rene Morgan, Jack Baker, Joe Elliot, Anette Haven. Producers/directors: Henri Pachard, Alex De Renzy. Writer: Rich Max. Caballero. 85 minutes.

This is a true sequel to *The Nicole Stanton Story,* part 1. We cannot imagine a man so besotted by lust that he doesn't notice his life being flushed down the toilet, but this is the movies, so we played along.

Poor Gerald (John Leslie) doesn't have a clue about what an unscrupulous woman he married, nor does he have a hint of the financial jeopardy his new bride, Nicole (Eve Allen), has put him in. Sexuality is power for Nicole. Using take-no-prisoners strategies of a female corporate raider and the weakness of Gerald's executive staff, she slowly secures her interests in his business empire. We liked the high-finance framework of this **Recommended** video.

Explicitness: 7;   Sensuality: 7   M,   2W,   2W/M

Nightdreams

INSOMNIA MATERIAL

Starring: Dorothy Le May, Loni Sanders, Jennifer West, Kevin Jay, Fast Steppin Freddie, Ken Starbuck. Producer: Rinse Dream. Director: F. X. Pope. Wonderful World of Video, 1981.

Mrs. Van Houten (Dorothy Le May) is in a psychiatric hospital, though we aren't sure why, since a failure to have orgasms (especially with a husband who "can't get it up") doesn't qualify most people for the lockdown ward. Her dreams, which the doctors somehow watch through a one-way mirror, are amazing. (If you've seen *Cafe Flesh*, with its rat-faced man going down on a sex positive, then you have the measure of Rinse Dream's intense imagination.) The bizarre images include Jack-in-the-Boxes popping up with huge erections, and a demon with a fetus coming out of his fly. It's the stuff of nightmares, fantastic and disturbing. Love it or hate it, you won't forget it.
Highly recommended.

Explicitness: 7;   Sensuality: 6   O,   2W

Nightshift Nurses

HOSPITAL FARCE

Starring: Lois Ayres, Keisha, Sheena Horne, Bionca, Lynn Francis, Dana Dylan, Siobhan Hunter, Louis T. Beagle, John Leslie, Peter North, Steve Hennessy, Jose Duval, Joey Silvera. Producer: Louie T. Beagle. Director: John Leslie. Writers: Jim Holliday, John Leslie. VCA, 1987.

Rumor has it that a mystery supervisor will be evaluating the performance of the night shift, and the staff is in a tizzy. The worry that they'll be caught with their pants down and their skirts up in no way curtails their usual activities—which are the usual activities—but it does give them something to talk about while they're doing it in every conceivable position and combination. If all you require of an adult movie is that it show as many acts of sex as possible without making the women look any sillier than the men, then you probably will find this raunchy, good-natured film satisfactory.

Explicitness: 8;   Sensuality: 5   M,   2W/M

Night Trips

MTV FANTASIES

Starring: Tori Wells, Porsche Lynn, Randy Spears, Jamie Summers, Victoria Paris, Ray Victory, Peter North, Tania Devries, Marc DeBruin. Producers: Patti Rhodes, Howard Klein. Director: Andrew Blake. Writers: Susan Philips, Andrew Blake. Music: Burk. Caballero, 1989. 80 minutes.

Tori Wells, with a diamond in her nose, is having trouble sleeping and has nightmares of a sexual nature in which her out-of-control urges shift wildly from hot to cold. Unable to remember her dreams, she checks into the Sexual Research Institute, where Dr. Lisa Jacobs (Victoria Paris) and her assistant Randy Spears diagnose her problem as repression by observing her dreams through the magic of technology. A feather, a leather glove (not O.J.'s), and ice are made good use of, and the music is listenable. Quintessential Andrew Blake with all the right Blake touches, plus some new moves and visuals.

Explicitness: 7; Sensuality: 7 M

Night Trips 2

MORE MTV FANTASIES

Starring: Paula Price, Randy Spears, Tami Monroe, Cheri Taylor, Brigitte Monroe, Lauren Hall, Erica Boyer, Cameo, Brianna Rai, Nina Alexander, Raquel Darian, Randy West, Eric Price, Jon Dough, Derrick Lane. Producers: Patti Rhodes, Howard Klein. Director: Andrew Blake. Writers: Montgomery Plum, Andrew Blake. Music: Rock Hard. Caballero, 1990.

In *Night Trips*, Tori Wells suffered from sexual repression. In this sequel, Paula Price's problem is nymphomania. We go with her for her cure at the Mind Scan Foundation. The W/Ws are the hottest segments in this video, though we felt one of the segments was a touch rough in the way women were handled with excessive biting, etc. Technically and visually sophisticated with plenty of high-intensity visuals and unusual treatments of color and lighting, we found the editing annoying and the intercutting between the dream and reality executed too fast for sustaining any erotic tension. Otherwise, an Andrew Blake video through and through. If you like his work, you'll like this.

Explicitness: 7;   Sensuality: 6   B,   C,   M,   T

9½ Weeks

SADOMASOCHISM GOES MAINSTREAM

Starring: Kim Basinger, Mickey Rourke, Christine Baranski, Margret Whitton, David Marguilies. Producers: Anthony Rufus Isaacs, Zalman King. Director: Adrian Lynn. Writers: Patricia Knop, Zalman King, Sarah Kernochan. From a novel by Elizabeth McNeill. Music: Jack Nietzsche. MGM/UA/PSO, 1986. 117 minutes.

He is the ultimate New York date—handsome, hip, rich, with enough personal problems to make him fascinating. She is the dazzling girl of his dreams—a talented artist, with a glamour job in a gallery to help pay for her designer clothes. Their romance begins like a garden-variety obsessive love affair—she looks at the watch he gave her and masturbates to orgasm; he blindfolds her, feeds her strange food, and rubs her bare body with ice. His strict rules about no background details, no friends, and his occasionally cruel and humiliating behavior add excitement to the relationship, right? (We guess her character hasn't seen *Last Tango in Paris.*) Kim's movie character draws the line far sooner than her counterpart in the book and past time for us.

This story is one of the two or three Hollywood movies most often mentioned as favorites by people who want something lusty but think they aren't ready for erotic films. For that reason, some of the sensuous details of this film have found their way into many couples' experiments with sexual variety. We can see that reason for renting it. There are some hot moments, and Kim and Mickey are beautiful to watch, but the movie is slow, slow, slow. Excellent sound track, including Joe Cocker, the Eurythmics, and Bryan Ferry.

Simulated

Nothing to Hide

COMIC ROMANCE WITH HEART

Starring: John Leslie, Richard Pacheco, Tigr, Erica Boyer, Chelsea Manchester, Misty Regan, Elizabeth Randolph, Holly McCall, Raven Turner, Aaron Stuart, Pat Manning, Eric Stein, Richard Dove, Nicole Adams, George Spelvin. Producer: Bernardo Spinelli. Director: Anthony Spinelli. Writer: Michael Ellis. Music: Ronnie Ramonovich. Cal Vista, 1982. 97 minutes.

Taking up where *Talk Dirty to Me* left off, the hypersexed Jack (John Leslie) and the slightly slow Lenny (Richard Pacheco) are friends who look out for each other. Jack, still compulsive about his sexual activity, is doggedly pursuing every woman who affords him an opening. Suffering from satyriasis of the soul, he denies his loneliness, claiming that loving a woman would only serve to make him a chump. In spite of his braggadocio, Jack shows himself to be a soulful guy in his heartfelt affection for Lenny, for whom he clearly cares very much. So much so that their relationship has been compared with that of Lenny and George in Steinbeck's *Of Mice and Men*.

Still a virgin, Lenny yearns for his first sexual experience and a soulmate. The latter is generously afforded him by Chelsea Manchester, who plays one of Jack's girls. Possibly the most honest erotic film we've seen, the narrative focuses on the relationship that develops when Karen (Tigr), on roller skates in the park, runs into Lenny. Wistful and sweet, their love is a refreshing contrast to Jack's detached encounters. Ending with a wedding, *Nothing to Hide* is a real winner. **Highly recommended.**

Explicitness: 7;   Sensuality: 7

Obsessed

(see *Anna Obsessed*)

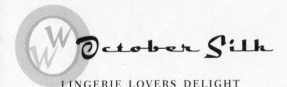

October Silk

LINGERIE LOVERS DELIGHT

Starring: Abigail Clayton, Lisa De Leeuw, Christine deSchaeffer, Christie Ford, Samantha Fox, Arcadia Lake, Merle Michaels, Candida Royalle, Tara Smith, Gloria Leonard, Jesse Adams, Bobby Astyr, George Payne, Biff Parker, Dave Ruby, Jeff Teague, Jake Teague, Tara Alexander. Producer: Cecil Howard. Director/writer: Henri Pachard. Command Video/A Wim Van Production, 1980. 76 minutes.

Gloria's Boutique—specializing in provocative lingerie, evening wear, and devices to enhance sexual pleasure—is the focus of this vignette video. Though the characters are in one way or another connected to each other, their relationships are irrelevant to the intent of the stories, which is to show a mélange of sexual sketches. All the stories are from the point of view of women, each of whom takes control of her sexual needs.

Two outstanding scenes make this superior entertainment. Lisa DeLeeuw, angry because her married boyfriend dumps her, shows up at his house and seduces his at-first-unwilling maid (Arcadia Lake) on the dining room table while enjoying a bottle of her ex's best champagne. Putting icy-cold hands and light bondage to good use, Lisa takes Arcadia from a shy and reluctant participant to an enthusiastic accomplice. Candida Royalle, who moved into the producer/director's chair at her company, Femme Productions (see pages 48 and 210), after performing in over twenty-five films, is here paired with Tara Alexander, a sex surrogate helping the married Eric and Abigail overcome his impotence. While not a teaching tool, *October Silk's* approach to impotence is enlightened, and the techniques these ladies use can be mimicked by anyone finding themselves in the same situation. And we say hurrah to Eric, who, for the love of Abigail, acknowledges and does something about his problem.

Our one caveat is about an extended scene involving two allegedly high school girls who set out to seduce an older man. Granted, they chase after him with intent, one of them having picked out just the right red slinky dress from Gloria's Boutique to capture

Dressing for Success

The power suit for mainstream erotic videos is not a Frederick's of Hollywood crotchless panty, nor a sheer black shortie nightgown. When the well-dressed erotic video star sheds her silk blouse and skirt, more often than not she's adorned in matching bra or bustier, garter belt, thong panties, stockings, and high heels. If there is no garter belt, the stockings are thigh highs with elastic lace tops. Pantyhose don't make the cut. The favored fabric is lace; the favored color is white, followed by pastels. More mature stars can wear black (indicating more sophistication?), and a daring few choose red. Occasionally the thong is adorned with ruffles on the hips, and white-eyelet bustiers are also seen. Bodysuits and teddies solve the problem of a little something to hide (in videos as in life, some tummies are rounder than others). The look is traditionally feminine and sweetly seductive, even when the behavior is aggressive.

Untroubled by real-life problems such as a white shirt and dark skirt, video stars never wear a white bra and colored panties, nor indeed any underwear that does not match. They can put safety pins in their noses but not on their bra straps. An errant lock of pubic hair curling out of the side of a thong is not permitted. And while you'll see plenty of silicone, as well as B- and even A-cup-size breasts, you'll never, never, never see a Wonder Bra.

her quarry. Leaving no detail unattended, she's prepared for the assignation by wearing a garter belt under her cheerleader outfit. We admit the scene has its funny moments, like showing a fully grown man panting like a dog in heat, but it did make us mighty uncomfortable.
Highly recommended.

Explicitness: 8; Sensuality: 8 A, B, SS, 2W

Ona Zee's Sex Academy

THERE'S NO BUSINESS LIKE SHOW BUSINESS

Producer/director: Ona Zee. Ona Zee Productions, 1994.

A mixture of nitty-gritty how-to and fiction gives us a look at people starting out in the business. Ona Zee, one of the bright and shining stars of adult videos, shares tips on subjects as varied as getting a first job, applying make-up, and having sex for the camera. She also gives some sound advice on assembling a provocative costume wardrobe (since low-budget films that hire the inexperienced expect them to provide their own wardrobes). Her "students" are a mix of the truly amateur and experienced performers. Ona's calm, self-assured manner and modulated voice would do credit to any practiced seminar leader, whether she's giving resume tips, modeling a leotard with cutout breasts, or demonstrating dildo insertion. The sex, when it happens, is humdrum. This is the first of many videos in Ms. Zee's new series.

Explicitness: 6; Sensuality: 6

Only the Best: Jim Holliday (vol. 1)

EROTICA HISTORIAN'S COMPILATION

Starring: John Leslie, Abigail Clayton, Annette Haven, Leslie Bouvee, Nina Hartley, Shana Grant, Joey Silvera, Fay Bird, John Holmes, Georgina Spelvin, Kate Harrison, Joanna Story, Jonathon Levi, Jackie O'Neill. Cal Vista, 1986.

Jim Holliday, the acknowledged historian of adult films, collected eleven of the sex scenes he considers to be the hottest ever made and put them on one video, together with a voice-over that gives the clips some context. For example, by the consensus of male stars who worked with her, Leslie Bouvee gave the best oral sex in the business. Watch her technique in a scene from *Eruption*—number 4 on the tape. The information and the opportunity to see a few legendary performers fascinated us. Understandably, but unfortunately for us, the sex scenes, chosen from a male perspective, include two rapes we would have left on the cutting room floor. On the other hand, there's a romantic beach scene from *Seven into Snowy* (a hard-to-find video) and a funky clip from *Outlaw Ladies*.

Jim Holliday's other compilation tapes—*Only the Best*, vol. 2 and vol. 3—contain more clips and narration in a similar format. We tend to prefer the whole story and not just the hottest sex scene, but if you don't, Holliday is the best.

Explicitness: 9; Sensuality: 5

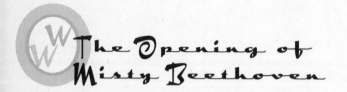

The Opening of Misty Beethoven

COMEDY IN EVERYBODY'S TOP TEN

Starring: Constance Money, Terri Hall, Jamie Gillis, Ras Kean, Casey Donovan, Jenny Baxter, Gloria Leonard, Mary Stuart, Cynthia Gardner, Helene Simone, Marlene Willoughby, Nancy Dare. Producer/director: Radley Metzger (aka Henri Paris). Music: Elephant's Memory. VCA, 1976 87 minutes.

Internationally known sex researcher Seymour Love (Jamie Gillis) sits in a Parisian theater watching a dirty movie when low-rent hooker Misty Beethoven (Constance Money) catches his eye. She is moving from seat to seat selling her merciful hands to movie patrons desiring relief. Curious, he makes her an offer. She takes him to an hourly hotel, where she recites a long list of things she wouldn't dream of doing and volunteers a rebate if he'll accept manual release.

"You're nothing but a sexual civil service worker," he announces. He's leaving, when he spies a very social woman friend having exuberant sex. They fall into each other's arms, and during their chatty gossip he bets her that he could turn any tacky girl into the new Golden Rod Girl, a sexual star. Guess who she points to? Yes, it's *Pygmalion* (or *My Fair Lady* without the music). A good story then and a good story now—well acted, too.

So the adorable Misty is groomed in almost all aspects of sexuality by the ruthlessly charming Dr. Love and his devoted staff of sexperts. We say "almost all" because as '90s women we can't help noticing that her lessons center on pleasuring men and achieving power and notoriety through her sexual proficiency, not in reaching her own multiple orgasms. We didn't let it worry us, since we found the combination of sex and laughter a great aphrodisiac. Maybe that's why this video is at the top of almost everybody's list of all-around, all-time best. **Highly recommended.**

Explicitness: 7;   Sensuality: 9   M,   3M/W,   O

The Other Side of Julie

COMEDY OF A DOUBLE LIFE

Starring: Susannah French, John Leslie, Jackie O'Neill, Paula Wain, Kristine Heller, Joey Silvera, Tracey O'Neill, Nancy Hoffman, Blair Harris, Michael Morrison, Richard Logan. Producer: Charles Gifford. Director: Anthony Riverton. Writers: Colin Davis, Anthony Riverton. Music: Oliver Mansfield. Cal Vista, 1977. 80 minutes.

By day, and frequently by night, Mike Robbins (John Leslie) runs Stag Enterprises. His ride around town is a Rolls Royce from which he checks in on his "escort" service for both sexes, his start-up investments with pretty young women who want to run their own businesses, and a profitable sideline in parting older women from their jewelry. Since these activities require his very personal participation, by the time he turns into Mr. Ordinary Suburbanite, with the help of metal-rimmed glasses and an Oldsmobile, all he wants to do is eat and sleep. His bewildered wife, Julie (Susannah French), who doesn't have a clue about his work, takes his neglect personally. Then her savvy Aunt Isabel (Jackie O'Neill) comes to town in search of her runaway daughter Kim (Paula Wain), and, my, oh my! Mike Robbins gets more than one unexpected lesson in management techniques.

Women may wonder why it took Julie so long to get a clue, but never mind. If you found the first viewing a turn-on, you'll enjoy the second even more. And as a bonus the Jackie O'Neill/John Leslie encounter is considered a classic.
Recommended.

Explicitness: 8;   Sensuality: 7

SECRET LIVES OF AMERICAN WIVES

Starring: Marlene Willoughby, Jody Maxwell, Juliet Anderson, Richard Bolla, Bobby Astyr, Samantha Fox, Veronica Hart, Merle Michaels, John Leslie, Candida Royalle, Joey Silvera. Producers: Eldon Byrd, Ron Sullivan. Director/writer: Henri Pachard. Music: Jhana Production. VCA, 1981. 83 minutes.

Husbands take note: Ladies who lunch aren't necessarily lunching. Populated by ladies well into their thirties, *Outlaw Ladies* begins by showing us what goes on in the morning in millions of upper-middle-class American households, presumably to make the point that these ladies are really quite ordinary. Husbands are getting dressed for work while giving instructions to their wives about the dry cleaning, complaining about the cost of educating the kids, and generally hiding behind *The Wall Street Journal* at breakfast and ignoring questions like "Will you be home for dinner?" no matter how many times they're asked.

Once their blokes are off to the office, the ladies set about pursuing pleasure in some very focused and unexpected ways. Wasting no time, two of the ladies hire a stud to share. Miss Cassie (Marlene Willoughby), a businesswoman by day, has a secret double life as a prostitute during her off hours. She beguilingly puts a pair of red panties to some unusual uses. Samantha Fox and Jody Maxwell, dressed in their best downtown clothes, pick up a low-lifer (Joey Silvera) and go to his seedy apartment for a little sexy slumming. Best of all, attorney Veronica Hart, wanting a new thrill, gets talked through first-time anal sex by John Leslie.

Of course the husbands are no innocents either. There's plenty of dirty talk, and be sure to check out what one of the women does to the other with a vibrator.
Highly recommended.

Explicitness: 8;   Sensuality: 8   A,   M

Pandora's Mirror

THROUGH THE LOOKING GLASS

Starring: Veronica Hart, Jamie Gillis, Candy Barbour, Marlene Willoughby, Heather Gordon, Merle Michaels, Tiffany Clark, Frederick Foster, Sandy Hilman, Annie Sprinkle, George Payne, Jerry Butler, Dave Ruby, Ron Hudd, Roy Stuart, Mark Valentine, Robin Sane, Ron Jeremy, Ashley Moore, Stuart Mitchell, Gordon O. Duvall. Producer/director/ writer: Warren Evans. Caballero/Warner Evans Film, 1981. 93 minutes.

Set in New York's West Greenwich Village, *Pandora's Mirror* revolves around an unusual pier glass that Pandora (Veronica Hart) comes across in a quaint though creepy antique shop. It's one of those dank and dusty stores that looks as if it's owned by Norman Bates's long-lost cousin, a place where you know you'll find an unclaimed treasure—if you don't disappear. Pandora's transfixed by the mirror, but the agitated shopkeeper won't let her look into it for long and refuses to sell it to her, claiming that it's been in his family for many years and, more to the point, it's dangerous. We know he's telling the truth because we have seen the secret of the mirror. When Pandora looks into it, she is transported back into time, where she witnesses what the mirror reflected. Her obsession with the mirror increases, and she cannot stay away. Are these episodes from Veronica's own past lives or a chronicle of the mirror's racey history?

Well paced and expertly performed, *Pandora's Mirror* would have made a perfect *Twilight Zone* episode were it not for the explicit sex. We wish it had a sequel—we want to know what happened next.
Recommended.

Explicitness: 8;   Sensuality: 6   C,   M,   2M/W,   2W, 2W/M

Passion in Venice

AND THEY CALL IT A BUSINESS TRIP?

Starring: Julie Ashton, Deborah Wells, Mark Davis, Anita Blond, Kelly Trump, Bernadette, Valentina, Sean Michaels, Frank Mallone, Valentino, Backey Jackie, Attila. Directors: Cameron Grant, Joe D'Mato. Writers: Cameron Grant, Elvis Betman. Music: Let's Play Music. Ultimate Pictures/Adam and Eve Production/Capital Film, 1995.

Of enduring interest as a vacation destination, the indoor and outdoor glories of Venice just about steal the scenes in this lavishly shot video. Having to do with a murky business scheme, the plot was ambiguous throughout, we couldn't always differentiate the good guys from the bad, so we quickly abandoned trying and just relished the gorgeous people (white and African-American), clothes, settings, and, of course, uninhibited sex Italian style. The opaque ending leads us to believe a sequel is in the making.
Recommended.

Explicitness: 8;   Sensuality: 7   M,   O,   2W

The Passions of Carol

MERRY CHRISTMAS TO ALL

Starring: Mary Stuart, Jamie Gillis, Kim Pope, Day Jason, Susan Sloan, Sonny Landham, Alan Marlow, Toni Scott, Ashley Moore, Marc Stevens, Kevin Andre, Arturo Millhouse, Steven Mitchell, Russ Carlson. Producer/director: Amanda Barton. Writer: Warren Evans. Video X Pics, 1975. 76 minutes.

Ms. Scrooge publishes *Biva*, a women's sex magazine. Bob Cratchit is her underappreciated and overworked art director. On Christmas eve he calls his wife: "I know Tiny Kim wants her daddy home. Miss Scrooge and her assistant are still auditioning the Biva Boy." In this retelling of Dickens's much abused *The Christmas Carol* the ghosts concentrate on showing Ms. Scrooge her disreputable sex life past, present, and future. Not as farcical as it should have been, after a promising beginning, the video runs out of steam and dwindles to a close, though not before Bob and his wife have one heartfelt Christmas celebration. We didn't much like the childhood Ghost of Christmas past scenes either. Bah humbug.

Explicitness: 7;   Sensuality: 4

Peril or Pleasure: Feminist Produced Pornography

DOCUMENTARY

Producer/director/writer: Andrea Torrice. Narrator: Julia Randall. 1989.

A documentary discussion of erotic films made by women for women, this well-meaning video tries for a balanced view of a controversial subject. On one side of the issue are Candida Royalle, former erotic star and head of Femme Productions, erotic films for women); Annie Sprinkle, former star, now a filmmaker and activist; Suzie Bright, a writer and editor who is an outspoken advocate of fantasy materials for women; and Mary Beth Nelson, a *Caught Looking* (magazine) artist. Opposed to them are members of Women Against Pornography, who take the position that women who make adult films are women doing it to other women instead of men doing it to women. The filmmaker tried to be even handed, and we found it informative, though we doubt anyone will change their mind on either side.

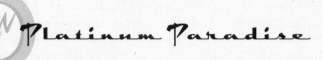

Platinum Paradise

TASTY VIGNETTES

Starring: Samantha Fox, Bobby Astyr, Hillary Summers, Christine Ford, Steven Mitchell, Robin Stores, Merle Michaels, Linda Vale, Vanessa Del Rio, Eric Edwards, Kandi Barbour, Maxine Charmin, Rico Estrada, Ashley Moore, Ellen Kain, Dave Ruby, Wally Seger, Marc Valentine, Peter

Waine, H. Oscar Ward. Producer/writer/director: Cecil Howard. Music: Siegfried & Schwartz. Command Video/A Scadro Command Presentation, 1980. 77 minutes.

It's a very early New York morning in 1980. The jogger is running, the ballet master is warming up, and the ballerina, rich lady, boss, secretary, and various other characters are absorbed in their morning rituals. As the day gets going, the folks at Paradise, a multisexual outcall service, are doing their best to supply the demand. Executed with a wink and a light touch, *Platinum Paradise* is unusually well written, amusing, and highly satisfying. Full of mistaken identities and unexpected assignations, this video will make for a fun evening.

Platinum Paradise has two exceptional scenes at opposite ends of the experience spectrum: The first is the slow, loving, gentle deflowering of the ballerina by the ballet master on the hardwood floor of the empty dance studio. Watch for the ballet master's unusual technique for undressing the ballerina. The second is a hilarious comedy of errors between two sex workers (Eric Edwards and Vanessa Del Rio), each of whom thinks the other is a paying customer. You'll love the pillow talk as each of these pros tries to outdo the other in technique and seductiveness. They work hard for the money.
Highly recommended.

Explicitness: 7;   Sensuality: 9 (two scenes)   2M/W,   T,   2W, 2W/M

Pretty Peaches 2

GIRL COMING OF AGE

Starring: Tracey Adams, Siobhan Hunter, Janette Littledove, Melissa Melendez, Ashley Bown, Tami White, Jamie Gillis, Peter North, Buck Adams, Herschel Savage, F.M. Bradley. Producer/director: Alex de Renzy. VCA, 1988.

Peaches (Siobhan Hunter) is a young girlish Candide figure, a trusting innocent who wanders unprotected through the world seeking sexual knowledge. She begins her search at home, but her mother is more attentive to the "lover's balls" of Peaches's boyfriend than to her daughter's questions, and her father tells her to "ask around the locker room." He does offer one piece of advice—"Don't be a tease." Peaches sees that there's no help to be had from them, so she dons her cutoffs and hitchhikes from LA to San Francisco, where her rich, sexually charged-up relatives welcome a newcomer to their domestic psychodrama.

Mom and Dad, though divorced, join forces to save their darling girl and briefly wonder why they ever left each other. After a while, Peaches's artless naïveté begins to look less like innocence and more as if her elevator doesn't go all the way to the top, but she finally gets her sexual initiation. An amiable if occasionally tasteless big-budget romp (we cite the father/son incest with Mom as particularly icky fast-forward material). After much research we discovered that *Pretty Peaches 1,* a favorite of those who know it, is out of circulation.

Explicitness: 8;   Sensuality: 7   2W/M

Pretty Peaches 3: The Quest

ON THE ROAD AGAIN

Starring: Keisha, Lynn Lemay, Tracey Adams, Marc Wallice, Eric Price, Rachel Ryan, Jamie Gillis, Victoria Paris, Pricilla Love, Vicki Blair, Tianna, Fefe, Jon Martin, Don Fernando, Jack Baker, Gene Carrera, Mike Horner, Richard Pacheco. Producer/director: Alex de Renzey. VCA, 1989.

The quest continues. A sequel to *Pretty Peaches 2,* in which Siobhan Hunter as Peaches searched for sexual enlightenment, the quest in *Peaches 3* is for spiritual enlightenment. Keisha replaces Hunter as Peaches.

Living with Mom (Tracey Adams) in a house trailer, Peaches has sexual nightmares that send her to famous psychiatrist Miss Thunderpussy, whose own excitable nature causes her to fling herself into the arms of an anatomically correct male blow-up doll. This is a "you have to see it to believe it" scene played with farcical zeal by Rachel Ryan.

The doctor's prescription to Peaches is to go on a quest for spiritual guidance, and so begins Peaches's brave and lonely quest at the feet of various supposedly wise teachers, most of whom require that you take your panties off to receive their wisdom. Her first stop is with a preacher cut from the same cheesy bolt of cloth as Jim Baaker and

Jimmy Swaggert whom she finds just as he's about to board a helicopter for South America to elude the IRS, cops, and angry parishioners. Jamie Gillis gives an over-the-top performance as the preacher worthy of the tacky originals. Peaches's disappointment doesn't deter her, and continuing her quest she travels to the Holy Repose Spiritual Retreat, a refuge something between a French country farm and an Amish village. From there she continues to the Realization Center, run by another horny guru. Peaches rejects all these holy perverts, finding herself, where else, in San Francisco, the end of the line for thousands of seekers. To her credit, Peaches is not fooled by any of these charlatans and discovers the "true" truth on her own, becoming a sort of guru herself.
Recommended.

Explicitness: 7;   Sensuality: 5   T,   2W/M

Porsche Lynn

We have Ronald Reagan to thank for Porsche Lynn's career as dancer, actress, and professional dominatrix. Out of funds after two years at Michigan State University because of cuts in student aid, she took a job as a peeler/dancer at an adult emporium with two auditoriums, a bookstore, peep booths, private video booths, and a pool hall. Finding herself in a community of "true genuine people, loving and caring who express themselves in an art form" as she describes the colleagues she met, Porsche left Michigan for California and a career in adult movies.

At the peak of her dancing career, she was on the road for thirty weeks a year. With the exception of San Francisco, which she describes as unique in the world for its progressive attitudes, dancing establishment are one of two kinds. If alcohol is served, the dancers are required to keep at least one garment on. In

Prison World

BEHIND BARS AND LOVING IT

Starring: Porsche Lynn, Sarah Jane Hamilton, Diva, Misty Rain. Producer/director/writer: Ernest Greene. Music: 506 Ciardia. Twist Production, 1994.

Bored silly with all the pampering attention you get at that expensive spa? Instead of being lavished with facials, massages, and low-cal meals, are you looking for a little poking and prodding in the right ways and places? If S/M is a delicacy you long for, check yourself into Prison World for an all-girl experience in light S/M. Relinquishing all rights at the gate, surrender yourself into the world of cuffed wrists and ankles,

juice bars, where no alcohol is served, everything can come off—except in Canada where the dancer must always keep some piece of clothing on even if it's her panties worn around an ankle. The decor in juice bars is nicer, usually replete with marble, velvet, and chandeliers. Fear of prostitution excludes women coming solo even on Ladies' Only nights.

Being a dancer and staying on the right side of the law is no easy task. At a club down the road from Churchill Downs in Kentucky, Porsche, who keeps her pubes shaved, found herself arrested and charged with a felony for "portraying child pornography." Determined to fulfill her obligation to the club, Porsche asked what she needed to do to be able to dance. "Draw it on with an eyebrow pencil or paste some hair" was the reply from the law. Guess which solution she chose? No, it wasn't a merkin. Though we did get a chuckle imagining a large black handlebar mustache a la Salvador Dali on her gorgeous blond self.

Porsche has in recent years cut back on her grueling schedule to concentrate on making movies and establishing phone sex lines and two domination studios complete with dungeons. Prison World, The Masseuse, Night Trips, and Sorority Sex Kittens are videos featuring Porsche that you will find reviewed in this book.

enemas, giant vibrators, gentle flogging, nipple rings, and leather swings. Your wardens are likely to be dressed in wet-look spandex, leather, and high high heels. Why not give a weekend at the prison as a birthday gift to your best friend?
Recommended.

Simulated   Sensuous: 5   B,   M,   S,   T,   2W

The Private Afternoons of Pamela Mann

WOMAN WITH A SECRET LIFE

Starring: Barbara Bourbon, Darby Lloyd Rains, Alan Marlow, Georgina Spelvin, Eric Edwards, Jamie Gillis, Day Jackson, David Savage, Sonny Landham, Levi Richards, Mark Stevens, Lola LaGarce, Kevin Andre. Producer/director: Radley Metzger (aka Henri Paris). Writer: Jake Barnes (aka Radley Metzger). TVX, 1974. 83 minutes.

Another carnal private detective movie, though it may not be fair to say "another," since this film is a classic on which many subsequent adult films were modeled. The by now familiar plot begins with a very successful magazine publisher/husband who hires a private detective to keep an eye on his wife, Pamela. She is a paragon of virtue with one eccentricity: She can't get enough sex. As might be expected in an erotic film, it's not for lack of trying. There is a brief kidnapping/rape scene with murky origins that may have been arranged by the husband, or perhaps by Pamela herself acting out a fantasy. Georgina Spelvin plays a hooker with a heart of gold whose big romance is with women. The very 1974 hipness of this video made it seem dated to us, although those into the history of adult films may want to take a look at this often mentioned trailblazer.

Explicitness: 8;   Sensuality: 4   M/W,   O,   2W,   2W/M

R & R

WARTIME DRAMA

Starring: Asia Carrera, Tiffany Minx, Tricia Yen, Victoria Andrews, Melanie Maslow, Vivian, Tony Tedeschi, Buck Adams, Sean Michaels, Steve Drake, Johnny Prober, Jack Mehoff, Austin Moore. Producer: Stuart Canterbury Production. Director: Stuart Canterbury. Writer: Nigel Crinch-Gibbons. Music: Greg Steel. VCA, 1994. 83 minutes.

It's Christmas Eve in Hell. The Vietnam War is raging, and the setting is atmospheric, with ceiling fans, mosquito nets, sounds of planes and choppers, and plenty of explosions. Though we don't know the year, stock jungle and war footage is used to suggest the heat of the combat. Soldiers gather at Al's Bar to drink, brawl, and screw. Tony Tedeschi, seriously wounded during a mission into Laos, is reflecting on his tour in flashback. He's been in Nam for eight months and has managed to keep his promise of celibacy to his girlfriend at home, a decision mocked and sabotaged by his fellow soldiers. Between intervals of Tedeschi's flashbacks we get episodes of what soldiers do to make life "in country" bearable.

Unable to resist temptation, Tedeschi finally succumbs to the lure of Asia Carrera. Shot along a river on a beautiful day with good music and lots of kissing, their union competes for heat with the fireworks of the war. Asia Carrera is one of our favorite performers, and we rented this video because her picture dominates the box. We felt ripped off. Asia doesn't appear until the very last scene. We know this industry isn't committed to truth in advertising, but this seemed a particularly egregious example of the practice of bait and switch. Her scene, when we finally got to it, is worth the wait once she gets over an attempt to be coy. You won't miss a thing if you fast-forward right to it.

The cast is multiracial, as you would expect it to be in a war zone on foreign soil. Sean Michaels, who is African-American, and Vivian, who is Asian, have a scene in which gorgeous Michaels is very effective, although Vivian is less so.

Explicitness: 9; Sensuality: 5 (except for Carrera scene, which we rate 8) A, C, T, 2W/M

Red Shoes Diaries series

Red Shoes Diaries 1

MADE-FOR-TV SOFT-CORE SUDS

Starring: David Duchovny, Brigitte Bako, Billy Wirth. Director: Zalman King. Writers: Patricia Louisiana Knop, Zalman King. Republic Pictures, 1992. Not rated. (**Soundtrack available on disc and tape.**)

Some women like this movie, and if you believe that a woman who cheats on the world's most perfect boyfriend with another incredibly good-looking man deserves to die, you might too. Since the movie begins with her funeral, we aren't giving anything away by telling you this. It's Zalman King's (*9½ Weeks, Wild Orchids,* etc.) familiar erotic theme of no name, no information, only-the-two-of-us-in-this-room sex, but anyone who has watched his movies knows it always goes wrong. The sport is in watching how. In this case Brigitte Bako, already engaged to the impeccable Jake makes her move on a really hip, incredibly hot-looking construction worker/shoe salesman. At the end, Jake the brokenhearted fiancé (David Duchovny, now on the *X-Files*), puts a personal ad in the paper. "Have you been hurt, betrayed, do you keep a diary?" The answers to this ad will appear in the sequels. Stay tuned.

Simulated

Double Dare

RED SHOES DIARIES 2: THREE SEXY SHORT STORIES

Starring: Steven Bauer, Joan Severance, Denise Crosby. Producers: Zalman King, Patricia Louisiana Knop. Republic Pictures. 92 minutes.

Jake (David Duchovny, the bereaved fiancé from the first *Red Shoes*), introduces each story. He's running a personal ad that reads, in part, "Have you been hurt, betrayed? Have you betrayed another? Do you keep a diary?" These stories are the answers he receives to his ad.

The heat varies in these episodes, depending on your taste. All three are handsomely shot, most of the people are attractive, and the first one is definitely hot.

Simulated

SAFE SEX (#1)
Starring: Steven Bauer, Joan Severance.

He is ruggedly attractive and has that dangerous male aura that women find irresistible. She has a classical face and a gorgeous body that looks like a gift from God, not a surgical alteration. After an accidental meeting escalates into incredible sex, the two arrange to meet twice a week in a typical Zalman King story of sex, only sex, no names, no histories, no problems. Equally typical King, life does not arrange itself so neatly. Some torrid scenes.
Recommended.

YOU HAVE THE RIGHT TO REMAIN SILENT (#2)
Starring: Denise Crosby, Robert Knepper. Director: Ted Kotcheff. Writer: Chloe King.

A woman admires men's bodies in her gym. One man pays no attention to her, so of course he's the one she wants. She's a cop and the simplest way to handle it is to pull his car over, kidnap him, and put him in a cage until he gets the picture. We understand the impulse. Sometimes a woman's got to do what a woman's got to do.

DOUBLE DARE (#3)
Starring: Laura Johnson, Arnold Vosloo, Michael Woods.

A happily married woman flirts through her office window with a manly fellow in the next building. She holds up a sign "Take off your shirt," then she takes off hers. They fax each other. Slowly they raise the stakes until he asks to meet in person. Wait a minute. Isn't she happily married?

Another Woman's Lipstick

RED SHOES DIARIES 3: THREE MORE SHORT STORIES

Narrator: Jake, played by David Duchovny. Executive Producers: Zalman King, Patricia Louisiana Knop, David Saunders.

The narrator of all three stories is Jake (David Duchovny, star of *X-Files*), who seems a little limp to keep on glooming around with his dead girlfriend's dog as his constant companion. But these are the best *Red Shoes* collectively so far—stop after the second one and you'll enjoy them even more.

Simulated

JUST LIKE THAT (#1)
*Starring: Matthew LeBlanc, Nina Siemazsko, Tcherky Karyo (as Phillip).
Director: Ted Kotcheff. Writer: Chloe King.*

Nina Siemazsko plays a young woman who goes to law school at night and works by day. Impulsively she has a hot, quick elevator fling with a bike messenger (Matt LeBlanc before he was in the cast of *Friends*) and shortly after that a different equally impulsive encounter with a successful businessman who looks rough in the way that Harrison Ford looks rough but who tenderly feeds her soup and takes care of her. She thinks she loves them both, but they each want an exclusive relationship. Her choice tells us that it really is a new day, baby.

ANOTHER WOMAN'S LIPSTICK (#2)
Starring: Maryann D'Abo, Christina Fulton, Kevin Haley. Director: Zalman King. Writer: Ed Silverstein.

Zoe (Maryann D'Abo) lives in a paradise of blissful married love until she has the sudden sickening realization that her husband is having an affair. She follows him and watches through the window while he spends the evening with his mesmerizing lover. Suddenly she understands, since she, too, finds the woman (Christina Fulton) completely compelling. Eventually Zoe dresses up as a most unconvincing man and seeks an introduction to her. Christina Fulton really is a knockout, and she does quite a hot strip thing when seducing Robert that suggests emulation, though it takes a lot of confidence to carry off the lamp-with-the-naked-light-bulb act. One of the best.

TALK TO ME BABY (#3)
Starring: Richard Tyson, Lydie Denier. Director: Rafael Eisenmann. Writer: Zalman King.

A long monologue from a down-market guy (signified by a tank top, hair that is short in the front and flows past his shoulders in the back, thick muscles) whose French girlfriend has caught him about to boink another woman in the ladies' room. He's driving and trying to apologize, recalling all the wild and outrageous things they've done sexually together (we see them in flashbacks). He threatens to kill them both if she doesn't talk to him. She has one line. This leaves you feeling as if you're listening to one of those dramatic monologues that high school students do for talent day.

Autoerotica

RED SHOES DIARIES 4

Starring: Ally Sheedy, David Duchovny, Sheryl Lee, Scott Plank, Marina Guilia Cavelli, Nick Chinalund, Caitlin Dulaney. Narrated by David Duchovny. Producers: Rafael Eisenmann, Avram Butch Kaplan, Jeff Young. Directors: Alan Smithee, Zalman King, Michael Karbelnikoff. Writers: Laurie Plank, Patricia Louisianna Knop, Ned Bowman, Ed Silverstein. 90 minutes.

Jake (David Duchovny) is back at the mailbox with communications from those who have "betrayed someone or been betrayed." Three more stories, one starring him. Story number 1 is the winner in this trio.

Simulated

ACCIDENTS HAPPEN (#1)

A yuppie husband and wife (Ally Sheedy) play games to keep their marriage spicy, with the help of an armoire full of toys and a remote-control camera over the bed. Their lonely Italian maid finds the key to this treasure chest and gets curious. She's also curious about the pool boy and decides to try a little red-wigged dress-up of her own, which leads to . . . an accident. We think this is the only intentionally funny *Red Shoes* we've ever seen. Who knew Zalman King had a sense of humor? *Favorite quote:* "I am a bright, beautiful woman and I am protecting my inner child."

AUTOEROTICA (#2)

A successful woman facing her thirtieth birthday and a marriage to someone "safe" gets involved in a race with a mysterious man in a desirable blue car. Pushing her red Corvette to the max, she learns to turn using the emergency brake and faces her fears of life while downshifting. The game is speed and power. May start your engines if you're a fast-car aficionada.

JAKE'S STORY (#3)

A mystery woman (Sheryl Lee) lies in wait for Jake at his diner/mailbox. The man has a gift for picking out the one who will do a real serious number on his gloomy head.

Weekend Pass

RED SHOES DIARIES 5: THREE MORE SHORT STORIES

Narrator: David Duchovny. Executive producers: Zalman King, Patricia Louisiana Knop, David Saunders. Producers: Rafael Eisenman, Avram Butch Kaplan, Jeff Young.

Three more stories linked together into one narrative by Jake, his post office box, and his faithful canine companion, Stella.

Simulated

DOUBLE OR NOTHING (#1)
Starring: Francesco Quinn, Paula Barbieri.

She's "kind of pretty" and has always been taken care of by men. Now she's on her own in LA with no cash and no skills except a talent for pool. She feels her choice is between hustling her body and hustling pool—she chooses the latter, something that doesn't always sit well with her victims, or with the man she links up with in partnership and love.

BOUNTY HUNTER (#2)
Starring: Clair Stansfield, Ron Marquette, Sue Kiel, Nicholas Love, Dee McCafferty.

A beautiful young woman comes into a lonely gas station/luncheonette. The handsome attendant/cook gives her a meal, and the two play sexual cat and mouse. The game heats up when the woman gets in touch with someone who hired her, someone who thinks that she'll be charmed into letting the man get away. She is charmed enough to play sexual games with him, and the handcuffs change wrists several times before the denouement.

WEEKEND PASS (#3)
Starring: Anthony Abbaddo, Ely Pouget, Shashawnee Hall.

A beautiful army recruit (Ely Pouget) goes on furlough with four friends and after many, many drinks in a bar brings a man back to the now-deserted barracks. What starts as a rough and tumble sexual fling resolves itself into a deeper and more interesting human encounter in this unusual tale of the Christmas season.

Revelations

FIRST-AMENDMENT DRAMA

Starring: Amy Rapp, Colin Matthews, Nicole London, Martin London, Ava Grace, Paris Phillips, Michele Capozzi. Producer: Per Sjöstedt. Director: Candida Royalle. Femme Productions, 1993. 75 minutes.

A slightly heavy-handed cautionary tale for those afraid of Big Brother. The censors have won. With the help of the military they have transformed the world into a dangerously unimaginative place, outlawing all sexual expression. Surrounded by dreariness, faces are gray and drab. Ariel (Amy Rapp) and Zane (Colin Matthews) (married to each other) mate only when she's fertile, as the authorities require. He pumps her with no interest or feeling. Procreation is the only purpose of sex.

One day Ariel discovers a hidden cache of videotapes showing a couple making erotic love—changing her life forever. The lovers in the video are deliberate and affectionate, slowly revealing the feelings of their hearts. Her pleasure is his focus, and, unlike so much in this genre, the director isn't just showing you umpteen rudimentary positions one after the other.

Candida Royalle's videos generally incorporate erotic force in a good story. The camera lingers on the expressive faces of the performers, showing the tenderness between them. We cheer what she has accomplished in an industry that ranks quality control low on its list of requirements. We were a touch disappointed in *Revelations*. The cinematography is at times disjointed, some of the close-ups are out of focus, and the narrative pace is too leisurely.

Explicitness: 6;   Sensuality: 8

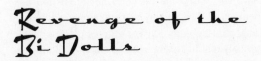

Revenge of the Bi Dolls

DOWN AND DIRTY

Starring: Ty Fox, Tina Tyler, Tony Idol, Cutter West, Dallas Taylor, Cort Stevens, Alec Powers, Vince Voyeur, Rob Baron, Crystal Gold, Vixxen, Sharon Kane (as Ceily Fontana), Gloria Leonard, and special guest star

178

Chi Chi La Rue. Producer/director/writer: Josh Eliot. Music: Rock Hard. Catalina.

With cat fights galore, *Revenge of the Bi Dolls* shows women at their absolute worst in relation to each other. And the men aren't so upright either. Two popular singers who only a year ago worked together have parted ways. One of them has gone into decline, while the other is on top of the pile. They despise each other with scenery-chewing verve. There's a dark savagery to their behavior that verges on buffoonery with dialogue that's so blatant, it's funny. Our favorite transvestite, Chi Chi La Rue, makes a special guest appearance as a maid in a grand house. She's brassy and sassy in a roaringly funny outdoor cat fight scene, which is a must-see.

Most of the video is set in a gorgeous house belonging to one of the singers, making for a high-style set. The performances are delivered with gusto. The sex scenes were too many to count, and like the best of Shakespeare's tragedies the stage is littered with dead bodies, but no one need cry since they all give as well as they get. **Recommended.**

Explicitness: 9;   Sensuality: 5   A,   C,   M,   2M/W,   SS

Rites of Passion

RED-HOT FEMINISM

Starring: Nina Hartley, Jeanna Fine, Robert Bullock, Scott Baker, Roger T. Dodger, David Sandler. Producers: Candida Royalle, Per Sjöstedt. Directors: Veronica Vera, Annie Sprinkle. Writers: Veronica Vera, Annie Sprinkle. Femme Productions, 1987. 70 minutes.

Featuring two short and very different stories, *Rites of Passion* has its moments. Each is written and directed by a former erotic film actress. "Shady Madanna," directed by Veronica Vera, takes place in a TV studio where moral majority preacher Mr. Morality (Scott Baker) is venting a parody of the usual far-right anti-everything-you-ever-liked-doing diatribe. In spite of his most sincere efforts he cannot keep his eyes off Nina Hartley's perfectly peachy bottom and is soon hallucinating an episode between her and Robert Bullock, the station's program manager, which eventually turns into a smoldering threesome.

The second segment, "The Search for the Ultimate Sexual Expe-

rience," is directed and written by an icon of adult cinema, Annie Sprinkle. Jeanna Fine, playing the role of Sprinkle, is having an entirely tedious encounter with hot body builder Roger T. Dodger, whose only apparent talent is pumping. She throws him out and succumbs to despair. Will she ever have the kind of love she deserves? Suddenly, a genie in a tacky green outfit and arm bracelets materializes, claiming to be her spirit guide bound to repay an ancient karmic debt by taking her to the place where spirit meets flesh. What follows is a very basic and rudimentary introduction to tantric sex. We wouldn't lie to you. The production has the ambiance of a K-Mart blue light special. Get past it. This introduces some simplified principles of tantric sex that are fun to try with a lover if you're lucky enough to have one who won't giggle. At this point it is useful to remember the immortal words of Annie Savoy "Men will put up with a lot if they think it's foreplay." He'll thank you some day.
Highly recommended.

Explicitness: 7;   Sensuality: 7   SS

Roommates

WAGES OF SIN

Starring: Samantha Fox, Veronica Hart, Kelly Nichols, Jamie Gillis, Gloria Leonard, Jerry Butler, Jack Wrangler, Bobby Astyr, Merle Michaels, Ashley Moore, Roy Stuart, Ron Jeremy, Ron Hudd, Phil Smith, Frederick Foster, Peter Andrews, Patricia Dale, Kurt Mann, Adam DeHaven, John Christopher, Henry Pachard. Producer/director: Chuck Vincent. Writers: Chuck Vincent, Rick Marx. Platinum Pictures, 1982. 90 minutes.

Samantha Fox stars in the tale of three roommates in a NYC apartment—young actress having an affair with a married man back home, a glamorous model with a coke habit, and the owner of the apartment, Billie, an ex-hooker whose past won't leave her alone. Their adventures and misadventures include rape, drugs, assault, and various kinds of sexual exploitation. The movie is on several recommended-for-women lists, and if you're turned on by the dark and gritty you may agree. We don't. The sex is explicit and more artfully photographed than some, but we found all but one scene joyless. In our opinion, if this movie was the only thing you knew about sex, you'd wonder why anyone wanted to have it.

Explicitness: 7;   Sensuality: 4

A Scent of Heather

PUZZLING FAMILY TREE

Starring: Paul Thomas, Vanessa Del Rio, R. Bolla, Lisa Bea, Neil Peters, Tracy Adams, Felix Krull, Christie Ford, Jessica Teal, Veronica Hart. Producer: Bill Eagle. Director: Phillip Drexler, Jr. Writer: Anthony Vincent. Music: Arthur Foote Jr. Video X. Pix, 1981. 99 minutes.

Heather (Veronica Hart), has been squirreled away in a convent until she's ready for her prearranged marriage to Frederick (Paul Thomas). Her isolation hasn't prepared her for the duties as wife and lover, but she's lucky to have Aunt Phyllis, who's eager to give her a quick and stimulating introduction to marital pleasure to heighten her anticipation. We should all have had such a generous aunt handy with her tongue and fingers. After just the right amount of feverish but fumbling foreplay, the happy couple are about to consummate their marriage when a letter from Heather's father arrives, revealing an altogether disconcerting relationship between Heather and Frederick: they're actually siblings! Through flashbacks, the particulars of their birth are revealed in a delectable scene involving mirrors. The rest of the video is taken up with cunning and ingenious resolution to this calamity.

In spite of an occasional anachronism, *Scent* follows the formula of love lost and found in a drama that's part Victorian, part comedy of errors. Set in a supposedly Victorian castle, it captures the atmosphere of another time, with great costumes, excellent dialogue, and nifty acting by Paul Thomas and Veronica Hart.
Recommended.

Explicitness: 8;   Sensuality: 8   M,   2W

Sea of Love

EDGY URBAN PASSION

Starring: Al Pacino, Ellen Barkin, John Goodman, Michael Rooker, William Hickey, Christine Estabrook, Barbara Baxley, Samuel L. Jackson, Lorraine Bracco. Director: Harold Becker. Writer: Richard Price. 1989.

Al Pacino plays a detective investigating a serial killer who chooses his victims through personal ads. Ellen Barkin plays the woman Pacino meets, suspects, and can't resist. The primo scene is the stand-up seduction by Barkin. Pacino leaves his undershirt on in bed, but that's OK. If he doesn't want to show it, chances are we don't want to see it. The rest is mighty fine.

Simulated

Secret Games 1

WIFE SEEKS EMPLOYMENT OUTSIDE THE HOME

Starring: Michelle Brin, Martin Hewitt, Dalia Sheppard, Billy Drago, Catya Sasoon, Sabrina Masko, Kimberly Williams. Producer: Walter Garnert. Director: Alexander G. Hippolyte. Imperial Entertainment, 1992.

The tried-and-true plot of a young, comely wife whose husband is so busy with the career that paid for the impressive house and deluxe car that he treats her like another expensive accessory is played out by Jacqueline (Michelle Brin) and Mark (Billy Drago). Jacqueline is persuaded by a more experienced friend to join a group of similarly underutilized housewives who are offered the opportunity to spend the afternoons selling sex and bondage to men who can afford to pay top dollar for their pro-am services. That's how Jacqueline becomes mistress to Eric (Martin Hewitt), a man whose seeming love and sexual obsession is a quickly shed disguise for his sick intentions. There is a plenty of tensely erotic simulated sex with both husband and lover.

The director of this movie makes explicit films as one of the Dark Brothers (see the review of *Devil in Miss Jones* 5 for a sample). The trade-off here seems to be nonexplicit sex for more violence than some of us found comfortable. There are several differently cut versions available apparently, from unrated to R. So far as we know, none are explicit.

Simulated

Secret Games 2

MALE MIDLIFE CRISIS

Starring: Martin Hewitt, Marie Laroux, Amy Rochelle, Sara Suzanne Brown, Thomas Milan, Holly Spencer, Jennifer Peace, Mark T. Paladin, Sherry Patterson, Gregg Christy, Bill Williams. Producer: Andrew Garroni. Director: Gregory Hippolyte. Imperial Entertainment, 1993.

Kyle (Martin Hewitt) is a performance artist, a broad term that covers a wide variety of art that takes place in front of an audience. He used to be an art critic with a big paycheck before giving up his day job to become "talent," a career choice that may be spiritually more rewarding but that doesn't pay very well. We don't see his art, so we don't know if he made the right decision. The money becomes

Nina Hartley, Actress

Onscreen, Nina Hartley's lively and likable enthusiasm makes her stand out in a crowded orgy, so when we met with her to discuss her life and new career behind the camera we were surprised by her glasses, softly combed hair, and long-skirt-with-loose-jacket outfit. Only her distinctive jawline and faint lisp reminded us of the glamorous queen of erotic movies we were used to seeing. She could have passed as any typical, pretty California young mom next door.

"Typical" is how she describes herself as a teenager. The youngest of four children, she grew up bashful, an overalls-and-Birkenstocks Berkeley girl, sexual only in her fantasies. But those fantasies were always exhibitionistic, and when she was eighteen and enrolled in nursing school she was also starting to dance onstage and then to work in live all-girl sex shows at the

quite an issue though, since Kyle's wife is unhappy enough about it to leave. Kyle immediately makes his move on two women—one married and one a hooker. The hooker leads him down the primrose path to seamy sexual adventures, including simulated twosomes and threesomes.

This is about as close to porn as you can find in a video that is available in Blockbuster, a chain that doesn't carry explicit movies. We've seen cable cuts of hardcore videos that had less action. Some of the simulated sex is well, sexy, but the story is cynical and emotionally bleak.

Simulated

Mitchell Brothers club in San Francisco. By the time she graduated from nursing school (B.S., magna cum laude), she had also graduated to making movies (Educating Nina was her first starring role). She says that people who worked in the hospital knew what she did, since several of them recognized her from films, but mention of it was shy, not confrontational. Even today, fans who recognize her in spite of the low-key "civilian" persona are respectful in their requests for autographs.

The unconventional exploration of her sexuality was encouraged by her boyfriend, Dave, now her husband of more than seventeen years, who functions as helpmate, protector, and cheerleader. Dave not only supported her wish to dance, he also found the person who introduced her into the adult movie business. They have a threeway marriage—Nina's female lover she refers to as her wife lives with them—they also are long-time swingers. Obviously, jealousy isn't a big issue in this relationship. Dave's only public appearance that we know of is in Nina Hartley's Guide to Cunnilingus: Under the Hood. *With true wifely enthusiasm, she says he's the best.*

Secret Games 3

SUSPENSE THRILLER

Starring: Woody Brown, Rochelle Swanson, May Karasun, Dean Scofield, Brenda Swanson, Bob Delegall. Producer: Andrew Garroni. Director: Gregory Hippolyte. Writers: Don Simmons/Tucker Johnson.

Here's yet another husband (this one's a doctor) who makes the mistake of leaving his attractive wife sitting around with too much time on her hands and not enough attention from him. Diane (Rochelle Swanson), possessor of tasteful plastic cupcakes and mall hair, has a magnificent house and no sex life. Bored, disillusioned, and a little whiny, she all but leaps to join Gwen, her neighbor, at a special "club" (read high-class brothel), where she's mesmerized by the action and begins to find expression for her fantasies. Her husband's interest in her is rekindled (and isn't that an old story), while her own attention is devoted to her new friends at the "club," particularly Terrell Baxter a "carefully screened client" whose passion for Diane quickly intensifies to obsession and is nearly her undoing. Lovely lingerie, simulated sex, and high production values make this the best choice of the three.
Recommended.

Simulated

The Secret Life of Nina Hartley

9-TO-5 FANTASY

Starring: Nina Hartley, Brittany O'Connell, Isis Nile, Kim Chamber, Sahara Sands, Anna Malle, Tom Byron, Mark Wallice, Alex Saunders, Kyle Phillips, Bernie Dix, Mazda Lee, Kaymen Stuart. Producer: Stuart Canterbury. Director: Nina Hartley. Writer: Robyn Pillage. Music: Les Noyce. VCA Platinum, 1994.

In 1994 Nina Hartley celebrated her tenth year as an adult film performer. In an industry where a three-year career for women is the norm (allegedly because of a very low boredom threshold among male viewers), Hartley's staying power is legendary. This video was shot after a slight but tasteful breast enhancement. Her firm and trim body is a testament to her commitment to physical fitness.

Working in an unpleasant publishing office environment, Nina copes with her In box by fantasizing situations in which she's a jailer, a secret agent, and a fortune teller. All result in sexual encounters, many of them with women. The most exuberant display of the glories of her body is our favorite scene in which she wears a seductive little red number and long red gloves.

Explicitness: 8; Sensuality: 6 A, B, S, 3W

Secrets

LIMOUSINE LOVE FOR SALE

Starring: Ashlyn Gere, Samantha Strong, Rocco Siffreddi, Saber, Nina Alexander, Fallon, Peter North, Randy West, Danelle Rogers, Jeanna Fine, Jon Dough, Sony McKay, Nicole Wild, Kristina King. Producers: Howard Klein, Pattie Rhodes. Director: Andrew Blake. Music: Rock Hard. Caballero, 1990. 90 minutes.

Though seldom burdened with a story line or plot, Andrew Blake's videos are nevertheless a feast for the eyes. Here, for example, one woman looks through a telescope focusing on intimate couples while someone else is taking photographs as though at a photo shoot. The constants in *Secrets* are marvelously toned and strikingly sculpted bodies, mind-boggling clothes, and dramatically furnished impressive settings.

The sex is cool and impersonal, and the music, with the exception of a segment that sounds a little like *Bolero,* is irritating. If you've ever turned off the sound on MTV and just let yourself be absorbed by the images, this movie is for you. Where, we want to know, does Andrew Blake shop for the clothes he dresses his ladies in?

If you pay close attention, you may note similarities between *Secrets* and the story of a certain high-priced Hollywood madam and her harem of harlots.
Recommended.

Explicitness: 8; Sensuality: 8 A, 2M/W, 2W, 2W/M

Sensations

TRAVEL IS SO BROADENING

Starring: Bridgette Maier, Veronique Monet, Tuppy Owens, Trixi Heinen, Frederique Barral, Robert Le Ray, Jean Villroy, Eve Quang, Dawn Cummings, Pierre Latour, John Wilson, Nicoe Velna, Walter Wolf. Producer/writer: Alverto Ferro. Director: Lasse Braun. (Producer and director are the same person.) Music: Richard Moore. Caballero, 1975. 81 minutes.

Margaret, a naive American beauty, meets two European students on a boat to Amsterdam and allows them to introduce her to a sophisticated, sexually liberated group of older men and women. "Experiences and sensations are the juice of life." This translates into a little coke, parties that become orgies, and obligatory free love. Did everyone do that in the '70s?

We usually find orgies about as spontaneous as a tag-team wrestling match, and the endlessly long one here is no exception. Because of the age range and variety of the participants, however, it's less boring to watch than some. We appreciated the focus on the pleasure Margaret receives instead of the pleasure she gives. This movie apparently was a big sensation at the Cannes Film Festival when it was released in 1975, and it's one of the few adult movies to receive mainstream attention. A book by Miss Tuppy Owens about the making of the film can be found in some specialty video stores.

Explicitness: 7;   Sensuality: 5   B,   O,   T

Sensual Escape

ROMANTIC LIAISONS

Starring: Nina Hartley, Siobhan Hunter, Richard Pacheco, Steve Lockwood. Producers/directors: Per Sjöstedt, Candida Royalle, Gloria Leonard. Music: Gary Windo. Femme Productions, 1988. 85 minutes. (Part 1, Fortune Smiles, starring Nina Hartley and Richard Pacheco, directed by Gloria Leonard, produced by Candida Royalle. Part 2, The Tunnel, starring Siobhan Hunter and Steve Lockwood, directed by Candida Royalle.)

Fortune Smiles introduces a couple at a restaurant who are at the critical will-we-or-won't-we moment in their budding relationship.

Willingness established, they skip dinner and rush home to commence. The sweet, sexy awkwardness of something new is deftly handled with voice-overs from both participants, and there is a really excellent condom scene. (A note at the end of the film says that Femme films use safe-sex techniques unless the lovers are a couple in real life.) One of the pleasures of this feature is that the playfulness doesn't stop after the orgasms. Worth renting for this episode.

In the second feature, *The Tunnel*, a neurotic artist with sexual hang-ups, played by Siobhan Hunter (the youngest sister from *Three Daughters*), obsesses about her recurring dream of a man in a tunnel and herself in a spider web outfit. Walking off her dream hangover in the park, she meets a man who looks familiar though she can't place him. As she leaves, he calls after her, "Come see me in the tunnel." That night her dream heats up—the man, a masseur, rubs and licks her to orgasm. She wakes to a bright new day and a new painting. There are strong elements here—the pace is languid, the emphasis on her enjoyment, with some intriguing massage techniques. We can't think of another video in which the man concentrates on the woman's pleasure with no attention on his own.
Recommended.

Explicitness: 7;   Sensuality: 7   SS

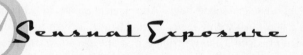

FINISHING SCHOOL FOR SEX

Starring: Kelly O'Dell, Raven, P. J. Sparxx, Deborah Diamond, Christine Tyler, Diedre Holland, Lana Sands, Kristi Lynn, Heather Hart, Melanie Moore, Paula Price, Mimi Miyagi, Devon Shire, Peter North, Marc Wallice, Joseph Verducci, Mark Davis. Producer/director: Andrew Blake. Writers: Andrew Blake, Raven Touchstone. Music: Let's Play Music. Blue Frame Films and Ultimate Video, 1993.

She's born for sex. We watch her being driven into the countryside as her voice-over explains how her lover insists that talent such as hers must be developed into skilled sensualism at a special school. As she enters the palatial, lavishly appointed house she sees a woman submit to a man and lick the floor. "Perhaps," she thinks, "the one who submits is in control." Next she sees pony girl training on the grounds (one woman in a harness pulling another woman in a light cart). "It is after all for their mutual pleasure."

You may recognize names in the cast if you've watched other re-

188

cent adult films, but chances are you'll have a hard time matching these polished high-fashion faces and expensively dressed bodies to the names you know. The flossy transformations of both men and women should have other producers and directors taking notes. The bluesy music on the soundtrack is pretty good. If Blake's your cup of tea, this is an excellent brew.
Highly recommended.

Explicitness: 7;   Sensuality: 6   B,   M,   SS,   2W

Sex 1994

BAD CAREER MOVE

Starring: Sunset Thomas, Tifanny Million, Debbie Diamond, Diedre Holland, Chasey Lain, Diva, Misty Rain, Asia Carrera, Gerry Pike, John Dough, Richy Razor. Producer: Jane Hamilton. Writer/director: Michael Ninn. Music: Dino Ninn. VCA Platinum, 1994. 80 minutes.

After the compelling credits comes the familiar angst-ridden story of small-town boy Gerry Pike turning his back on golden true love for the tinsel lure of worldly success and slick, big-city women. We witness all his foolish sins, and quite photogenic some of them are, including one high-heeled scene with Asia Carrera and "a woman brought in on a leash" bit with Chasey Lain. There is also an interlude with the breast-enhanced Tifanny Million that she swears was a genuine personal-best orgasm. Please notice that Ms. Million takes her vibrator along wherever she goes.

Often the flamboyant production re-creates the main character's drug/alcohol problems and his sexual experiences with dreamy intercut scenes and chaotic camera angles guaranteed to baffle anyone seeking a story line. Lest the viewer get the idea that some of these activities might be jolly despite Gerry's relentless self-destructiveness, the doleful voice-over narration disabuses us of that notion. The best way to watch may be the same way we look at an Andrew Blake: turn off the sound, put on your own choice of music, and go with the visuals.

Explicitness: 9;   Sensuality: 7   A,   B,   C,   T,   2W,   3W

Sex 2: Fate

MORE OF THE SAME

Starring: Unset Thomas, Tifanny Million, Gerry Pike, John Dough, Zach Thomas, Debi Diamond, Steve Drake, Misty Rain, Diva, Shayla LaVeaux. Producer: Jane Hamilton. Director/writer: Michael Ninn. Music: Dino Ninn. VCA Platinum, 1995. 95 minutes.

A sequel to the 1994 award-winning *Sex*, *Sex 2: Fate* underlines the erotic film business's motto that any film worth making is worth making twice. In the first video, Gerry Pike made it big as a model only to lose everything. This sequel returns to the openings of the first video and retells the rise and fall of Pike as a model through those ubiquitous handy flashbacks. Fate seems, to us, to be less about sex than the ways in which sex is used as an instrument of power, pain, and destruction by corporate movers and shakers. Like its predecessor, the message here is that the price of fame and fortune is high and there's no success without selling out.

As a condition of his servitude, Pike is coerced into giving Jon Dough a blow job. Before you get too excited, we must add that this scene is shot from Dough's back. Except those established by law, taboos are virtually unheard of in the straight adult video business. The only "thou shalt not" of straight videos is male/male sex, making the presence of this scene queer. Homophobia, at least as far as men are concerned, is alive and well in adult entertainment.

The muddled, quasi futuristic plot of *Sex 2: Fate* isn't easy to follow, but, like the original, the production values are high, the girls opulent, the sets and music hallucinogenically futuristic, and the music a touch wearing.

Explicitness: 8;   Sensuality: 5   A,   2W,   2W/M

Sexcapades

CASTING COUCH COMEDY

Starring: Sharon Mitchell, Ashley Welles, Joanna Storm, Sharon Kane, Lee Carroll, Eric Edwards, Michael Bruce, Tiffany Clark, George Payne. Producer: David Stone. Director: Henri Pachard. Story by R. Allen Leider. Screenplay: Henri Pachard. Music: Ian Shaw. VCA, 1983. 90 minutes.

Poor Harry Crocker (Eric Edwards) retired from erotic films to work in real Hollywood pictures, but financial reality caught up with him, and he's unhappily returning to the old profitable grind. His social-climbing wife (Sharon Mitchell) is shocked, especially when Harry tells her their chicly decorated townhouse will be the set of his new production. Their marriage isn't in the best of shape anyway. *Harry:* "My little cock is ready to doodle doo." Less-than-thrilled-to-hear-it *Wife:* "Watch out Harry. You know I'm very sensitive down there." *Harry:* "Aren't we all." The handwriting is on the wall for this couple, and sure enough before the movie ends Harry changes his mind about many things, including whether a man would choose the bathroom as a place to have sex. (Since bathroom sex is a signature of the film's real director, Henri Pachard, this is a tiny in-joke.)

Sharon Mitchell's performance gives the wife such a divinely disagreeable edge we didn't sympathize with her even when we saw her point. A little tougher to take is the W/W scene (excerpted in one of Jim Holliday's best of the best compilations) between Lee Carroll playing Harry's first wife, Lorraine, the tough producer of his movie, and Sharon Kane as an ambitious wanna-be star. These unevolved portrayals of wife and working women taken into account, we were captivated by the strong story and comic point of view and rate it **Highly recommended.** (*Great Sexpectations* is something of a sequel to this movie.)

Explicitness: 8;   Sensuality: 8   A,   T,   2W/M

Sex Freaks

OF POLITICAL INTEREST

In German. Approximately 40 minutes.

During the Clarence Thomas/Anita Hill hearings we heard an earful about the notorious Long Dong Silver. Now get an eyeful of the famous black man whose penis reaches to his knees when it is semierect. You won't see it in action—mostly he capers around, swinging it like a fire hose. (It looks to us as if he might have used a pump—see *How to Enlarge Your Penis,* page 240.) He is only one of several strangely endowed people who appear in this short film. Among others are a blonde fellow with a penis nearly the length of Long Dong's, a woman who ties her extra-large labia into a knot, and two persons of the persuasion made famous by that other Thomas—Jay—the possessors of both cocks and breasts. The people are presented in a casually clinical way, invited one by one to show us their wares. It's in German without subtitles, but we got the whole weird picture. More strange than erotic.

Frontal nudity,   Explicit byplay,   No intercourse

Sexophrenia

MEDIA PARODY

Starring: Debi Diamond, Beatrice Valle, Joey Silvera, Rocco Siffreddi, Brittany O'Connell, Tom Byron, Nikki Shane, Cody O'Connor, T.T. Boy, Hank Rose, Dick Nasty. Director: John Leslie. VCA Platinum, 1993. 85 minutes.

Sometime in a bleak, puritanical, not-so-distant future, two investigative TV reporters in a van try to gain the trust of a known sexophreniac by leaving a sandwich on the sidewalk. "Thirty percent of these people would rather have sex than eat." This sad, grungy mock-u-drama, which looks modeled after a PBS show on schizophrenics, reflects deep concerns about the sexually repressive direction our society is taking. Unfortunately, the story offers way too much message and not enough entertainment. Director John Leslie is preaching to the choir here and has momentarily forgotten that his greatest strength lies in seduction, not rhetoric. Alas, a pass.

Explicitness: 8;   Sensuality: 2

Sexual Fantasies, the Video

SHARING FANTASIES WITH EACH OTHER

Starring: Aja, Julianne James, Champagne, Carol Cummings, Nina De Ponca, Cheri Taylor, Rene Morgan, Tom Byron, Peter North, Ray Victory, Jon Doe. Producer/director: Paul Thomas. Writer: Bryce Britton. mfm Home Video.

Five women in a hot tub share their fantasies in five individual episodes. Once you get the gist of what's going on, you might want to

192

push the mute button on your VCR to avoid the annoying voice-over lec-
ture on the importance of fantasy in your life. The scenarios are woman
driver and black motorcycle cop, husband and wife with a woman they
pick up in a restaurant, husband and wife in a posh public ladies' room,
two women (one plumpish) in the shower after workout class, and
woman "raped" by masked intruder. Some of us disliked the last one,
even though the segment ends satisfactorily for the woman and is her
fantasy. Others thought it one of the best in the video.
Recommended with caveat.

Explicitness: 7;   Sensuality: 6

Sexual Response

BAD FAMILY VALUES

*Starring: Shannon Tweed, Catherine Oxenberg, Randy West, Emile
Levisetta, Vernon Wells. Producer/director: Yaky Yosha. Columbia/Tri-
Star, 1992.*

Married to a violently jealous husband, radio talk show therapist
Eve (Shannon Tweed) listens to the sexual secrets and problems of her
call-in radio audience. Pursued by a persistent caller who throws some
of her advice back at her and poses some provocative questions to her,
she's both attracted and repelled by the idea of responding to the lure
of a total stranger whom she suspects of being a nut case. She cannot
help but be tempted by this wildly passionate man. Desire wins over
logic. Asking for trouble is what we'd say.

Her pursuer is a skilled lover with a slow, deliberate pace. A sculp-
tor, his name is Edge, and the first thing he does is sculpt her torso,
setting it in her front yard for all—particularly her jealous husband—
to see. More trouble, wouldn't you agree? As her husband Philip's
(Randy West) suspicions and rage intensify, her lover's obsession overwhelms her. Unexpectedly, she begins to see a spooky and violent
essence in Edge and recognizes the peril all around her. The plot takes
unexpected twists and turns evocative of Hitchcock's style, hurtling
toward a bizarre and surprising end.

Randy West's performance as Phillip is outstanding. He captures
perfectly the demeanor of a man on the edge of losing control and just
barely able to contain his rage.
Recommended.

Simulated;   Sensuality: 8

Sex World

LIBIDO SPA

Starring: Leslie Bovee, Annette Haven, Sharon Thorpe, Kay Parker, De-
siree West, John Leslie, Kent Hall, Jack Wright, Amber Hunt, Abigail
Clayton, Cris Cassidy, Joey Silvera, Johnnie Keyes, Carol Tong, Roberto
Ramos, Peter Johns, Maureen Spring. Producer: Billy Spinelli. Director:
Anthony Thornberg. Essex Picture Co., 1978. 90 minutes. (Best erotic
score, 1979; Screw's Best 10.)

An all-star big-budget extravaganza that opens on a tour bus, complete with tour leader and microphone. Destination: three fabulous
days and nights at *Sex World,* the ultraprivate resort dedicated to making your personal fantasies come true. We meet, in flashbacks, a very
sexual couple looking for a thrill, a dysfunctional couple looking for
help, and a lonely woman looking for human connection. Much more
to come, but the bus has arrived and the white-coated professional
staff—equipped with tests, gadgets, and video cameras for every
room—is working hard to ascertain each person's secret fantasy, perhaps the one they didn't suspect themselves, and make it a reality.

The set-up is an elaborately worked out variation on a typical
erotic movie scenario serving to link many different sex acts into a
story, but just as the details and the cast are superior, so are many of
the politically semicorrect fantasies. A lesbian woman wants to know
what she's missing by dissing men (we're not telling). A white racist
male (John Leslie) is paired with the divine Desiree West ("Take a
chance, white boy. I'll prove your spigot ain't no bigot.") She's way better than he deserves, and though eventually he figures that out, the
scene isn't exactly a Spike Lee Joint point of view. Johnnie Keyes,
wearing the crotchless white tights he made famous in *Behind the*
Green Door, does a star turn for a shy woman desperate for someone
to like her. A sissy guy watches his itchy, bitchy wife dominated by
rough trade. Well, you get the picture—opportunity for outrage on all
sides. We took the Sex World host's statement ("We're not here to
judge you. We're here to pamper you.") seriously and enjoyed almost
everything, even incest, and that's one of our big no no's. **Highly**
recommended, but don't complain that you weren't warned.

Explicitness: 7;   Sensuality: 8   T

Sherlock Homie: In the Mysterious Case of Isabella the Man Eater

PARODY

Starring: Lana Sands, Janet Jacme, Jeannie Pepper, Sabrina, Julian St. Jox, Sean Michaels, Mr. Marcus, Valentino. Director: Sean Michaels. Intropics Video, 1995.

In a comical spoof of Sherlock Holmes with a mostly African-American cast, Sean Michaels plays Sherlock Homie, with his sidekick, le Fool. Men are disappearing. There are no clues to their fate. Sherlock Homie quickly deduces that it must be an act of revenge by Isabella the Man Eater. She strikes men who have been hostile to women, inflicting on them the injury they've inflicted on women. Indefatigable in her holy mission, she's been on the hunt for one hundred years, and shows no signs of slowing down. Michaels revels in his tale and makes the most of every opportunity to relish the sumptuous bosoms and bottoms of the women in the cast.

Playful and farcical. We hope we're not taking too much for granted by assuming that stupid lines like "You're not supposed to think. You're a woman" and "I am your husband. And you are my prize" are meant to be tongue in cheek.

Explicitness: 7;   Sensuality: 8   3W

She's So Fine

HERE COMES THE BRIDE

Starring: Jerry Butler, Sharon Mitchell, Gloria Leonard, Taija Rae, Paul Thomas, Joey Silvera, Rachel Ashley, Melanie Scott, Johnny Nineteen. Producers: Bill Turner, Dick Thomas. Writer: Dick Thomas. Director: Henry Pachard. Music: Barton Leslie III. VCA/BlueBird Productions, 1985. 83 minutes.

Jim Holliday, in his book *Only the Best*, called this "Wedding for Godot." That's right. The groom doesn't seem likely to show, but everyone else has a grand time hanging out at the bride's home. This farce (supposedly set in Motor City, though we know it was filmed on Long Island) was made when weddings had moved out of the chapel and onto mountaintops, meadows, and beaches and wedding dress codes had been chucked along with the idea of virgin brides.

The bride's agitated mother (Gloria Leonard), has never met the groom and calms her anxieties with a nearby brandy bottle, finding comfort in the arms of Paul Thomas, the manager of a rock band. Thomas does a hysterical parody of Alice Cooper (or maybe it's Kiss, or, more likely yet, a combination of the two). The bride, Angela (Taija Rae), hasn't seen her groom in months, and even she begins to doubt that he's going to show. She's not a happy girl.

A raucous and funny video full of outrageous characters, entertainment industry jokes, credible acting, and plenty of impromptu sex among the wedding party, including the mail-order preacher. *Best moment:* Sharon Mitchell's leather punk rock girl takes on suburban horndog Jerry Butler. We'd rent it again for that scene.
Recommended.

Explicitness: 7;   Sensuality: 8   T

Skin

NO PAIN, NO GAIN

Starring: Carol Lynn, Nadine Bronx, Jolla Petinot, Julia Snow, Isabelle Le Voix, Elodie Gander, Richard Largin, Marrnelle Phalle. Producer: Toshi Gold. Erotique, 1995. (**A European film, badly dubbed in English.**)

A dominatrix dressed in black leather lounges on a chair, drinking champagne. She orders a man to lick her vinyl-booted feet, read to her, and have sex with a submissive woman who is present. Other leather-wearing minions act out the story he reads. Whips exist mainly as accessories. One man has his balls tied up in a way that looks excruciating. The outfits are what mesmerized those who viewed this video—studs, aprons, pants with the front and back cut out, masks, hoods—fashion notes from a different world.

If you want a peep into S/M but have issues about power and violence, this may provide an acceptable introduction. The film is harshly lit and very explicit, but with the one aforementioned exception the kink is limited to costumes and bossiness. Our honorary WW,

who possesses a highly developed sense of style, named this as one of the few X-rated films she found involving.
Recommended.

Explicitness: 9;   Sensuality: 5   B,   S/M,   T,   2W,   2W/M

Skin Too

CHECK YOUR INHIBITIONS AT THE DOOR

Starring: Carol-Lynn, Maheva Dream, Cindy, Barbara, Valerie, Herve, Stephen, Richard, Phillipe. Producer: Toshi Gold. (**German, dubbed in English.**)

Kinky, Kinky, Kinky! Set in a German sex club, with minimalist metal sets, *Skin Too* has a Rem Kolhaas look. Cages surrounded with lots of aluminum tubing, high-ceilinged warehouse space, way cool black-and-red wet look costumes on snarling, writhing women with no restraint or inhibitions and plenty of dominatrix attitude; this and *Skin* are examples of German porn. Fun in small doses or for the right occasion (like National Dominatrix Day).

Explicitness: 9;   Sensuality: 3   A,   B,   S/M

Sleepyhead

RELIGIOUS MUMBO JUMBO

Starring: Georgina Spelvin, Tina Russell, Darby Lloyd Rains, Judith Hamilton, Davy Jones, Jamie Gillis, Mark Stevens, Jason Rusell, Lvi Richards. Producer/Director: Erik Anderson. Video X Pix, 1973. 93 minutes.

Bernice (Georgina Spelvin) and Tracy (Tina Russell) are sisters sharing an apartment in New York. Bernice is a writer whose sexuality has been dormant for fifteen years. Tracy is a fanatical religious zealot who works as a "religious suffragette," carrying a large cross and Bible wherever she goes. Each disapproves of the other's values, guilt being their operating system. Bernice, egged on by friends, gives Tracy, who was nicknamed "walking chastity belt" in high school, the opportunity to get over her prudishness in an orgy scene that begins as an unwelcome advance but evolves into a raucous episode in which Tracy abandons herself to the fun and is quickly converted to hedonism.

Full of secondary subplots and characters who provide occasions for varieties of sexual experience and melodramatic plot twists, the main themes of *Sleepyhead* (where did they get this title?) are sex, religion, and the dangers of extremism. Because of the period in which the video was made, the bodies aren't quite as buffed, tuned, and tidy as in videos made after 1985, but the performances and the nuances of character and plot make it a compelling watch.

Explicitness: 7;   Sensuality: 7   O,   M/2W,   W/2M,   2W

Smoker

CULT CLASSIC

Starring: Veronica Rocket, Diane Sloan, Troye Lane, David Christopher, Sharon Mitchell, Joanna Storm, John Leslie, Eric Edwards. Producer/director: Veronica Rocket. Music: Gerry Gabinelli. VCA, 1984. 75 minutes.

Weird and kinky, *Smoker* is set in a sex shop with a B/D dungeon in the cellar run by Madame Suque (Sharon Mitchell), who doubles as a potential destroyer of worlds. The bombs she needs to achieve her evil ends are hidden in a recent shipment of vibrators, one of which accidentally gets sold to a customer. A game of who's got the vibrator turns into a comedy of errors, terrors, and perversities of a sexual nature, including a scene in which Mme Suque is strung up upside down in her own dungeon.

Everyone, including the married transvestite janitor, gets to perform twisted sexual hostilities, the most outlandish of which take place at a kitchen table while the spouse of one of the parties disinterestedly eats his dinner as his wife (Joanna Storm) gets the best of John Leslie, who plays the "faceless dick" pursuing Mme Suque.

If you find following the plot too taxing, just focus on the goings on above- and belowground, especially the solo self-entertainments of Diane Sloan and Troye Lane.
Recommended.

Explicitness: 7;   Sensuality: 6   B,   M,   S,   S/M,   T, 2W

Soft, Warm Rain

MEMORIES

Starring: Tracey Adams, Sheri St. Clair, Siobhan Hunter, Keisha, Randy West, Buddy Love. Producer/director: Eric Edwards. Writer: Rene Summers. Vidco, 1987.

Flashback with old prospector Randy West as he tells you about what happened when he was a young man looking for gold. He has heard a legend about an Indian tribe that adopted a white baby they named Ky-rie, or Soft, Warm Rain. And lo, just as he is about to die of thirst, a beautiful Indian maid saves his life and takes him to a place where a fountain flows and so does the lovemaking. A romantic tale. **Recommended.**

Explicitness: 7;   Sensuality: 7   M,   2W

Sorority Sex Kittens, Part I

RIBALD CAMPUS COMEDY

Starring: Ashlyn Gere, Victoria Paris, Bianca, Madison Flame, Selena Steel, Angela Summers, Melanie Moore. Also starring: Alexis De Vell, Kelly O'Dell, Shayla LaVeaux, Shawnee Cates. Costarring: Teri Diver, Lacy Rose, Tiffany Minx, Summer Night, Stacy Nichols, Lana Sands, Alicia Rio, Tin Lindstrom, Tim Lake, T.T. Boy, Jon Dough, Peter North, Mike Horner, Nina Hartley, Porsche Lynn, Tami Monroe, Lacy Rose. Special guests: Sharon Kane and E. Z. Ryder, based on characters created by Amanda Hunter and Christine Savage. Screenplay: Jim Holliday. Producer: Michael Craig. Directors: Michael Craig, Jim Holliday. VCA Platinum, 1992. 85 minutes.

The licentious women of Upsilon Sigma sorority put the S in Sex, and the enthralled male students of Lost River College are so busy thanking their lucky stars they haven't noticed that their best and brightest keep disappearing. We know because Dr. Easy Ed, a pear-shaped '60s' flower child, is spying on the sorority—a hard job when their jamming equipment is more up-to-date than his. He brings the full-blown hippie paranoia usually reserved for government plots to bear on the activities of Upsilon Sigma. Those women are up to something, he rants, and surely they are, but you'll find only a hint of the answer at the end of part 2.

Much of the noisy, all-action-no-emotion sex, featuring blondes with over-enhanced breasts, looks like other mainstream adult films we'd advise avoiding. What sets *Sorority Sex Kittens* apart is the skewed point of view and offbeat humor with which the women initiate and control the goings on. *Favorite scene:* Pledge mistress tells pledges that while most Upsilon Sigmas are Cajun, the sorority accepts right-thinking women from all parts of the country except east of the Susquehanna. "That means you New York Girls and New England Debs." We New York girls are way too bad even for this group.

The video works equally well with a mate (our experience suggests you'll laugh and he'll get turned on) or a girls-night-out group of friends if no one flinches when it gets down and dirty. **Recommended,** but not for beginners.

Explicitness: 9;   Sensuality: 7   O,   SS,   T,   W/3M,   2W, 2W/M

Sorority Sex Kittens, Part 2

THE STORY CONTINUES

Starring: Ashlyn Gere, Bionca Madison, Selena Steele, Angela Summers, Victoria Paris, Melanie Moore, Alexid DeVell, Kelly O'Dell, Shayla La Veaux, Malia, Teri Diver, Lacy Rose, Tiffany Minx, Summer Knight, Stacey Nichols, T.T. Boy, Jon Dough, E. Z. Ryder, Sharon Kane, Joey Silvera, Mikala, Tina Lindstrom, Porsche Lynn, Tammy Monroe, Steve Drake, Jim Holliday, Nina Hartley. Producer/director: Michael Craig. Writer: Jim Holliday. VCA, 1993. 85 minutes.

The most believable theory we have heard for the annoying practice of making a rambling two-part movie instead of one coherent feature is the filmmaker's need to delete all the hard-core sex to sell the movie to lucrative pay-TV channels such as Adam and Eve, Playboy, and Spice. If they shoot a two- or two-and-a-half-hour movie and split it for the rental market, you pay twice. Then they can cut out the explicit stuff for cable. Whatever the reason, we're irritated and we're not going to help them do it, so if you decide you must watch part 2 for yourself don't read the last paragraph of this entry where we give away the ending.

Fifteen minutes into this disappointing sequel, Nina Hartley bounces onto the screen and demonstrates what has been missing. She actually seems to enjoy her lighthearted romp with Ashlyn Gere. And the usually fierce Gere drops her tougher-than-leather attitude and comes across as warm and even, dare we say it, giggly. Sorry Ashlyn, but we saw you.

After Nina's all-too-brief appearance, glazed boredom set in, though we wanted to know what happened to those missing men from part 1. For that we endured an endless jumble of gymnastic sex, including the famous twenty-five-women orgy in the Upsilon Sigma House. The answer, if it was an answer, is so quick and elusive we ran it again. Are the Upsilon Sigma girls Cajun maenads? Anything is possible. If you feel a need for personal closure rent part 2 and read no further.

Ending: After the secret sorority ceremonies and the circle orgy, the leader holds up a sign that reads "The strongest power in the world is Pussy Power." Mike Horner, who was led away blindfolded in the very first scene of part 1, is brought out by his captors. The women run forward shrieking, and he disappears under a pile of blondes. That's it.

Explicitness: 9; Sensuality: 5 O, SS, T, 2W, 2W/M

Stairway to Paradise

KARMA DRAMA

Starring: Nina Hartley, Aja, Tianna, Victoria Paris, Heather Lere, Lee Carol, Randy Spears, Joey Silvera, Peter North, James Lewis, Chi-Chi-La Rue, Kay Parker, Sharon Kane, Jeff James, Bhagwan Bob. Producer: Abigail Beacher. Director: Sharon Kane. Story/screenplay: Sharon Kane, Jim Holliday. Music: Original Song, Sharon Kane. VCA. 90 minutes.

In her first directorial effort, Sharon Kane (see *Urban Heat* and *The Swap*) has fun mocking faux spiritual buffoonery. After climbing to the top of a mist-shrouded spiral staircase, Susan Moore (Nina Hartley) finds herself in limbo before the throne of guru Rainwater (Randy Spears), where she's greeted as a long-lost friend. Spears plays the part of Rainwater with tongue firmly in cheek, never letting the opportunity for a double entendre pass him by.

Susan is given potions to help her relax and remember all her former lives. This is supposed to be a purging experience. Though she's told it's not a dream and she's not dead, we suspect she didn't get to limbo of her own free will. She's just moved to another level of existence. Rainwater is there to help her turn three hundred lousy years of unpleasantness around with the help of "cosmic flashes" and sessions with Morning Star, the "regression sessionist," who takes her on a past-lives journey from Salem witch hunts to the Civil War to Bhagwan Bob of the psychedelic '60s. It's Rainwater who finally breaks her string of bad karmic luck, with the best scene in the video. With the right amount of kissing and caressing, Rainwater makes love to Susan with intense focus and concentration, and she's no slouch either, so skip the earlier mumbo jumbo and head right for paradise after the opening sequence, which is also of a high caliber. **Recommended** for the two hot scenes.

Explicitness: 6;   Sensuality: 6 (except for the scenes mentioned above, which we rate 8)   2W

Steamy Windows

DON'T GET MAD, GET EVEN

Starring: Rachel Ryan, Danielle Rogers, Sunny McKay, Debi Diamond, Tianna, Rocco Siffreddi, Joey Silvera, Peter North, Randy West, Randy Spears. Producer/director: Alex de Renzy. VCA, 1990. 80 minutes.

Katherine (Rachel Ryan) owns an art gallery successful enough for her to buy a posh new red convertible with a certified check. She also owns a bad attitude that keeps her loving and leaving men just to show them she can. Sometimes those she likes or wants to reward get, as a consolation prize, one of the decorative women who work in her gallery. In a flashback we see the reason she is unhappily punishing everyone around her: high school football star Tommy (Randy Spears), who used her trusting love and left her crying.

Then the phone rings. Tommy, a football hero no more, has read about her gallery in the newspaper and wants to reignite the old flame. Guess who's top dog now?

The ending is abrupt, and we gather (from an old review) that a cut has been made since the video was issued. If you get an older rental, you may also get a rougher scene between Rachel and her long lost love than the version we saw. As it is, the real victims of her displeasure with life are the female employees who get handed out like lollipops. We suppose when they accepted positions in a gallery where eyelet bustiers, frilly panties, garters, and stockings are worn to pass the hors d'oeuvres trays, they knew what the job entailed, but we ex-

pect better behavior from women bosses. *Best scene:* Joey Silvera and the lovely Sunny McKay.
Recommended with caveat.

Explicitness: 8;   Sensuality: 7   M,   2W,   2W/M

The Story of O
(the series; ten volumes available)

LAVISH MASOCHISTIC CLASSIC

Starring: Claudia Cepede, Paulo Reisas, Nelson Freitas, Gabriela Alves, Mauro Jasmin, Jacqueline Sperandio. Based on The Story of O, *by Pauline Reage. Screenplay: Ron Williams, Jennifer Field. Music: Sergio Saracenis. Producer/director: Ron Williams.* (**The series was produced in South America, set in France, and dubbed in English. The cast is the same in all the volumes, though everyone does not appear in each video.**)

For those unfamiliar with the famous erotic novel of S/M on which this ten-part video series is based, the story concerns O, a photographer who becomes so obsessed by her lover, Rene, that she abdicates her will and responsibility to him.

The production looks sumptuous, with elaborate costumes, rich interiors, and expensive cars. We see the women naked, not the men; all the sex is simulated; and the floggings that O endures are less graphic than many Hollywood movies, though the welts from the whippings are visible and are part of the gestalt. Sexy, yes; disquieting, also yes. One thing is certain—S/M has never been more romantically photographed than it is in this series.

Each video begins with O sitting at a desk, writing her story. We hear a male voice-over, her lover, speaking: "What I have read so far in your *Story of O* is the most fiercely intense love letter a man could receive. It is also a fairy tale and a dream." O's voice-over replies, "It's more than a dream—you've got to understand. Love is no joke. There's no freedom in it. My love, listen and live my dreams—if you dare." The video will remind us throughout the series that the story is O's fantasy and the action O's choice. If you're curious but don't want to deal with all ten volumes, we suggest 1, 2, 8, and 9 as the best in the series. We have found it shelved in video stores' regular racks, not the adult section. **Highly recommended.**

Simulated (all in series)

The Story of O, vol. 1

Here we are given the background—O's love affair with Rene and the fateful evening during which he delivers her to the mysterious castle called Roissy, where she is initiated into the rites of the inhabitants. She becomes a sexual slave, available to any of the men at any time. Her clothes, her habits, her whole being are now controlled by their sexual practices, which include elaborately ritualized beatings among other humiliations. To state these things baldly does not convey the hypnotic power of the work.

Most original sex: on horseback. *Most compelling image:* blindfolded O in Roissy, breasts bare, wrists chained to a leather collar, red cape billowing, led by two attendants also dressed in red capes.

The Story of O, vol. 2

Life at Roissy continues. O is beaten, chained up, and brought to new heights of pleasure. Rene, the man who brought her here, watches her make love to another man and tells her he loves her. A pleasurable preoccupation with the welts the whips make on her thighs is one of the new features of this episode. The pace is slow as molasses in January and deeply, profoundly, exhaustingly serious. If it turns you on, you won't care. All the volumes after the first one begin with O writing her fantasy and a brief recap of events in the previous episode.

The Story of O, vol. 3

O's training at Roissy castle ends with a special effort made to enlarge her rear opening. She returns to her apartment, her job as a fashion photographer, and her friends, but she now lives according to the training of Roissy and the rules of her lover, Rene. These rules include a new wardrobe, on the surface demure, even dowdy, but made to specific erotic requirements, and worn with no panties. People at work are beginning to notice, as indeed they might, since the rules also require that she lift her skirt as she sits down.

The Story of O, vol. 4

O finds a beautiful model who reminds her of erotic adventures she had as a naughty schoolgirl. She suggests the model as a possible recruit to Rene. He rewards O by taking her to see Sir Stephen, an older man he idolizes and tries to please. Rene's mother was once Sir Stephen's stepmother, so the two men refer to each other as brothers, and in a show of brotherly solidarity Rene leaves O with Sir Stephen. What seemed like a kinky game is turning dark.

The Story of O, vol. 5

The next morning, when the stern black housekeeper, Norah, lets her leave Sir Stephen's house, O knows she will be back. She loves Rene, but the bearded, professorial Sir Stephen is her master. As if her love life weren't complicated enough, O is more and more attracted to a model in her studio, the sensuous Jacqueline. Sir Stephen orders her to seduce Jacqueline and bring her to Roissy "by betrayal if necessary."

The Story of O, vol. 6

O keeps trying to seduce the elusive Jacqueline and reports some progress to Sir Stephen, though she says Jacqueline will never go to Roissy. "Then she will be taken by force," he replies. Jacqueline accepts O's offer to become her roommate and allows O to seduce her. When O tells Sir Stephen she had an orgasm, something she never has with him because she "concentrates on his pleasure," he announces he is taking her to visit his friend Ann Marie, an experience he promises will be unpleasant. Rene orders O to tell Jacqueline he loves her. Jacqueline gets a movie role. This volume, possibly the slowest in the series, provides narrative information.

The Story of O, vol. 7

Sir Stephen takes O back to Ann Marie's country house for a ten-day visit. It's full of young women whose tight, ruffled pink bustiers leave their breasts, rear, and pubic area exposed. O is given a costume and told at the end of the stay, designed to enhance her sense of femininity, she will wear a ring and chain on her private parts and be branded on the buttocks with a hot iron. Meanwhile, her regime involves having the inside of her thighs whipped while a harp is played. Some of us found this volume over the top.

The Story of O, vol. 8

This episode is worth renting even if the S/M content of the series doesn't turn you on. Sir Stephen invites two friends to use O as they please, and one does so immediately. The other, played by the young and divinely handsome Mauro Jasmin, asks to take O away with him for a night. Will romance save O? Does she need to be saved? Is Mauro Jasmin, Prince Valiant haircut and all, one of the most delectable men ever to appear in a woman's erotic video?

The Story of O, vol. 9

Rene, who has seduced Jacqueline, invites her to visit Sir Stephen's country house. He tells her, "O's not possessive of me and I'm not possessive of you so you'll be well taken care of." The plan of Sir Stephen, Rene, and O is to take Jacqueline to Roissy on the way home, willing or not. When Jacqueline asks if she can bring her fifteen-year-old sister with her, the girl is included in the plan. Jacqueline, even more beautiful than O, can be capricious, though she makes love to O, among others. Her little sister (who may meet the legal requirement of eighteen but who looks younger) finds O captivating and begs to be her slave. The encounters between Jacqueline and O are some of the most erotic in the series, but the presence of the supposedly young, innocent sister, despite no one paying her any sexual attention, makes volumes 9 and 10 uncomfortable for those who believe teenagers should be completely off limits.

The Story of O, vol. 10

O is given an owl mask and prepared for a public humiliation. She tells Sir Stephen she loves him. Both O and Jacqueline must make choices about their futures. If you are drawn into the story, these final scenes are intriguingly ambiguous, though perhaps it's one of the least sexy of the ten volumes, as an erotic story becomes a moral tale.

Suburban Dykes

LESBIAN LIFE

Starring: Sharon Mitchell, Nina Hartley, Pepper. Producer: Nan Kinney. Director: Debi Sundahl for Fatale. 50 minutes.

A cuddly lesbian couple calls in to a phone sex line. During the ensuing conversation it is revealed that one of them has a dildo fantasy, so after they hang up they place another call to a specialty service requesting a "big bull dyke." When Sharon Mitchell shows up at their front door dressed in the requisite black leather, the couple is astonished, like a pair of open-mouthed children who are wondering how to get the genie back in the bottle. Much safe sex then takes place in various twosome and threesome combinations—even the large lavender dildo gets a condom. *Best moment:* Sharon stylishly puts on her latex glove; her attitude transforms safe sex into foreplay. Fatale has been specializing in lesbian erotic videos since 1984, but heterosexuals who are open to the fantasy of a same-sex scene will also find their films exciting. **Recommended.**

Explicitness: 7;   Sensuality: 7   M,   S/M,   SS,   T,   3W

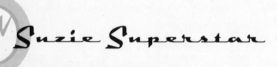

Suzie Superstar

SHOW BIZ MUSICAL DRAMA

Starring: Shauna Grant, John Leslie, Tara Aire, Laura Lazare, Ron Jeremy, Sharon Mitchell, Gayle Sterling, Laurie Smith, Joey Silvers, Jan Martin, Mai Lin, Tigr, Ross Roberts. Producer: Sam Norvell. Director: Robert McCallum. Writer: Toni Jackson. Music: Horizon. Cal Vista, 1983. 81 minutes.

The lead singer of her successful band, Suzie Mitchell (Shauna Grant) is kept on a short leash by her sleazy manager/lover Z. W. McCain (John Leslie). As the hottest entertainment game in town, she's hired by Priscilla, the lawyer daughter of mobster Lorenzo Loducca (Ross Roberts) to perform at her father's birthday party. Priscilla's price is $100,000 per performance, but Z.W. will knock $30,000 off if Priscilla will honor him with the gift of her body.

Depressed over her love-hate relationship with Z.W., Suzie goes to her friend and band member Rick (Joey Silvera), for comfort. He sings to her and makes her body quiver with satisfaction. This is one of the sweetest and most affecting love scenes we've seen. For his trouble Rick gets beaten up by the jealous Z.W.'s chauffeur/bodyguard and groupie appeaser Raul (Ron Jeremy), who's a feast if you happen to be a size queen.

Determined to evade Z.W.'s hostility and regain control of her life, Suzie cleverly manipulates her performance for Loducca, freeing herself of Z.W. once and for all. This being the movies, Z.W. loses no time in bouncing back.

This makes both of our personal top twenty list for its strong story line, music, and tender love.
Highly recommended.

Explicitness: 7;   Sensuality: 9   S

The Swap

FERTILITY DANCE

Starring: Jennifer Stewart, Sharon Kane, Jerry Butler, Joel Schults, Ameiko, Madison, Bridget Monroe, Axel Wolf, Max Steed, Tom Byron, Terry Richardson, Patricia Kennedy, Paula Price, Heather St. Clair. Producer/director: Paul Thomas. Writer: Ariel Hart. Music: Barry Boxx. Vivid Video, 1990.

Judy (Jennifer Stewart) and Steve (Joel Schults) find themselves in the contemporary dilemma of trying to have a baby in spite of his low sperm count. Thermometers and sex on a schedule aren't doing much for their love life or their dispositions. When Judy explains to her best friend the source of her crankiness, Claire (Sharon Kane) confides that they are in the same boat, only in their case she's the infertile one, not her husband, Greg (Jerry Butler).

After several intense discussions, the couples agree that the fertile Judy and Greg should get together and make a child for them to share. Judy agrees reluctantly—she doesn't really like Greg, a feeling he reciprocates. When the thermometer says it's time, they meet but can't go through with it, though she makes him promise not to tell. Next month they'll try again. Meanwhile their other halves are spending a lot of restless time together speculating on what's going on.

The film has a believable story and sex that arises naturally out of the situations. Even the hilarious orgy works. Good job, Paul Thomas.
Highly recommended.

Explicitness: 7;   Sensuality: 7   O

The Swap 2

SWINGING IN THE SUBURBS

Starring: Lene Hefner, Leena, Dyanna Lauren, Misty Rain, Isis Nile, Asia Carrera, Christina Angel, Veronica Lake, Marc Wallice, Jon Dough, Tony Tedeschi, Alex Sanders. Producer: Bud Lee. Director: Paul Thomas. Vivid, 1994. 72 minutes.

If you're hoping to find out more about the baby-making couples in *Swap* you'll have to wait. The second *Swap* features two different "best friend" couples and a far different problem. Jon Dough and Leena, the husband of one couple and the wife of the other, both want to experiment with swapping, swinging, or *something,* and their dull old mates Lene Hefner and Marc Wallice vote thumbs down. Leena keeps after the subject, and in due time the much-harassed mates see no option except to permit Leena and Jon to wander on a carefully limited basis. (Note: Those who haven't seen *Swap* surely want to know that the orgy on the television is from that movie.)

Again, the sex arises from believable situations, and, unusual for the genre, sexual actions have realistic consequences. **Highly recommended.**

Explicitness: 7; Sensuality: 7   O,   2W,   2W/M

Talk Dirty to Me

NO DOWN TIME

Starring: Jesie St. James, John Leslie, Richard Pacheco, Cris Cassidy, Sharon Kane, Juliet Anderson, Aaron Stuart, Dorothy LeMay, Holly McCall, Anthony Spinelli. Producer: Jerry Ross. Director: Anthony Spinelli. Dreamland Entertainment/Four Rivers Releasing, 1980. 80 minutes.

John Leslie won a Best Actor award for his performance as the irrepressibly confident and audacious Jack, a womanizer whose only close relationship is with his slightly retarded and socially immature virgin-friend Lenny (Richard Pacheco). Jack tries to appear dapper and suave but succeeds only in looking slightly oily and slick. He lightheartedly scores and scores. More comedy than drama, the scene in which two women pamper and groom each other's pubic hair is price-

less. The most affecting scene is the one in which Sharon Kane sensitively initiates Lenny in the pleasures of the flesh. Departing from the laundry list of "must include" elements, there is no 2W in *Talk Dirty to Me*. Although the promised dirty talk of the title is no more than normal sex talk, film fans will enjoy the Hollywood trivia throughout, which serves to enliven the dialogue. For more of Jack's and Lenny's adventures, see the sequel, *Nothing to Hide*.
Highly recommended.

Explicitness: 7;   Sensuality: 7

A Taste of Ambrosia

TWO FANTASIES WITH A LIGHT, ROMANTIC TOUCH

Starring: Jeanna Fine, Randy Paul, Alexis Firestone, Rugby Rhodes, Michele Capozzi. Producers: Për Sjöstedt, Candida Royalle. Directors: Veronica Hart, Candida Royalle. Writer: Veronica Hart. Music: Gary Windo, E. Boy. Femme, 1987. 70 minutes.

Instead of cutting a single story into two separate videos like in *Things Change: My First Time,* and *Things Change: Letting Go,* Candida Royalle gives two different stories for the price of one. Both are slice-of-life vignettes with unpredictable plots. Royalle expertly sets the scene in context, giving the viewer time and information to get invested in the characters and stories.

It's a lazy morning. Even though Jeanna Fine, "In Nine Lives Hath My Love," isn't in the mood, she obliges her lover, Randy Paul. While he's making love to her she gives loving attention to her cats, stroking them and letting Randy know she's really not interested. Her passive-aggressive behavior is not lost on him, and he bursts out in a jealous tantrum, prompting her to do something *very* special and magical for him.

In "Pickup," directed by former adult actress Veronica Hart, Alexis Firestone tidies up her home at the end of the day. After putting away the children's tub toys she takes a luxurious and erotically charged bath, puts on slutty makeup and a revealing dress, paints her nails, and steps into high heels, transforming herself from a mom to a street walker. Across town Rugby Rhodes showers, grooms himself, and puts on fresh clothes. When we next see them downtown Alexis is walking the streets and Rhodes is cruising her vin his car. They make their deal and after a quick stop at a liquor store they're back in her apartment relishing each other.

Royalle's approach to sex is lovingly sensuous and erotic. The conventional couples in these vignettes take real pleasure in each other as the camera captures the elusive sexual dynamic between them, lingering on delicious long kisses and foreplay. Both stories end in unexpected surprises. A *Taste of Ambrosia* is one of our favorites and **Highly recommended.**

Explicitness: 6;   Sensuality: 9   2W

More Candida Royalle

Candida Royalle moved to San Francisco to pursue an avant garde artistic life. As a serious student of art and music, her passion lay in performing and singing in jazz clubs. The decision to make adult movies merely seemed a daring way to pay her bills, one that required only a few days a month of her time. She little suspected that she was making a career choice that would shape her life. "The '70s was the sexual revolution. Sex was open and free. Acting in explicit movies seemed outrageous and rebellious, but at the time it felt like a short, bold hop from an experimental life-style."

She didn't tell her parents about her X-rated career until she was getting married (to Për Sjöstedt) and retiring, temporarily as it turned out, from the business. She says that they were shocked but accepting. Her stepmother said, "You're my daughter, and I love you." Most recently, her father, who enjoys having business conversations with her about Femme Produc-

The Tease

THE LADY RUNS THE SHOW

Starring: Lauren Hall, Selena Steele, Ashlyn Gere, Rayne, Randy West, Randy Spears, Tom Byron, Peter North, Marc Wallice, T. T. Boy. Producer: Louie T. Beagle. Director: John Leslie. Music: Bill Heid. VCA, 1990.

The three-way sex starts under the opening credits with Randy Spears and Marc Wallice entertaining a blonde (Rayne) in an electric

tions told her that with all the corrupt politicians' industrial pollutants causing pain and suffering in the world, he thought she should be proud that she only wanted to bring people pleasure. She is proud of that, and proud of the letters she gets from couples (from young marrieds to senior citizens) thanking her for her movies and the effect they have on their intimate lives.

Now divorced after nine years of marriage, she said she had a chance to experience the positive effect of videos herself when she began to seriously date a new man. She was reviewing movies for AASECT (American Association of Sex Educators, Counselors and Therapists) and had a stack of them beside her VCR. "After he made it past my bedroom door he was like 'Wow, movies.' I had never watched recreationally with a man, and viewing the videos strictly as a consumer was fascinating. We come to relationships with such a disparity between our sexuality and our fantasies. I think videos demystify sex in a positive way—it made me more tolerant of his sexuality and more aware of some of my own turn-ons that I hadn't consciously considered."

We thanked her for her time without asking her what those turn-ons were, but for an erotic filmmaker it isn't a big leap from conscious consideration of a fantasy to a new video, so we'll all find out the answer to that question soon enough.

blue teddy. The minimal storyline takes only a few moments to establish. Paul (Randy West), an unsuccessful writer, is introduced to Marie (Lauren Hall), a rich woman who "collects" artists, and seductively hires him to write her book. Paul will have a month of first-class room and board, and at the end of the month, not a day sooner, he will also have Marie. She gives his ear a nibble just to seal the bargain. For the next month Marie will tease Paul any way she can as she acts out her fantasies for him to turn into a book of personal erotica.

The video slides from one sex scene to another without much conversation, and offers a sampler of men now working in adult films from buff T. T. Boy to softly boyish Tom Byron. Randy Spears plays a wise guy whose character has limited appeal, but he has an amazing body and when he stops leering at the camera and settles down to business with Rayne in their threeway (with Marc Wallice), we were impressed. On the other hand, women who prefer smooth to hairy male chests vote a slight edge to T. T. Boy in the physique department. *Best scene:* seasoned pro Randy West's torrid blue light encounter with Selena Steele. Rewind! Rewind!

Some men apply the unerotic word *cockteaser* to the lovely Marie. If you have partner viewing in mind, you first might want to check this out on a solo spin.
Highly recommended.

Explicitness: 7;   Sensuality: 8   A,   2M/W,   2W/M,   2W

Tequila Sunrise

A MAN CAN CHANGE

Starring: Mel Gibson, Michelle Pfeiffer, Kurt Russell, Raul Julia, J. T. Walsh. Director/writer: Robert Towne. 1988.

Mel Gibson is a retired drug dealer, and his oldest best friend Kurt Russell is a cop whose superiors don't believe drug dealers ever retire. They order Russell to investigate. Michelle Pfeiffer is the woman they both love. The plot is routine, but Gibson and Pfeiffer in the hot tub are worth a rental any day. Wow then and wow now.

Simulated

Thelma and Louise

GIRLS HIT THE ROAD

Starring: Susan Sarandon, Geena Davis, Harvey Keitel, Michael Madsen, Christopher McDonald, Stephen Tobolowsky, Brad Pitt. Producers: Ridley Scott, Mimi Polk. Director: Ridley Scott. Writer: Callie Khouri. Music: Hans Zimmer. UIP/Path Entertainment, 1991. 129 minutes.

An exhilarating feminist road movie in which a couple of nondescript women turn into vigilantes. We mention it here for the carnal sweaty scene between Geena Davis and Brad Pitt loved by so many women.

Simulated

Things Change: My First Time

SEXUAL IDENTITY CRISIS

Starring: Diedre Holland, Nikki Dial, Paul Harlow, Francesca Le, Flame, Woody Long, Mickey Ray, Jon Dough. Producer/director: Paul Thomas. Writer: Bella Feega. Cal Vista/Metro Home Video, 1993. 74 minutes.

What determines our sexual preferences and, more to the point of this video, how do we really know what our true sexual nature is without the benefit of experimentation?

Lisa (Nikki Dial) has been living with Denise (Diedre Holland) in a committed relationship since Denise rescued Lisa from the gutter after her father remarried. A relationship with a hint of who-owes-whom-what, the balance of power between the ladies is not equal. Lisa is unprepared and surprised by her own response when she finds herself enjoying the attentions of a man who, challenged by her "virginity," tutors Lisa on some of the delights of making love to a man. Of the two, Denise more emphatically identifies herself as a lesbian, committed to Lisa. Not only does she make no move to seduce a client's willing husband, she declines the attentions of a straight woman curious about loving a woman.

At this point the film loses some of its nerve, and the next time we see them, Lisa has decided she needs to explore her sexuality and wants to move into her own place. In their final, near-flawless tumble, the ladies talk, laugh and cry in the way you might want to when leaving a lover you like but no longer love.

This and its sequel, *Things Change: Letting Go,* may sound familiar to you. They bear close resemblance to the Hollywood feature *Three of Hearts.*
Highly recommended.

Explicitness: 7;   Sensuality: 6   SS,   2W

Things Change 2: Letting Go

THE CRISIS CONTINUES

Starring: Nikki Dial, Diedre Holland, Paul Thomas, Kim Wylde, Steve Drake, Francesca Le, Jon Dough, Paula Harlow, Heather Hart, Lili Xene, Kelli Dylan, Woody Long. Producer/director: Paul Thomas. Cal Vista, 1992.

The sequel, or more likely the second half of *Things Change: My First Time,* has the same theme of indecision concerning sexual preference. Denise (Diedre Holland) was left to nurse her wounds after Lisa (Nikki Dial) left her for hetero adventures. On the loose, she turns up in a lesbian bar, where Steve Drake tries to pick her up. A guy trying to pick up a woman in a lesbian bar? Now that takes real nerve! Turning him down, Denise goes for Francesca instead, and together they visit the ladies' room for a raucous 2W involving beads not used as jewelry. Staying in the john, Francesca entertains all comers, exhibiting some of the seamier sides of the lesbian scene.

Unable to accept Lisa's desertion, Denise successfully manipulates a situation in which Lisa falls for a guy only to "discover" that men are scum and return wounded to Denise's waiting arms. A short-lived reunion ensues, and both women come to the conclusion that they're not yet ready to choose their sexual identity. One of the better movies with a lesbian love theme, even if it does give too much credence to the male fantasy that all gay women need is the right man. The location shots are good, and the dialogue is realistic and conversational.
Highly recommended.

Explicitness: 8;   Sensuality: 6   A,   M,   S,   T,   2W,
2W/M

 3 AM

FAMILY TRIANGLE

Starring: Georgina Spelvin, Charles Hooper, Claire Dia, Rhonda Gallard, Sharon Thorpe, Frank Maura, Rob Rose, Judith Hamilton. Producer/director: Robert McCallum. Writer: Tony Trelos. Music: Peter Van Den Beem. Cal Vista, 1975. 90 minutes.

3 AM is the beginning of the end for Kate (Georgina Spelvin), a lonely, unattached woman who's been living with her sister Elaine's (Rhonda Gallard) family. She and Mark (Frank Maura), her brother-in-law, have been having an affair for fifteen years. In a scene that has occurred in bedrooms around the world, Elaine and Mark are making love and without warning Mark declares his unhappiness in their marriage. He gets half a woman, he claims. What she married was the beach house, not him. He's decided to get out; his midlife crisis is right on schedule. The rest of the film unveils the repercussions of Mark's decision and the significant role Kate plays in this family drama.

By far the best classic film in the noir-erotic genre, 3 AM has all the elements of a great film in both its erotic and dramatic content. The sex scenes are in the context of the story, with the exception of a shower scene in which a total stranger joins Kate for a sensuous W/W. All are erotically charged and arousing, and their focus involves whole bodies, particularly hands and faces instead of the usual concentration on organs. Extended foreplay gets a front and center spot in the love scenes. The beach locale is beautifully exploited in a horseback riding sequence that's breathtaking. Combined with excellent writing, solid character development, credible motivation, high dramatic content, and thoughtful explorations of love and guilt, 3 AM is an exceptional and very watchable film.

Our one reservation is about the development of an erotic relationship between Ronnie (Charles Hooper), Mark and Elaine's young son, and Vicki (Sharon Thorpe), their fortyish neighbor. We appreciate the fantasies young boys have about older women, but we don't appreciate situations in which older women make themselves available and take advantage of all that hormone eruption in underage boys. Charles Hooper definitely looked underage.
Highly recommended.

Explicitness: 7;   Sensuality: 9   M/2W

Three Daughters

GIRL COMING OF AGE

Starring: Siobhan Hunter, Gloria Leonard, Robert Bullock, Carol Cross, Nina Preta, Annette Heinz, Johnny Nineteen, Ashley Moore, Clark Sharp. Producer: Për Sjöstedt. Director/writer: Candida Royalle. Music: Gary Windo, E. Boy. Femme Productions, 1986. 108 minutes.

Three Daughters is an affectionate spicy slice of life. Writer/director Candida Royalle treats her characters with respect and especially looks out for the women. It's the feminist age of adult movies." Jamie Bernard, *New York Post*

The three Clayton girls are home for spring vacation. The oldest, Michelle, is torn between accepting a proposal from a man she loves and going to London for a job she's worked hard to earn. The next daughter, Jennifer, is in college studying piano. The youngest, Heather, is an eighteen-year-old high school student who is experiencing sexual awakening as the events unfold.

The people are affectionate to each other, the bodies are good but real (A and B cup), and the lovemaking feels tender, playful, convincingly intense. Even the parents have their moment. The overall impression is wholesome—kind of like the Partridge Family with sex instead of singing—and if that weren't enough, in Candida Royalle's films the men do not come all over their partners! She said that she made this as an idealized girl-coming-of-age film—the way she *wishes* it had been. If you've been holding back from explicit videos, this is a great place to begin.
Highly recommended.

Explicitness: 7;   Sensuality: 7   B,   2W

Throat
12 Years After

COUPLES AT PLAY

Starring: George Payne, Sharon Mitchell, Eric Edwards, Michelle Maren, Sharon Kane, Jerry Butler, Joey Silvera, Joanna Storm; cameo appearances by Annie Sprinkle, Gerard Damiano, Marc Stevens, Margot Dumot. Producer/director/writer: Gerard Damiano. VCA, 1984. 85 minutes.

Two couples, unlikely friends, are both having trouble with their marriages. Jerry Butler stops on the way home from work to have sex with hooker Sharon Mitchell. Meanwhile his sweet, suburban wife, Michelle Maren, is giving one of her homemade muffins to Eric Edwards, the meter reader, and telling him her marital woes. "I'm afraid to ask for the things I want and ashamed to do the things he wants." With an attitude closer to compassion than lust, Eric encourages her to model her secret stash of see-through nighties and shed some inhibitions.

Meanwhile in another part of town Joey Silvera and Sharon Kane, a rich semialcoholic couple with an open marriage, are each having their own adventures. Hers is with a stud for hire; his is with a bubbly blonde he takes to a sex club called The Sewer (based on New York's infamous '70s club Plato's Retreat), a place his swinging wife dislikes. "When someone sticks a cock in my face I at least want an introduction." People there are tied and chained in painful-looking ways, though everyone is smiling. Are we having fun yet?

Eventually the couples are reunited, all the more satisfied with their mates after their extramarital flings. Gerard Damiano, the man who made the original *Deep Throat,* has acquired a much more complicated view of human sexuality over the years.
Recommended.

Explicitness: 8;   Sensuality: 7   O,   S/M,   2W

The Tiffany Minx

HEROINE IN PERIL

Starring: Crystal Synk, Robin Storrs, Carter Stevens, Jeffrey Hurst, Jennifer Jordan, Marlene Willoughby, Richard Bolla, Samantha Fox, David Morris, Candida Royalle, Candy Smith. Producer: Robert Walters. Director: Roberta Findlay. Music: Brandon Harris. Solid Gold Video, 1981. 84 minutes.

Paul (Jeffrey Hurst), is the sleazy husband of the rich and apparently naive Jessica (Crystal Synk). Paul manages to keep his mistress, Anne (Marlene Willoughby), with his wife's money, which he shamelessly admits to Anne. One night, while Paul is with Anne, a prowler gets into Jessica's house and rapes her. A real fighter who won't go down willingly, she manages to stab the intruder in the back with a pair of scissors, dispatching him to meet his maker. Was this a random act of violence, or does Paul have it out for Jessica? And why doesn't he muster even a little sympathy for his wife?

To recover from the assault and the experience of having killed a man, Paul and Jessica go to their isolated beach house on Long Island. Which is what you probably wouldn't do if you were smart. In jug-wine land, she's befriended by a neighbor, who is herself being taken advantage of by a gigolo (R. Bolla) with eyes on Jessica. The complicated plot, sprinkled with red herrings, closes with a satisfying surprise ending.

Directed by a woman, Roberta Findlay, who was, according to Jim Holliday, an early behind-the-camera woman pioneer. **Recommended.**

Explicitness: 8;   Sensuality: 7

Tokyo Decadence

JAPANESE BONDAGE AND S/M

We open with a man strapping a girl into a chair and tying a gag with a hole over the mouth in place. He blindfolds her and gives her an injection. She is afraid. He sings and fondles a red high-heeled shoe. The credits roll. This is a slice of life about a young call girl in a Tokyo establishment that looks as efficiently businesslike as a quality office temp agency but specializes in S/M workers "to go." Most of the scenes are woman submissive, though occasionally one of the men wants to be whipped or strangled. Since in the United States it is illegal to show S/M with penetration (separately is OK), leather is the whole story. This is shot from the young woman's point of view, and she looks alternately resigned and terrified, certainly not pleasured by what's going on. Even the successful and sophisticated call girl who befriends her escapes into drugs when she's at home. Some of the visual effects are striking, and no one gets lasting physical wounds, but the psychic pain is evident. More of a cautionary tale than a turn-on, *Tokyo Decadence* offers a fascinating glimpse of another culture's erotica. *Best moment:* A client tells the girl to stand on a window ledge and pose against the night sky. We see her from the outside, one figure in a lighted window high up in an anonymous skyscraper.

Explicitness: 8;   Sensuality: 3

Traci, I Love You

TOO MUCH TOO SOON

Starring: Traci Lords, Marilyn Jess, Gabriel Pontello, Alban Ceray. Producer/director: Jean Charles. Caballero Home Video/Traci Lords Productions Inc., 1987.

After Traci Lords revealed her real age, she went to Europe, where she produced and starred in this, her only legal erotic video. The story is simple. An American girl needing a change of scene goes to France. There she meets a handsome Frenchman who introduces her to the local hot sex club. When she leaves him after an intense night of pleasure, he gets even by pretending to ignore her while watching from afar to make sure she doesn't have a pleasant time. The last third of the film is an extended marathon in a minimalist setting (mattress on a pedestal) as Traci is lovingly prepared for sex and then introduced to a kaleidoscope of lovers.

Traci is a magnetic performer, and we caught an impression of her youth and vulnerability in the strip club and the encounter, set in a cellar, with her French lover. To us, the rest has interest for curiosity, not erotic value. The scene in which a producer, supposedly interviewing Traci for a "real" movie, ended up with his pants around his knees looked too pathetically true. We were pleased that she

220

No Girls Allowed

Traci Lords seemed made for erotic films. Large natural breasts, slim hips, long legs, blonde hair, and an I'll-try-anything-once enthusiasm. After she signed on with the World Modeling Agency in 1983, she quickly made more than seventy films and was considered one of the industry's brightest stars. So it was with a genuine sense of shock that her producers woke up on May 8, 1986, to the news that Traci (born Norma Kuzma in Steubenville, Ohio) had just celebrated her eighteenth birthday.

Federal law firmly and implacably states that no one may perform in explicit movies unless they are at least eighteen years old—no exceptions, no excuses. The Feds yearned to send some people to jail over Traci's exploits, but after it was revealed that

didn't pretend to enjoy it, but it's the opposite of a turn-on. The film has been edited in various ways and released under the following names: *Traci, Je T'aime; I Love You Traci; P.S. I Love You;* and *A Taste of Traci Lords.* Whatever the title, it's more or less the same video. **Recommended with caveat.**

Explicitness: 8; Sensuality: 6 B, 2M/W, O, 2W, 2W/M

her false identification had been good enough to get her a U.S. passport, their case dissolved.

Hurriedly, all of the Traci Lords movies and videos were withdrawn from the market. (Dan Abend has compiled an on-line list of more than one hundred appearances: abend@cis.ohiostat.edu.). Whenever possible, her presence was clipped and an edited version reissued, accounting for the unexplained, abrupt transitions in movies where she made a brief appearance, such as The Grafenberg Spot. Movies in which she starred, as in Traci Lords' Fantasies, made just before her birthday, had to be destroyed.

What made her tell? One speculation is that the announcement came as part of a mother/daughter fight over her mother's share of Traci's hefty income. Another is that Traci hoped to put out her own line of videos without competition from her younger self. Whatever the reason, Traci made only one legal erotic movie before retiring from the field. She now has a mainstream career, has appeared in films, and was a regular on Melrose Place. A television series is rumored to be in development.

Troublemaker

BAD TO THE BONE

Starring: Aura Palmer, Eric Price, Rocco Siffreddi, Celeste, Tammi Ann, Crystal Gold, Tony Tedeschi, Mark Davis, Ian Daniels, Asia Carrera (though she's inexplicably not listed in the credits). Producer: Bud Lee. Director: Paul Thomas. Writer: Maria LeMans. Music: Barry Boxx. Vivid. 120 minutes.

One of those people who's mean for the hell of it, Shayne (Asia Carrera), insinuates herself into the life of Rita (Celeste) and George (Eric Price). Rita and George, who marry in the course of the video, have a wonderful sense of fun and adventure and frequently include Shayne in their activities. Easy targets, they somehow remain innocent of Shayne's shameless manipulations and offense to the friendship they offer. The sex among the three of them is spontaneous and frequent and one of the best examples of a cunninlingus episode takes place during a birthday party Rita and George throw for Shayne.

Regrettably, *Troublemaker* is a missed opportunity. Paul Thomas, whose skills are tremendous, would have made a better video if he and the rest of the crew had given the same attention to motivation and character development, especially that of the despicable and contemptible Shayne, that they gave to the many and varied sex scenes. All we're left with is the image of a woman who lies, cheats, and, for no reason made apparent in the script, tries to come between a couple.

Explicitness: 8; Sensuality: 7 A, M, 2M/W, 2W/M

Two Hearts

LIFE IS A FOUNTAIN

Starring: Randy Spears, Raquel Darian, Ona Zee, Kim Wylde, Derrick Lane, Steve Strong, Veronica Hart. Producer/director: Gloria Leonard. Writer: Raven Touchstone. Vivid, 1991. 70 minutes.

A concoction that is memorably bizarre for its shaggy-dog-story improbability, *Two Hearts* is more about money than sex. David (Randy Spears) has been left a pile of cash by his father, who out of some perverse notion tattooed a secret message revealing the meaning of life on David's penis. David cannot get his hands on the loot unless he can read this message. All his efforts to get his toolie to rise and shine are to no avail. Enter Trish (Racquel Darian) and Ivy (Ona Zee) to the rescue. What is the secret of life? And, more important, which of the ladies—the pretty young one or the more mature experienced one—has the right technique for success? And you thought the only reason for getting it up was pleasure! No, we're not going to tell you the message on the penis. Rent the movie and learn the secret of life for yourself.

Explicitness: 7; Sensuality: 6

Up 'n' Coming

COUNTRY WESTERN BACKSTAGE DRAMA

Starring: Marilyn Chambers, Lisa De Leeuw, Herschel Savage, Cody Nicole, Loni Saunders, John Lazar, Clay Tanning, Ferris Weal, Tiny Mary, Doug Rossi, Tom Byron, Jay B. David, Donna Capris, Brandy Monique, Winston Cleft, John C. Holmes. Producer/director: Godfrey Daniels. Writer: Jim Holliday. Music: Mike Lyman/Haywire Band. Caballero, 1983. 86 minutes.

Written by Jim Holliday, a veteran of the adult industry and its acknowledged historian, *Up 'n' Coming* turns *All About Eve* on its head. The movie shows the underside of Nashville's music trade. Cassie Harland (Marilyn Chambers) and Althea (Lisa De Leeuw), two country western singers, collide and behave like rabid animals as one is making her way up the success ladder and the other is in a free fall about to crash.

Althea has been sabotaging herself with booze, not showing up for performances, reading her lyrics off of 3" × 5" cards, and living off former glory. The ambitious Cassie, about to put out her first single, is a back-up singer catching everyone's eye. In the background are the usual movers and manipulators—the men who run the business of the music business and require special services from performers to give them the breaks they need. Singing her own songs, Chambers' performance is seamless in the sexual and nonsexual scenes. De Leeuw plays her role just to the edge of ridiculous but not over. Like other Chambers's videos, homage is paid to her role as the Ivory Snow girl.
Highly recommended.

Explicitness: 7;   Sensuality: 6   A,   O,   2W/M

Urban Heat

CARPE DIEM

Starring: Marita Ekbert, Klaus Miltia, Sharon Kane, David Farel-Sandler, Taija Rae, Scott Baker, Chelsea Blake, K. Y. Lee, Casandra Lee, Davic Scott, Tish Ambrose, David Ambrose, Carol Cross, Bernard Daniels. Producer/writer of concept: Candida Royalle. Director: R. Lau-

ren Neimi. Music: George Socaras, Philip Goetz, Sharon Stone, Vicki Genfen, Rich Productions. Femme Productions, 1985. 78 minutes.

With no plot or dialogue to follow but lots of original music to listen to, Candida Royalle's second video is a pure celebration of libido. The episodes take place in elevators, dance clubs, gardens, and beaches on a lovely blue sky summer day in and around New York. Relieved from come shots and gratuitous clinical close-ups, enjoy the pleasures of foreplay and the affectionate loving of couples. With the soul of a woman, the roving camera definitely captures the heat. **Highly recommended.**

Explicitness: 7;   Sensuality: 8

LEARNING THE RIGHT MOVES

Starring: Victoria Paris, Diedre Holland, Cameo, Randy Spears, Jon Dough, Cal Jammer, Ariel Knight, Staci Lords, Axel Wolf, Jacqueline, Jennifer Stewart, Chaz Vincent, Jon Dough, Randy Spears, Axel Wolf. Producer/director: Paul Thomas. Vivid/Paul Thomas Production, 1994.

A disparate group of women gathers in a classroom. One by one they stand up and tell the invisible teacher why they want to learn to dance and strip. They show him what they can do while he videotapes them and coldly asks very personal questions. (If you saw *A Chorus Line,* you get the scenario.) The women represent a range of life experiences—some look like seasoned pros in the flesh business, others like the girl (or mom) next door. Victoria Paris plays a private dancer who humbly fears something is wrong with her act because men don't get excited. Diedre Holland says she wants to learn something new to spice up her marriage.

The teacher, arrogant but knowing all the right moves, gives them lessons in steps, stripping, and the all important tease, including the constant awareness of your profile on stage and how to take your bra off under a feather boa. Sex is included in the story line, but the real draws are the striptease lessons. (It's also fun to see the responses of the husbands and boyfriends in the audience when the class puts on their graduation "recital.") Watch it today; use it tonight. **Recommended.**

Explicitness: 7;   Sensuality: 7

Virtual Sex

CYBER SYNTAX

Starring: Kelly O'Dell, Tiffany Minx, Tina Tyler, Deborah Wells, Laurie Cameron, Tanya Summers, Jalynn, Ariel Daye, Mark Davis, Tony Tedeschi, Eric Starr, Matthew Sebastian. Producer: Derek Graeyson. Director/writer: Nicholas Orleans. Music: Weley Evans. VCA Platinum, 1993. 90 minutes.

Good color, good music, good cinematography, great sets, and normal-sized breasts aren't enough to lift this video out of the category of rudimentary in-out. The concept of "virtuality" seems to give filmmakers permission to abandon all notions of narrative integrity and any kind of linear plot, not to mention dialogue that's something more than stupid. What does work in *Virtual Sex* is the stylishness of the sets and clothes and the electronic paraphernalia. Reminiscent of the work of Andrew Blake, it can be used as background sight and sound for a rousing bachelorette party.

Explicitness: 9; Sensuality: 5   C,   M,   O,   SS,   T,   2W

The Voyeur

REKINDLING THAT MARITAL ROMANCE

Starring: Kim Dawson, Sean Abbananato, Swen Somers, Joe Schuster, Leonore Andriel (as Aunt Lydia). From "Other Men," by Edward Buskirk, a short story from The Erotic Edge, *edited by Lonnie Barbach, Ph.D. Producer: Lynn Larkin. Director: Deborah Shames. Writer: Udana Power. Script and sexuality consultant: Lonnie Barbach, Ph.D. Music: Jim Purcell.*

Brenda (Kim Dawson) and James (Sean Abbananato) head for a romantic weekend at a country inn to put the spark back in their ten-year marriage. He's worried about business; she wants to call home and check on the children. When she does, her sexy Italian Aunt Lydia, who is babysitting, tells her the kids are fine and scolds her for calling. "Who teaches you American women about men? TV sitcoms and women's magazines? You are there to seduce your husband, not talk him to death." Taking her aunt's advice to heart, the ever-so-blonde Brenda changes into a semisheer dress that plays peek-a-boo with her revealing new underwear and goes down to lunch. When she teases the confession from James that he once fantasized about watching her make love to another man, she sets out to make his dream a reality.

Brenda is a cotton-candy blonde with a good, though not buff, body, and she is shown wearing a suit and running an office before she goes to the country with her husband, so you won't get confused and consider her an airhead. Deborah Shames, the director, is one of the several women making films especially directed toward women. (If you keep a sharp eye on the backgrounds you can catch a glimpse of her playing Brenda's secretary.) Together with sexpert Lonnie Barbach, who acts as a consultant on these films, she makes lighthearted comedies with situations and foreplay that are way above average. Unfortunately, Brenda's husband comes across as a sweet, worried wuss—a little like Darren in *Bewitched*. If he had more energy, the movie would be sexier than it is.
Recommended.

Simulated

The Voyeur 2

EROTICA VERITÉ

Starring: Liquid Slater, Eva, Kylie Ireland, Shane Tyer, Lana Sands, Melissa Hill, Kitty, Valentino Rey, Jon Dough, Joey Silvera, Chad Thomas, Damien, Sean Michaels, Tom Chapman, Kyle Stone, Ricky Ricardo. Producer/director/writer: John Leslie. Evil Angel/John Leslie Productions, 1994. 110 minutes. **(This is a John Leslie video, not a sequel to the Deborah Shames video.)**

Peeping pervert David (John Leslie) and his hand-held video camera spend days and nights shooting singles, couples, and threesomes doing the wild thing. The most successful of the seven scenes, which range from the scary to the comical, are the ones in which Leslie himself is a presence as the voyeur giving direction to his sometimes willing and sometimes not performers. The middle segments, especially one in which Leslie hires a feisty prostitute, are the best. We found the first and last vignettes problematical and suggest you skip them unless assault and rape are part of your fantasy reel. The first shows two mechanics forcing a bossy customer who's come for her car to have sex. We found this gang rape too brutal and scary, even though the subject gives in to the man. We thought the last segment particularly egregious. It's evening and Leslie is watching a woman undress through her uncovered bedroom windows. Noticing an intruder, she invites him into her house and after their sexual encounter he proceeds to attack her. Leslie interferes and saves her life, after which she asks him to spend the night with her. Please! This sends all the wrong messages to men and women. And in addition, need we remind you to draw your shades before getting undressed?

For the record, most of the women in *Voyeur 2* are small breasted. Could we have stumbled on a John Leslie preference? The verité camera work is sometimes distracting, and the sound is occasionally poor, but Leslie's audacious personality works its usual magic. **Recommended with caveats.**

Explicitness: 8;   Sensuality: 7   A,   M,   S,   T,   2W/M

Where the Boys Aren't

LIGHTHEARTED SPOOF

Starring: April West, Barbara Dare, Summer Rose, Joey Silvera, Tori Wells, Paul Thomas. Producer/director: Judy Blue. Writers: Paul Thomas, Mark Cushman. Vivid.

A day in the life of P.T. Video. The writer (Paul Thomas as himself) and director (played by Joey Silvera) are trying to make a video. The women stars are present and ready to work, but not one suitable male is available. Joey Silvera begs Paul Thomas to change the scenes to girl/girl, but he says, "I hate girl/girl. Girls don't do that in real life. If I wanted to get artsy I would have taken out the come shots." Meanwhile all around them the women are showering, trying on lacy panties, and making their own movie—girl/girl, of course. This is a simple, good-natured comedy, on the level of a TV sitcom with sex. If you're into "girl/girl," you'll probably enjoy this.

Explicitness: 7;   Sensuality: 5   2W,   3W

228

Where the Boys Aren't 2

WASTE O' TIME

Starring: Jamie Summers, Barbara Dare, Diedre Holland, Cheri Taylor, Kelly Royce. Producer/director: Judy Blue. Writer: Mark Weis. Vivid, 1990. 62 minutes.

The set looks borrowed from a junior high drama club—a painted ocean backdrop, stones made of Styrofoam, and a sandbox beach. A blonde showgirl stumbles up and falls in the sand. Shipwrecked. Before you can say *Gilligan's Island* four other blondes wash ashore along with a trunk containing such life-sustaining necessities as makeup, clothes, a dildo, plenty of batteries, and stuffed grape leaves. The blondes get cranky with each other until Nature takes her course and they become very intimately acquainted.

We thought this was a truly stupid film and would bet a large sum of money that should these blondes ever find themselves castaway they prove more resourceful and entertaining than their film counterparts.

Note: There is now a whole series of *Where the Boys Aren't* movies. The premise—no man/woman sex—remains constant. The quality varies.

Explicitness: 7   Sensuality: 3   T,   2W,   3W

White Palace

UNLIKELY COUPLE FINDS SEX AND ROMANCE

Starring: James Spader, Susan Sarandon, Eileen Brennan, Jason Alexander, Kathy Bates, Steven Hill, Rachel Levin, Renee Taylor. Producers: Ark Rosenberg, Amy Robinson, Griffin Dunne. Director: Luis Mondoki. Writers: Ted Tally, Alvin Sargent. Based on the novel by Glenn Savan. Music: George Fenton. UIP/Universal/Mirage/Double Play, 1990. 103 minutes. Rated R.

He's a twenty-seven-year-old yuppie widower, a neatnik advertising executive with an affectionately concerned circle of friends and family.

She's a forty-three-year-old waitress in a hamburger joint, messy, disorganized, with a sister who is an itinerant fortune-teller. They fall into improbable lust and then even more improbable love. Especially if you're a woman of a certain age, it's an agreeably sexy film, not profound, not particularly believable, but we can go with the fantasy. Hey, we liked *Pretty Woman*.

Not everyone agrees with us, but an English WW reports, "I saw this with three women friends who go out once a week for dinner and a movie. At our next meeting we all confessed we had, without discussion, gone home after the movie and shown our men a very good time." *Best scene:* Susan Sarandon gives James Spader a wake-up call. *Best line:* James Spader on why he isn't attracted to a perfect girl his friends want him to date: "There's no dust in her Dustbuster." Yep. Whatever turns you on, James.
Highly recommended.

Simulated;   Sensuality: 8.5

Whore

DRAMA VERITÉ

Starring: Theresa Russell, Benjamin Mouton, Antonio Fargas, Sanjay, Elizabeth Moorehead, Michael Crabtree. Producers: Dan Ireland, Ronaldo Vasconcellos. Director/writer: Ken Russell. Music: Michael Gibbs. Palace/Trimark, 1991. 85 minutes.

Ken Russell holds nothing back in this look at a night in the life of a prostitute, made the same year as *Pretty Woman*. Theresa Russell (*Black Widow, Impulse, Track 29*) stars as Liz, the cynical beauty who's seen it all, done it all . . . and tonight she tells it all.

Her story begins with the dream many girls have—to live happily ever after. But her hopes shatter when her husband begins to drink and sleep around. Hurt and betrayed, she leaves him but becomes trapped by poverty. She struggles to support herself and her baby on a waitress's inadequate pay. One night a customer offers her $100 to go out with him. That's more than she makes in a week! She agrees . . . and ends up sleeping with him. It's the first step on the slippery slope that takes her to the streets.

It's dangerous on the street. After a vicious assault nearly ends her life, she realizes she can't work without protection. A pimp named Blake is the guy she picks. Bad move. She gives him everything she has, but he always wants more. Tonight, Liz is determined to make a new life for herself. She runs away from Blake. She's terrified he'll find her, knowing the brutal punishment she'd face. Again and again she manages to evade him. Still Blake is relentless . . . and out for blood. At last, he captures her and has her at his mercy. This time she's ready to fight back!

Though this is a remarkably slow and boring movie for such a hot subject, we include it here because it's frequently lauded in articles as a mainstream effort that explores the true nature of prostitution, possibly as an antidote to the *Pretty Woman* point of view.

Simulated

Women in Love

D. H. LAWRENCE ON FILM

Starring: Glenda Jackson, Jennie Linden, Alan Bates, Oliver Reed, Michael Gough, Alan Web. Producer: Larry Kramer. Director: Ken Russell. Writer: Larry Kramer, from a novel by D. H. Lawrence. Music: George Delerue. UA/Brandywine, 1969. 130 minutes.

Ken Russell was crowned the enfant terrible of British cinema about the time he made *Women in Love,* the first of two (the second is *The Rainbow*) D. H. Lawrence novels he adapted to film. Though Glenda Jackson, who later became an MP, won an Academy Award for her role, what everyone remembers is the provocative nude wrestling scene between Alan Bates and Oliver Reed. Erotically charged and saturated with glowing light from a blazing fireplace, it oozes with sexuality. Feverish with eroticism (Rex Reed called it *Women in Heat*), *Women in Love* celebrates the connections of body and spirit in a lushly photographed movie that holds up very well indeed after twenty-six years.

Simulated

X-Factor

NEW-AGE ROMANCE

Starring: Pamela Mann, Danica Rhea, Eric Edwards, Paul Thomas, Kristara Barrington, Erica Boyer, Karen Summer, Rick Stevens. Producer/director: Hal Freeman. Writer: Red Newsom. Music: John Gonzales. Hollywood Video, 1985. 90 minutes.

Teddy (Eric Edwards) and Susan (Pamela Mann) qualify as genuine soulmates. The first time they make love a sickly plant in the next room grows luxuriantly green and leafy. The second time a downstairs neighbor (Paul Thomas) takes off his bandages and neck brace—healed. Awesome. But when it's Susan at death's door, how will Teddy alone be able to save her?

More plot than usual, sex that is an unforced part of the story line, and a heartfelt relationship redeems the lackluster shot-on-a-shoestring look of this film. An excellent choice for couples. ***Highly recommended.***

Explicitness: 7;   Sensuality: 7

X-Factor: The Next Generation

THE STORY CONTINUES

Starring: Heather Hart, Gail Force, Tracy Adams, Taylor Wayne, Raven Richards, Jamie Lee, Marc Wallice, Ron Jeremy, Jim Southm, Jon Dough, Eric Edwards, Buck Adams. Producer/director: Charles Grey. Hollywood Video, 1991.

Teddy (Eric Edwards) stands by Susan's grave with their two grown-up children. It's been several years since she died in a car accident, but he can't stop grieving. The accident also left their son, Marc (Marc Wallice), bitter and angry, but their daughter (Heather Hart) has grown to be as gentle and loving as her mother. When she meets Mr. Right she finds that her mother's healing gift unexpectedly is her gift, too. But will she be able to save her family? Hold tight, new agers. You knew all the time that love was the answer.

This is a true sequel, though you don't have to have seen the first one to make sense of the story. As before, the sex scenes flow from the situations, and the characters' goals and actions are believable, no matter how fantastical the plot device. Another winner for couples. ***Highly recommended.***

Explicitness: 7;   Sensuality: 7

Instructional Videos and How-to Series

Explicit sex and simulated sex are noted, but these videos are not rated on a scale of recommendedness. We have made the descriptions detailed so that viewers can choose according to their own needs and preferences. Series are listed at the end of the section and are available only through direct-mail purchase. Addresses and phone numbers are provided.

Instructional Videos

Acts of Love

Narrator: Paul Thomas.

Paul Thomas, the amiable narrator and guide in this video, spent more than ten years as a top male star of adult videos and is now a director. He doesn't do the authority-figure-medical-expert-thing that is usually seen in how-to videos. His attitude is more that of a deeply cool older brother sharing his experience as he introduces and comments on five short episodes of dramatized information.

The participants talk to each other, not the camera, so it is less self-conscious than some of the other how-tos. Since the suggestions are directed to experienced adults, there are no charts and this-is-the-penis-this-is-the-vagina lectures. It offers ideas and points of view that might not be on every couple's regular sexual menu, though it's the attitude and presentation, not the material, that make it stand out.

The film begins when Alexis Grecko comes home and catches her husband getting ready to masturbate. He's embarrassed, but she calmly strips down to her underwear, gets out her vibrator, and shows him how she pleasures herself. When he gets used to that idea she asks him to share his own favorite techniques with her. Soon they have moved to mutual masturbation, and she gives him directions to increase her satisfaction. She's direct but breathless, not bossy. Her verbal techniques are a real how-to bonus if you feel hesitant about giving suggestions to your lover.

The other four vignettes include putting romance into a long-term relationship, women who make love together who are not lesbians, toys that include a penis enlarger used not only to make the penis bigger but also to delay orgasm, and a demonstration of first-time anal sex for both the man and the woman (she uses a dildo on him).

The backgrounds are attractive, and the attitude low key. These people aren't trying to sell anything, just show you a good time.

Explicit

Art of Touch 2: A Taoist Erotic Massage

Starring: Espen Tontor, Aiden Shaw, Steve Lycette, Richard DuPont, Gabor Marko, Istvan Keri. Producer: Gary Wicks. Director: Mike Esser. Writer: Layne Derrick. Pride Greenwood/Cooper Video Production, 1993. 50 minutes.

An all-male international cast discusses and demonstrates the efficacious application of massage in hightoned British-accented voices. The techniques are basic and not particularly inspired. Emphasis is on mental and psychological preparation by giver and getter imbuing the massage with ceremonial importance. The subjects of the massage are laid on various beds that are surrounded by revolving decorated backgrounds, not unlike sets for a play. The backgrounds change with each new pair of participants, but all of them turn round and round during the entire video, putting the observer (you, the watcher) on the verge of dizziness or motion sickness, making it nearly impossible to actually glean any relevant or useful techniques. Just when you think you've got it, a plant or latticework twirls past and obscures the view. We were inclined to think of this as soft-core Tao-babble.

Complete Videoguide to Safe Sex

Institute for Advanced Study of Human Sexuality, Dr. Clark Taylor. Directors: Laird Sutton, Clark Taylor. 1988.

The intention of this video is to eroticize sexual health via the use of condoms and other safe-sex practices. After a few testimonials, including one by Mike Horner, who says he wants safe sex to feel natural, a few safe activities like massage and bathing are mentioned, followed by everything you ever wanted to know about using condoms—how to put it on, what to do once it's on, and how to enjoy the difference. The video clearly states that no one is safe from a disease like AIDS, but scary stories are eschewed. This is an excellent video to show a reluctant partner and for adults who want to educate their sexually active children (erections are shown, but not sexing). While this doesn't have the latest information on female internal condoms and safe-sex condoms for latex-sensitive people, there is much useful information here. The bottom line is that asking someone to put on a condom is like saying, "I care about you as much as I care about myself."

Explicit

Couple's Guide to Great Sex Over 40 (vols. 1 and 2)

Narrators: Dr. Culley Carson, certified sex therapist, urologist, and former cochair of the Sexual Dysfunction Unit at Duke University, Diana Wiley, licensed psychotherapist, board-certified sex therapist, and member of the President's Council on Aging. Sinclair Institute, 1995. 60 minutes each.

The clear message of these excellent tapes is that age and failing health need not be hindrances to a satisfying, pleasurable sex life. Three middle-aged committed couples, ranging in age from mid-forties to late sixties, discuss and demonstrate the strategies (some ingenious and some not), they use to continue to pleasure themselves and each other. Past the concerns of child raising and career building, they creatively face the changes that age brings. Mature and sophisticated, with bodies and faces that don't disguise the years, the participants share their issues and solutions, including the discoveries they continue to make about their own and their partners' bodies and needs.

Everything about these videos is outstanding. The narrators are attractive, knowledgeable, and articulate. In language that doesn't patronize, they explain the inevitable physical and psychological modifications our bodies and minds undergo after the age of forty. Penile injections, menopause, and postmastectomy sexuality are among the subjects discussed. Carson and Wiley, with the help of the couples, demonstrate that the best is yet to come.

Explicit

For Couples Who Want a Better Sex Life (includes A Ripple in Time)

1. FOR COUPLES WHO WANT A BETTER SEX LIFE
Producer: Ted McIlvenna. Director: Laird Sutton. 1991.

Several couples demonstrate how they have put variety into their sex lives. Couple number one shops together for groceries and plans where on each other's bodies they will try out their purchases. Whipped cream on your guy's penis sounds better than it looked to us, but hey, this couple obviously gets off on their inventive uses for cheese food, maraschino cherries, and peanut butter.

Couple number two shops together for expensive erotic books and tries out some of what they see. Others play fantasy games or find a secluded alfresco setting for love. The look is Birkenstocks and body hair—multigenerational counterculture.

2. A RIPPLE IN TIME
Filmmaker: Laird Sutton. 1991.

Ed and Sally are mature (over sixty) sex-positive lovers (she's in somewhat better shape than he is). The video chronicles their erotic afternoon. Okay if what you want is encouragement or if you are of the seeing-is-believing school. Otherwise, the *Sex Over Fifty* video has more useful information for older men and women. Because Ed and Sally are amateurs, the video left us feeling we had been peeping in the windows of the intellectual older couple down the block. If that idea thrills you, they don't mind.

Explicit

Encyclopedia Sexualis, The Video

Starring: Jessica Wild, Buddy Love, Francois Papillon, Angel Kelly, Jeff Scott, Tiffany Blake. Voice-over: Bryce Britten. Writer: Bryce Britten, MS. MFM Video, 1986. 60 minutes.

This is an instructional video illustrating a medley of sexual pleasures. A couple is in bed—he's sleeping and she's reading *The Encyclopedia Sexualis*. As she reads, she slips into various fantasies, which are performed by others, including an interracial couple. The feeling you get from her is that her sex life is less than satisfactory and perhaps her husband is less than enthusiastic and accommodating. Information is power, and, armed with the power of knowledge, she wakes her husband at the end of her reveries and shows him what she's been boning up on.

Much of this video is done in voice-over, including the listing of euphemisms for words like masturbation, penis, breasts, intercourse, etc., making this video great for expanding your dirty-talk vocabulary. Herewith some samples for your amusement: anal sex—dot dig, old back door, corn hole, peak sticking; masturbation—flog the bishop, paddle the pickle, pinch the cat, pull the wire; oral sex—blow the whistle, cake eater, muff diver, Peter eater, yodel the canyon; vagina—black velvet, cock pit, hidden treasure, honey pot, jelly roll, middle sister.

Explicit

Erotic Massage (vol. 2)

Producer: Kenneth Ray Stubbs, Ph.D. Director: Frank J. Tsacrios. Music: Gymnosphere Music. 1990.

Not a massage video in the strictest sense, this is a feast for the eyes and the libido. With the help of a feather and the biggest, softest, whitest rabbit-fur mitten you've ever seen, a man softly strokes an undressed woman and she returns the favor. Exquisitely shot with great color, moody lighting, pretty bodies, and no sound except music, this video can be treated as wallpaper for a seduction. We

…d like those mittens, and we can imagine just how fine they'd feel! Hard as we searched, we could not locate the first volume of *Erotic Massage*.

Good Vibrations Complete Guide to Vibrators

Producer: Good Vibrations, 1993.

If you've been wondering how on earth to choose among the many vibrators available, help has arrived. A thirtyish woman sits on a sofa, undresses, and demonstrates the self-pleasuring use of a range of vibrators—how they work, the advantages and disadvantages of each one, and what feels best to her. Along the way she experiences about ten orgasms of varying intensity, barely pausing to draw a deep breath before she continues her cheerful instructions. Not a fancy production but useful, direct, and to the point. (Available by mail order from the Good Vibrations catalog [see "Mail-order Sources"] and rental in some video stores.)

How to Enlarge Your Penis

Starring: Scott Taylor. Writer/producer: Scott Taylor, John Stagliano.

Scott Taylor displays his penis to the camera, meeting the U.S. standard (2–4 inches at rest) with room to spare, but of course the national average is not the subject of this tape. So Scott greases up to the pubes and claps a long plastic tube over his poor, defenseless member. The pump he demonstrates and recommends is a bilge pump sold at most shipyards and marine supply stores and approved by the U.S. Coast Guard for more customary uses. All the while he's talking, he's pumping, pumping, pumping. After two hours (not real time) we have an unveiling. His penis temporarily ranks as a genuine huge guy, much thicker than before and three inches longer. *Best and most believable quote:* "There is some pain involved if you can take it."

The finished product flops around like a top-heavy tulip when Scott and his girlfriend prop it up for a lackluster demonstration. Unequivocally grotesque to view. However, should you find yourself considering breast enlargement or some other painful process designed to make you more attractive to a man, watch this video and ask yourself what self-respecting admirer would be foolish enough to go through even this temporary procedure for you.

Explicit

How to Reawaken Your Sexual Powers

Playboy, produced in association with the Sharper Image, 1993. 53 minutes.

Five couples give your fantasies visual stimulation against resplendent backgrounds of beach, waterfall, and ferny woods that leave you longing to pack your bags and visit the Hawaiian locations first-hand. The suggestions encompass exercising together, massaging each other, learning from nature (the power of water, air, and fire), using your mind and thoughts in a positive manner, and developing the power of words to become aware of and communicate your feelings. Featured are frontal nudity for both men and women; trim, good-looking black and white couples; slightly soft-focus slow-motion kissing, stroking, cuddling; and a soothing female voice-over rather than dialogue. Drawbacks include the suspicion that most of the women received their breasts from the same talented plastic surgeon. Opinions split between romantic and saccharine. If you have enjoyed other Playboy advice films, you'll probably like this one.

Simulated

Intimacy Skills: A Sex Therapist's Guide for Couples

Dr. Michael Perry, Mary Simone. Access Instructional Media, 16161 Ventura Blvd., Suite 328, Encino, CA 91436; 818-784-9212.

Intimacy. A word of the '80s that's made it into the '90s. To help couples develop intimacy skills, the narrators walk through the various stages of lovemaking: communicating, sensual massage, sexual massage, manual lovemaking, oral lovemaking, intercourse, and afterplay.

We thought of this video as Sex 101. It is specific, clearly stated and demonstrated. Many other instructional tapes cover the same territory. What we liked about this one was the understanding that intimacy begins long before you get to the bedroom or take off your clothes. The narrator demonstrates that giving can be as big a turn-on as getting pleasure and that sex can be enjoyed without intercourse. Safe sex is emphasized.

Attractive locations, the use of unusual camera angles, and a minimum of talking heads made the advice easy to take. Considerable segments of this video seem to be directed to men as the surrogate is a woman working with men.

An Intimate Guide to Male Genital Massage (aka Fire on the Mountain: Taoist Erotic Massage)

Starring: Joseph Kramer, Matthew Simmons, Steve Davis. Writers: Joseph Kramer, Carol Leigh. Music: Into the Dreamtime. Body Electric, 1992.

Joseph Kramer introduces himself by sharing some of the many titles of his adult life—sacred initiate, sexual healer, erotic shaman, visionary, erotic revolutionary, massage instructor. Then he offers step-by-step instruction in the "caress of the cock," a massage that has its basis in Taoist and Tantric sex practices. The ultimate goal is relaxation and stimulation without ejaculation. It's recommended as an alternative to intercourse, a way to be emotionally close and sexually intimate in the age of AIDS. The intended audience for the video is gay men, but it can be instructive for women, too, especially at times when they want to do something loving with their partner but penetrative sex is not possible.

The tape begins with two men affirming that each one is special—they breathe and groan, which, even if you are familiar with Tantric sexual practices, can leave you rolling your eyes. You won't miss anything important if you fast-forward through the drums and chanting and go right to the science of cock reflexology, which incorporates several familiar massage techniques with some strokes we hadn't seen before. The massage takes at least one half-hour and should leave the recipient profoundly relaxed. An interesting option for women.

Jewel in the Lotus: The Art of Tantric Union (vols. 1–3)

Starring: Lorin and Parker, Prabhakar and Maha, Vandano and Maya. Producer/director: Bodhi Rathel, Andre Rathel. Teacher: Goswami Sunyata Srawati. Narrators: Bodhi Avinasha Rathe, Marvin Lincoln. Music coordinator: Suzanne Doucet. Tantric International, Taos, New Mexico/Kriya Jyoti Tantric Society. 1986.

A three-volume series covering the principles and practices of Tantric sex through specific theoretical and practical teachings. The theoretical teachings take place in the context of a classroom setting in which technical aspects are covered in significant detail with a lot of charts and graphs that are hard to comprehend and absorb. The teacher, Goswami Sunyata Srawati, cannot be well understood, and the diagrams aren't always clearly seen. We found the teachings and rituals engaging and were ourselves captivated by the principles of these ancient practices and wish the production values had been equal to the material. In spite of the difficulties, we recommend that you begin by renting the first two videos to help you understand the principles of Tantra and purchasing the third to help you through the movements.

Volume 1: The sources and history of Tantra are discussed and a number of positions demonstrated. The performers move from position to position naturally and elegantly, giving the perception of a beautifully choreographed dance.

Volume 2: A continuation of the first volume, focusing on explanations of the shakras and cobra breath, with exercises for enhancing sexual energy.

Volume 3: A discussion of the importance of stimulating internal orgasm and the use of sexual energy throughout your entire body. A couple demonstrate, step by step, the sacred *mintuna* rite and demonstrate Karana Kria exercises. This is the most practical of the three volumes in this series.

Explicit

Kama Sutra: The Art of Making Love

Penthouse, 1993. Distributed by A'Vision entertainment. 60 minutes. Not rated.

This is an explicit but tasteful (no funky close-ups) demonstration of more than thirty positions described in the *Kama Sutra,* a 2,000-year-old classic of erotic instruction. The *Kama Sutra* has been in print in countless editions and has been illustrated by Chinese, Japanese, and Indian artists. According to the makers, this is the first film version of the secrets of the mysterious East.

The lovemaking (illustrated for some reason solely by white people, odd for a tradition whose source is in India) concentrates on position, explaining how and why each is effective. The cool, clipped male voice that narrates the film says, "The shifting, ever-changing postures flowing like dance figures one to another are only meant to express the tenderness of the controlling mind. Kama Sutra is especially valuable to couples who are married or in a long relationship." We agree and think this is a terrific video for couples to watch together. Some of us liked this video for the attention and instruction it gives to the needs of women. The voice-over suggests, "Do what she likes" and "Whatever you're doing, slow down—better at half the speed." *Favorite scene:* a romantic Victorian claw-footed tub full of bubbles and love. The lighting flatters the comely participants, and the backgrounds are lovely—even the tree the couple leans against for support is an especially well-grown tree. If you're flexible and want a challenge or are looking for new ideas to add spice to your love life, this is the tape for you.

Explicit

Learning the Ropes (9 volumes)

Starring: Ona Zee, Frank Zee. Ona Zee Productions.

We hear that bondage and S/M have become more mainstream in the age of AIDS since many practitioners don't depend on penetration for their satisfactions. The range of participation is broad, from silk ties to massive coils of rope, from spanking to torment. Some people are just in it for the cool leather outfits. If you're new to the idea, be warned that this is an area of sex in which the pursuit of pleasure can lead to real physical damage if you don't know what you're doing. Our own strongly held opinion is that when it stops being a game, it stops.

Ona Zee is an established adult star who openly practices domination in her private life. Her husband, Frank Zee, is a willing and inventive partner in the games. This couple switches roles, which means sometimes one is the dominant, sometimes the other, though many other players have preferred roles and do not depart from them. According to one author, there are ten want-to-be-submissive men for every woman willing to be a dominant.

Frank and Ona put together a series of ten films that stress safety as they provide an ever more challenging introduction to this usually underground world. These films are not meant to be a turn-on, and both participants freely stop the action to instruct the viewer on how to do it right. In spite of the dominant/submissive aspect, remember, *this is a consensual activity in which both partners must agree.* There is no explicit activity in these tapes, since federal law permits showing either penetration or bondage S/M but not both.

Vol. 1: Male submissive. Frank demonstrates his own home-made restraints that open quickly in case of emergency and explains how you too can make them. The couple talks about the importance of establishing a code phrase that means "No more!" since saying "No" and begging for mercy is part of the game. Ona spanks Frank, and he licks her high vinyl boots. At this early stage it's apparent that being ominant or submissive is very time-consuming—the submissive does-n't just put on an apron and do the housework while the dom takes in a movie—they interact. We were forcefully reminded of an afternoon at the swimming pool with a group of seven-year-olds. "Look at me." "Watch me." "Now watch me." "Did you see me?" If you're a mom you'll know what we mean. 85 minutes.

Vol. 2: Male submissive. Bondage that includes tying up the cock and balls in painful-looking ways, cross-dressing, and various whips and their differences. She tells the slave what to do. He says, "Yes, Mistress. . . . Is this right, Mistress?" 79 minutes.

Vol. 3: More male submissive. Ever more painful. 78 minutes.

Vol. 4: Female submissive. This time it's her turn for spanking, bondage, and restraints. We'd like to see better costumes here; we won-

Safe Sex 2

Almost all adult erotic movies we have viewed begin with the same safe-sex message. It recommends "monogamy and/or absti-nence" (we wonder if the and/or is ironic) "and at a minimum the use of a condom and a selective choice of sexual partners." So why is there so little evidence of safe sex in the videos? With a few no-table exceptions (see the Safe Sex list in the "Index of Videos by Category"), the utilization of condoms is a furtive now-you-see-it-now-you-don't business, generally used at the insistence of a per-former.

"Aren't they worried about disease?" we asked. The answer, it seems, is not in public. Mike Horner told us that in a small community word gets around quickly if you're involved in things that could lead to a dangerous problem, and no one will hire you. And what if you ask to use condoms? "If you insist, you can," he said. "But you won't work as much."

"Women seldom get to choose their partners," Nina Hartley said, "but they're allowed to say no." She also said that the out-

der why so many sexual accessories look so badly made and unesthetic—it's not as if they're inexpensive. 79 minutes.

Vol. 5: Female submissive. More whips, canes, feathers, pain. Yikes. 79 minutes.

Vol. 6: Lesbian bondage. As it says, woman to woman bondage, though some of the stuff is not limited to one sex. Toys, hanging sex chair, and an introduction to a pro. 77 minutes.

Vol. 7: At Lady Laura's. A field trip to a bondage parlor and dungeon, with accessories for all tastes, including racks, hoists, etc. Rather amazing to the uninitiated, known in this subculture as "vanilla." 75 minutes.

Vol. 8: Slaves in training. Hanging, whipping, hot wax, and the ever-popular pony girl training. This last is shown more briefly but se-

side come shot we dislike so much is now her preference because it seems safer.

All performers are required to get an HIV test once a month and a test for STDs (sexually transmitted diseases) every three months. Certificates must be presented the first day of shooting. If you "forget" to bring it, perhaps you'll be allowed to work for a day using a condom. And, to be fair, there doesn't seem to be much incidence of HIV in the community of performers.

There are exceptions to the prevailing laissez-faire attitude. Femme Productions announces at the end of each video that everyone in their films either practices safe sex or is working with their real-life partner. We applaud that point of view and wish that some of the industry giants—such as PHE, which is in the mail-order condom business—would use their influence to see that more videos incorporate this positive role modeling. We don't mean to pick on PHE, but since it has a board of therapists who scrutinizes films to see if a bottom is too red after a playful spanking and rules a ball gag too sexually coercive, we find it paradoxical that safe sex doesn't rate equal concern. Until there is a cure for AIDS, safe sex should be the only way to have nonmonogamous sex. Remember, you can't catch anything from your television set—except an attitude. We think that attitude ought to be the one that saves your life. End of message.

ductively in Andrew Blake's *Sensual Exposure,* in case you're curious but don't want to sign on for the whole package.

Vol. 9: The training continues. More slave training.

Love Potions

Starring: Anastasia Alexander, Carl Ross, David Barr, Toni Culen-Barr, Steven Diebold, Leslie Meenen. Producer/director: Sweet Vision. Writers: Ken Segall, Cynthia Mervis Watson, M.D. Music: Arthur Barrow, Scott Morgan. Narrator: Paula Mann; additional narration by Bill Wilson. Based on the book Love Potions, *by Cynthia Mervis Watson, M.D., published by G. P. Putnam, Inc. A Sweet Vision Productions presentation, 1993.*

The video, based on a popular book of the same name, begins with exercises to improve sexual performance, including testicular breathing to postpone orgasm in men and Kegel exercises for women. It goes on to massage—sensual Swedish massage (one of the better short introductions we've seen of this form of massage), acupressure points you can stimulate that work on your partner's sexual energy, and chakras.

Having delved into touch, we move to the sense of smell, with aroma therapy. Did you know that neroli is a natural tranquilizer that may be rubbed on arms and legs for sexual magnetism? Then we're on to fascinating taste tips about food for love, erotic play, fantasy, and medicinal uses of herbs. A lighthearted introduction that offers some original ideas for playful experimentation. We found this as a rental, but it can be ordered: 1-800-927-0158.

Simulated

The Magic of Female Ejaculation

Featuring: Dorrie Lane. Producer/writer: House o' Chicks. 1993.

Do women ejaculate? According to this short film, Masters and Johnson say no, but Dr. Grafenberg (of G-spot fame) and women's health centers say yes, some women do. Ancient records from sources as diverse as rabbinical lore, Native American tradition, and William Shakespeare are quoted to prove that this is not a recent preoccupation. A woman testifies that she repressed her ejaculations for twenty years but finally in a loving relationship began to ejaculate and had complete orgasms as a result.

The presenter then introduces some of the best charts we've seen of female reproductive bits and shows us the urethral sponge, paraurethral gland, and paraurethral ducts, from which the ejaculate comes. (By the way, onion and garlic lovers, it smells of what you eat.) The tape is recommended for those who want to explore the idea further.

Explicit

Masturbation Memoirs (vol. 2)

Featuring: Juliet Carr, Anna Marti, Annie Sprinkle. Producer: House o' Chicks. Director: Carol Leigh. 1995.

Here's a tape on how to be your own best friend. The opening song tells it all—"If you're lost and blue, give yourself a helping hand. . . ." Juliet Carr, post-fifty and still classically beautiful, is a former adult movie star who had a hysterectomy. Orgasms help her chronic intestinal problems and arthritis, but vaginal sex doesn't feel great, so she now touches her whole body in a way that gives her what she calls "orgabumps."

Anna Marti talks about getting her breasts augmented and how women should be free to make their own choices. Annie Sprinkle, the third speaker, wears a large flower wreath on her head and says she imagines the earth as her lesbian lover. She likes to do what she calls "metabation," a cross between masturbation and meditation. While sitting and talking beside a woodland stream surrounded by redwoods, she revs up her Hitachi magic wand vibrator and lets out an orgasmic cry that echoes through the woods. Really echoes. Annie yodels, "Ai ai ai ai ai." The echo answers, "Ai ai ai ai ai." Annie always pushes the envelope, but here she's way past that. If you find it liberating to watch someone else heading for outer space, take a peek.

Nina Hartley's Guide to Anal Sex

Starring: Nina Hartley, Anna Malle, Hank Armstrong, John Decker. Producer/director: Nina Hartley. A Nina Hartley Production. Adam and Eve, 1996.

The very reassuring Nina Hartley takes on another difficult topic. She begins by saying that anal eroticism does not have to include sex. "The majority of people who play with anal eroticism don't have penetration—anal intercourse."

Her advice covers the gamut from charts and diagrams to diet (enjoying anal sex is yet another reason to eat more fiber). The cleanliness concern is mentioned, but not in depth. She suggests proceeding slowly, at your own pace and only as far as you want to go—"If your mind is saying yes, yes, and your heart is saying no, no, your anus will always follow your heart." Nina says that in her marriage they discussed anal sex for at least a year before they got around to actually doing it.

Then she settles down to demonstrate—first a slow, relaxing massage and detailed chat with her friend and subject, Anna Malle, about Anna's physical sensations. After getting warmed up, the two women join male partners for a long session of sex that includes anal intercourse. There's too much "Oh yeah" for us, but overall it's the gentlest of introductions.

Explicit

Nina Hartley's Guide to Cunninlingus: Under the Hood

Producer/director: Nina Hartley. Music: tje 506. Adam and Eve/Nina Hartley Production.

With infectious charm and enthusiasm, Nina Hartley gives a complete tour of the geography of feminine organs. Thorough, intelligent, and entertaining, Nina offers very specific instructions and advice to both men and women, urging playfulness for the sake of lust, passion, and arousal. And thanks to her training as a nurse, she doesn't stumble over the words. From the totally resistant to the guy who's a hair from getting it right, she'll inspire a new willingness and expertise. *Favorite line:* "The clitoris is not a doorbell."

Nina Hartley's Guide to Fellatio

Starring: Alex Sanders, Nina Hartley. Producer/director: Nina Hartley. Writer: Ernest Green. Adam and Eve, 1994. 45 minutes.

Nina Hartley, drawing on more than ten years of adult movie star experience, shows how to treat a man right. "Get them by the balls and their hearts and minds will follow." She doesn't demonstrate a deep throat technique but uses her mouth and hands in several different ways to give Alex Sanders pleasure. Among her tips are: "You can never tell the size of a woody by a softy" and "Wetting the penis magnifies the sensation." Alex Sanders, who shows an amazing amount of patience when Nina stops what she's doing to chat with the viewers, offers a unique tip of his own—eating kiwi and celery makes your come taste sweet.

Nina Hartley, Filmmaker

When we talked to Nina she had just returned home from a grueling weeks-long dance tour. Even after ten years as one of the biggest and best known stars in the business she said it isn't possible to make a living as an erotic actress. Competition from several thousand amateur films that each year flood the market has lowered the sales—and budgets—of mainstream erotic film-makers and the pay of actors and actresses.

Within the business, the producers think the public wants to see new faces and three years is the average length of a time a woman is able to command a large paycheck. Nina works to stay in front of the camera, making phone calls, reminding people of her enthusiasm and availability. For her, like most of the women stars, it's dancing not acting that pays the bills. Acting

Nina Hartley's Guide to Swinging

Starring: Anna Malle, Hank Armstrong, Cristy Lake, Sahara Sands, Dic Tracy, Luc Wilder, Ariana, Shannon Rush, Magnum, Duane, Dallas. Producer/director/writer: Nina Hartley. Executive producer: Jay Galt. Adam and Eve, Nina Hartley Productions, 1996. 60 minutes.

With warm encouragement for the timid, Nina Hartley introduces the pitfalls and pleasures of swinging, or opening your relationship up to others. She and her husband have been "in the life" for many years, and she straightforwardly says that "swinging will strengthen a good relationship and tear apart a bad one."

Anna Malle and Hank Armstrong act the curious couple. First they discuss swinging and use the fantasy as foreplay, then they try a three-

in movies boosts your popularity and marketability as a dancer, and she told us, regretfully many of the young woman coming into the erotic film business these days aren't doing it out of love for the work, but as a dancing career move to enhance their marquee value.

The decision to move behind the camera seems a natural evolution, not only so she can keep doing the work she loves but also to make videos that include her vision of strong, healthy, sexually emancipated women.

The money for her videos is advanced by PHE/Adam and Eve, in return for distribution rights. She is responsible for hiring, production, packaging, and making it all come together on time and within a very tight budget that includes everything from camera rental, tape, lights, set, editing time, props, and talent, to her salary. Budgets range from $15,000 to $30,000 dollars, and filming must be accomplished in two or three very long days.

Articulate and intelligent, she has become one of the most visible spokespersons for the business and an effective defender of her first amendment rights to represent her lifestyle choices and point of view to the public and have a good time time while she does it.

some with experienced swinger Cristy Lake. "So Ann tells me you're quite the social person," Hank says as he sits awkwardly on the end of the bed with the two women. Indeed. Finally the couple attends a party with Nina as hostess (her husband is listed in the credits but not in evidence on camera). This turns into one of the few convincing orgies we've ever seen on camera. For a change, the participants really looked as if they were enjoying themselves. Nina's message is that this must be a comfortable decision for both members of a couple.

If anyone could persuade us that swinging looks like fun, it would be the optimistic Nina Hartley, but we admit to doubts. Nina says that's okay—swinging isn't for everyone. Use the idea to fuel your solo fantasies or as foreplay on Fantasy Night with your mate. Act it out. Live it up. The two of you can stage a swing all by yourselves, and your friends will never suspect the roles they played.

Explicit

Over Forty: The Best Sex of Your Life

Starring: John Martin, Rosalin Javier, Roberta Harte, Danielle Brittania, Jason Brittania, Walter Electric, Janet Tyrone, Rene Morgan, Ona Zee, Jonathon Lee, Kay Place, Frank Place, Nina Hartley (as surrogate), Bryce Britten. Producer/director: Paul Thomas. Writer: Bryce Burton. Home Video/Cinnamon Production, 1989.

This helpful little video shows real over-forty bodies (some *way* over forty) graphically working through a number of sexual issues. There are four different but related episodes, including one in which a man and his wife are making love for the first time since his heart attack (he looks like Christopher Torville gone to pot). Several physically undemanding but satisfying positions are demonstrated, useful not only to the convalescent but to stressed-out baby boomers whose spirits are willing but whose bodies are tired.

In a second episode, an older couple works with a surrogate (played by Nina Hartley). She begins their instruction with hand-holding and progresses to a guided tour of their genitals. She demonstrates cunnilingus (with a gentle attitude adjustment for the husband) and the squeeze technique for delaying male orgasm.

The other two episodes revolve around sexual fantasy and keeping the thrill alive—in both, third parties are invited to join the couples. We liked this video because it deals with real-looking people and problems. Of course, people this age could have used more flattering lighting. Still, the movie has its heart in the right place.

Explicit

Sensual Fantasy for Lovers: How to Experience Your Secret Desires

Executive producer: Hugh Hefner. Playboy, 1994. 55 minutes.

Five couples explore games, film fantasies, risk taking, romantic settings, and secret desires. The sequences are romantically filmed, with no visible erections or intercourse. The people are awe inspiring, with superlative sculpted bodies and flawless skin, hair, and teeth. What's to complain about? To us they seem inhuman, not a turn-on, but those who find most erotic videos too realistic and gritty may find this better suits their aesthetic sensibilities. The fantasies offered could give you a few ideas of your own.

Simulated

The Sensual Massage Video

Starring: Tracy Adams, Gina Fine, Randy Paul, Breezy Lane, Keisha, Jack Gaske. Producers: Bryce Britten, licensed sex therapist, J.P. Howard. Director: J.P. Howard. Writer: Bryce Britten.

Since this video begins with a couple in bed making love, it will take you no time at all to come to the same conclusion we did—that it's about massage as foreplay. There's an attempt to introduce a few basic strokes and massage oils, but the training session with the therapist, her girlfriend, and two other couples spends more time on tacky-looking group sex than massage techniques. We've seen better videos on both subjects.

Sex after Fifty

Dr. Lonnie Barbach, Ph.D., with Helen Singer Kaplan, Md., Ph.D., Betty Dodson, William Masters, M.D., Virginia Johnson, Sc.D., Bernie Zibergeld, Ph.D., Mary Lake Polan, M.D., Robert Kessler, M.D., Joani Blank, Ph.D. Producer: Focal Point Productions. Director: Deborah Shames. c. 1991.

Just because you're in your thirties or forties, don't think this video has no message for you. If you know what to expect and what to do about the physical changes of aging (such as a shift in sexual desire, erections, or lubrication difficulties), problems will remain manageable and in proportion. The spirited Dr. Lonnie says we can enjoy sex into our nineties—God willing—if we don't give up. She proceeds to interview a number of men and women of all colors, shapes, and sizes, from fifty to over seventy, who talk openly (without demonstrations) about obstacles to be overcome and satisfactions to be gained as bodies change.

Problems include desire, health, and arousal difficulties. Solutions discussed are hormones, lubricants, oral sex, and vibrators, as well as visits to a sex therapist for mental problems and a doctor for physical ones. And best of all there are suggestions for prevention—how to keep from having sex problems in the first place. Everyone we know who watched this film thought it was fantastic and "my older friend would enjoy it"—though some of these Wise Women were already in their seventies. Boogey on, bright spirits.

No visible sex beyond hand holding

Sexual Positions: The Video

Lewis E. Durham, Ph.D. Starring: Aurora, Greg Johnson, Claudia Miss, Francois. Director: K. J. Ellison. Narrator: Kelly Brennan. Writer: Marilyn Lawrence, Ph.D. Based on a book by Hans Richter. Home Video, 1985.

A cool woman's voice-over describes the action as couples work out, one at a time, running through the positions as if they were a brightly lit animated sex manual. "In this position the couple can mutually caress each other's bodies," or, "Anal sex can satisfy dominance needs for men, providing control over his and her sexuality." No atmosphere here, no emotion, just acrobatics. If you prefer a detached presentation, this authorized film version of the acclaimed best seller by Hans Richter is the video for you.

Sluts and Goddesses

Starring: Annie Sprinkle and many women (friends, not professional film actresses). Producers/directors: Marla Beatty, Annie Sprinkle. Writer: Annie Sprinkle. Music: Pauline Ollveros. 1992. 50 minutes.

Annie Sprinkle appears looking for all the world like an impersonation by Lily Tomlin (dowdy '50s dress, hair piled in a flat bun on top of her head) and instructs us in awakening our inner goddess and slut. Her program has a handmade, loving, amateur look, as if the rainbow coalition of women who appear also pitched in to do costumes, makeup, and camera work. It includes both goddess and slut tips on choosing your name for each persona, fantasy makeup and costumes ditto, sexercise for all occasions, positions, knowing your body, toys. The faintly new-age slant is established by the names of the sex positions: Quenching Five Desires, Charming the Serpent, Paying a Karmic Debt, etc. The tone is earnestly lighthearted, and the intended audience appears to be sapphic counterculture, though there's nothing to keep straight women from picking up a few tips. As Annie says, "Never knock something until you've tried it for yourself."

Explicit women

The Tantric Guide to Sexual Potency*

*and Extended Orgasm

Starring: Diedre Holland, Sharon Kane, Laurie Cameron, Ariel Daye, Jonathon Morgan, Mike Horner, Jon Dough, Steve Drake. Host: Kay Parker. Producer: Wesley Emerson. Directors: Wesley Emerson, Kay Parker. Writer: Martin Brimmer. Adam and Eve, 1994. 85 minutes.

The Tantric yoga techniques shown here look similar to hatha yoga positions you may have learned for health. Tantric yoga emphasizes delaying the orgasm, channeling the energy up the spine, and prolonging the pleasure for both parties. (The Tantric sexual practices of Aly Kahn, a legendary playboy of the '40s, supposedly enabled him to be an amazing lover even though he had an actual orgasm only a few times a month.) This video gives an introduction and shows basic yoga postures and breathing techniques. (Just in case you wonder how easy it is, Mike Horner, who appears in this tape, has been a practitioner of yoga for about twenty years.) We would have been happy with less sex, which looks, when all is said and done, just like sex, and even more instruction. Couples who have tried this talk about feeling a connection on spiritual as well as physical levels. A good beginning.

Explicit

Ultimate Massage: The Art of Sexual Touch

Dr. Michael Perry. Access Instructional Media, 16161 Ventura Blvd., Suite 328, Encino, CA 91436. 818-784-9212. 1994. 60 minutes.

Stroke by stroke, a male and female narrator demonstrate massage techniques. Don't expect relief to aching muscles and bones, as *sensuous* is the operative word here. Do expect arousal, as the focal points are sexual organs as much as the specific massage strokes. The goal is arousal; mood, environment, and attitude get lots of attention. The many details, like warming the massage oil, will enhance your experience. For your first try you might want to make a list of the strokes to make transitions smoother, but let's face it, even a bad massage is pretty good.

What Men Want

Narrator: Dr. Michael Perry. Access Instructional Media, 1994. 60 minutes.

What do men want, and what do they think makes a woman good in bed? Pretty much what women want and what they think makes a man good in bed. Though there are no big surprises in the man-in-the-street-style interviews of this video, the vignettes (with explicit sex) are exceptional and will give you lots of inventive and smart ideas for turbocharging your honey's libido. They'll liberate both of you from the routine sexual two-step that's so easy to fall into when you're busy. Plus, it's fun to hear average Americans express their sexual cravings.

Explicit

Women Who Love Sex

Out of Line Production. Writer: Gina Ogden. 24 minutes.

Worthless drivel is just about all we can say about this video, which is supposed to make you feel good about your surging libido. We were promised help in creating new images of our sexuality. We got the same old, same old: women like two-way nurturing, they want to be connected, etc. etc. etc. Yawn. If you have a forty-year-old virgin in your life who's about to get married, this is the perfect gift to make her feel better about her deflowering. Otherwise, this video bears no consideration.

World of Good Safe and Unusual Sex: The Video

Starring: Lois Ayres, Taja Rae, Angel Kelly, Jerry Butler, Jerry Heath. Producer: MFM Video. Director: David Wolk. Writer: Joyce Burnham. Home Video, 1987. 60 minutes.

A laundry list of sexual practices ordinary, unusual, and bizarre that works as a tour guide and would probably work best for watching alone, especially if you're looking to surprise someone special with your enlightenment. There is an emphasis on safe sex, with good information on how to use a dental dam and advice on making condoms more effective with the use of spermicidal jelly.

There's lots of foreplay and kissing, also, some cool straddles are demonstrated for which better-than-good muscle tone is needed. A three-way is shown with two women and one man, raising the question: Why is it so seldom two men and a woman? The practices covered in-

clude exhibitionism, fetishism, G-spot stimulation, lesbianism, masturbation, mud wrestling, oral sex, phone sex, prostitution, rubbers, safe
sex, sex toys, shaving, swinging, three-way, transsexualism, trans-
vestitism, voyeurism.

Explicit

How-to Series

Behind the Bedroom Door

Educational Video Corporation, 3600 Park Central Blvd., Suite #3635, Pompano Beach, FL 33064.

Billed as what couples do in bed, *Behind the Bedroom Door* is a forty-volume series whose premise is that the viewer can learn something from other people having sex. Proposing that even the best sexual relationship can become routine with time, each video tells a story and shows the solutions to the issues of the relationship. We couldn't manage more than nine of the volumes and found them too slow going and tedious for our taste. After the first few, the couples and their issues became confused in our minds. We're convinced that these would have been far more effective if less time was spent with the couples and more issues and couples were covered in the individual tapes.

All but one of the couples is under forty, and, being "real" people, though fit, they have their fair share of blemishes and soft spots. This aspect can make them less intimidating for the rest of us to watch.

Well made from a production point of view, everything about these tapes was too modulated and slow to hold our interest for long.

Vol. 1: The Sexuality of Jim and Patty. A couple in their late thirties and married for twenty years, Jim and Patty are looking for ways to incorporate fantasy, new locations, and edibles in their sexual practice. 65 minutes.

Vol. 2: The Sexuality of Rod and Linda. In their second marriages, Rod is dealing with the psychological complications of not being circumcised and Linda shares how she uses toys to enhance her experience. 56 minutes.

Vol. 3: The Sexuality of Annie and Eric. Both under thirty-five, Anna and Eric are uninhibited, playful, and orally fixated. To add excitement, they toy with light bondage. 62 minutes.

Vol. 4: The Sexuality of Liz and Tom. Liz is ten years older than Tom (he's twenty-five). They love sex al fresco in an apple orchard, play together in the shower, and amuse themselves with "nasty sex." 59 minutes.

Vol. 5: The Sexuality of Shane and Stacy. At twentysomething, Shane and Stacy have been together for four months. They practice safe sex and love the woman-dominant position. 55 minutes.

Vol. 6: The Sexuality of James and Carol. Carol is working on overcoming the inhibitions resulting from a religious upbringing, and he's recovering from surgery to correct an undescended testicle. 60 minutes.

Vol. 7: The Sexuality of Karen and Michael. Fans of the G-spot, Karen and Michael incorporate fantasy in their love play and practice analingus. 55 minutes.

Vol. 8: The Sexuality of John and Heidi. Taking their play outside the bedroom, this twentysomething couple experiments with a variety of positions. 66 minutes.

Vol. 9: The Sexuality of Donna and Gary. Donna likes to arouse Gary with an anal stimulator, and Gary demonstrates how to use a cock ring. 56 minutes.

Better Sex Video Series (3 volumes)

Dr. Judith Seifer, assistant clinical professor, Dept. of Psychiatry and Obstetrics and Gynecology at Wright State University School of Medicine; fellow of the Masters and Johnson Institute; certified by the American Association of Sex Educators, Counselors and Therapists.

Dr. Michael Kollar, member of the National Board of Directors of the American Association of Sex Educators, Counselors and Therapists; certified sex therapist in private practice. Volumes 1 and 2.

Dr. Roger Libby, elected fellow of the Society of the Scientific Study of Sex at the prestigious International Academy of Sex Research; he is certified as a sex educator and sex researcher with diplomat status from the American Board of Sexology and an invited member of the Academy of American Sex Research. Volume 3.

Consultant on AIDS issues: Marilyn Volker, MA.Ed. Producer/director: American Video Productions.

Three videos stressing verbal communication and open-minded sexual experimentation are produced as a series, but they can be viewed independently. Volume 1 introduces the backgrounds of the five couples who appear throughout the tapes and explains the reasons they wanted to improve their sexual relationships. This may be useful for couples who want someone to identify with, but it isn't necessary to understand the material presented.

Dr. Judith Seifer, who presents the information with the help of two male colleagues, has a pleasantly earnest, well-groomed, middle-American look, and her demeanor is both warmly encouraging and professional. Depending on how you respond to authority figures, this can be either reassuring or a turn-off. She doesn't overwhelm the viewer with charts and lectures, preferring to let the couples demonstrate her points.

The couples are in their early twenties to late thirties, with attractive, natural bodies. They talk to the viewer in voice-overs—interspersed with comments and directives from the two experts—while we watch them make love. The sex, while explicit and often experimental, is restrained and discreetly photographed. The overall attitude is: No matter how good your genitals feel, remember that we communicate romance best with our hands and loving kisses.

Vol. 1: Better Sexual Techniques

We get acquainted with five attractive couples who talk about their relationships and the changes their new knowledge has brought, and they demonstrate the techniques of making love they find most satisfying. These include mutual masturbation, the most usual sexual positions, and oral sex.

The subjects include a young wife who didn't find much pleasure in sex with her husband, a second marriage where both partners had divorced over sexual problems, a couple in which the woman's sex drive is much stronger than her husband's, a woman who grew up in a very religious atmosphere and didn't know how to show her sexual pleasure to her husband, and a couple in a formerly open marriage who wanted to make their newly monogamous relationship exciting.

The audience for this tape seemed to us to be primarily young couples just starting a relationship. Older couples might also find the stress on communication and experimentation useful, but the didactic tone of voice was experienced as condescending by viewers who had been in a sexual relationship for a number of years. One person we know gave *Better Sexual Techniques* to a college-age daughter who was in her first committed relationship. There's a long safe-sex text at the end of this video, although the actual safe sex, unfortunately, is shown only in *Advanced Sexual Techniques*.

Vol. 2: Advanced Sexual Techniques

The same five couples move on to more advanced techniques. They demonstrate and discuss their experience of masturbation, mutual masturbation, foreplay, G-spot stimulation, fellatio (including developing a version of deep throat and how to pleasure the man if he can't get an erection), cunnilingus (with several techniques and preferences), "69," and intercourse in different positions. Anal intercourse is presented as an option, accompanied with circumspect visuals. Couples who want to try anal sex might be reassured by Dr. Seifer's matter-of-fact presentation but seek out one of the other more detailed introductions. The thorough safe-sex demonstration includes latex gloves, dams, condoms, nonoxynol 9, water-based lubricants that can be used with latex gloves, and condom options for oral sex and regular sex. The new safe condoms for latex-sensitive people are not included.

Vol. 3: Making Sex Fun with Games and Toys, 1992

Dr. Seifer says that she encourages couples to incorporate a vibrator into their sex play for the pleasure of the man as well as the woman. Various participants are shown using vaginal barbells, intravaginal vibrators (can be worn all day at work or play), modern plastic versions of ben wa balls to be inserted into the vagina, vibrators, cock rings (using a ring with a vibrator results in a very hard erection for some men), and dildos (both vaginal and anal).

The video concludes with sex games—alternatives to the bed, such as a swimming pool (with a good, sensible point of view about vaginal lubrication); the office on Saturday; outdoors; light bondage; romance and fantasy. The fantasy section comes with a caution about sharing more than a partner wants to hear, though "for people who enjoy it, sharing fantasies can be very arousing." This tape could enrich the repertoires of more experienced couples as well as beginners.

The Lover's Guide to Sexual Ecstasy

Starring: Raven von Bergen, Don Fischer, Shannon Wright, David Michaels, Nicole Greiner, Rod Hopkins, Elizabeth Cole, Nick Douglas. Producer/director: Edward Holzman. Writer: Jessica Stewart. Music: John Gonzalez. A Sexual Enrichment Series™ Production Pacific Media Entertainment in association with Holiday Pictures, 1992.

We purchased this tape in a store. Mail-order catalogs often group it with the two following *Lover's Guides* as a three-part set; however, this first volume is quite different from the two that follow, first and foremost because the sex in this one is simulated, and in the other two it is not.

A beautiful young couple dressed in evening clothes enter a room and begin a dance of seduction. We see them, but we hear another unnamed woman's gentle voice, backed by saxophone and jazz guitar, giving orders: "Push them [brassiere straps] off her shoulders and kiss the spots where they were. Wait before reaching around to undo the hooks of her bra. Her arms are now immobile because the straps are still around them." It's very leisurely, very seductive for a tape of instruction. As the low voice goes on explaining step by step how to arrive at each of the Four Plateaus of Sexual Excitation™, culminating in the Grafenberg Orgasm™, several different couples take turns illustrating her points. Their lovemaking is stylized and balletic rather than passionate, but it did convince us that these couples know each other. We see breasts, legs, the curve of a derriere as the positions are demonstrated, but no sweat, no heat, and certainly no unsightly genitals. A very tasteful introduction to sex.

While we liked the tape very much, we want to know who trademarked a name for the orgasm women have been enjoying since time began. Please tell us it wasn't a man. What's next? An advertising campaign? Accept no substitute. Always demand a genuine Grafenberg Orgasm™. Satisfaction guaranteed.

In the spirit of fair play, we propose the Wise Women Ejaculation™—that's the one men have when they watch erotic movies with their wives and lovers.

Simulated

Lover's Guide to Advanced Sexual Techniques (vol. 2)

Presenter: Dr. Andrew Stanway, MB, MRCP.

We rented volumes 2 and 3; volume 1 of Dr. Stanway's tapes was not available in any store we visited or any catalog we saw.

This guide is the only one we know of that recognizes that short-term relationships exist, though it keeps an emphasis on long-term couples. It begins with a chapter on communication, because, as Dr. Stanway says in his brisk English accent, "I have helped more couples to happier sex lives by improving their communication skills than I ever have by improving their bedroom ones." While the next eight sexually explicit chapters concentrate on the bedroom skills, communication is an ever-present theme. The subjects covered are: time together; massage; tips for stimulating the penis and clitoris; the act (basic and not so basic); positions; varying locations; taking vacations; sex games (such as doctor and nurse, vicar and nun [English film, remember]); and tips for starting a relationship on the right foot and keeping romance alive in long-term relationships. There are various body types—young to middle aged, thin to plump, all Caucasian, no silicon. Fans of Masterpiece Theatre may find that this combination of dignified presentation and flatteringly lit demonstration works for them.

Lover's Guide to Better Orgasm

(vol. 3 in *Lover's Guide* series)

Now that one has mastered the basics, the dignified gray-haired Dr. Stanway is ready to show the way to higher bliss. With the help of six different couples, young to middle aged (one racially mixed), he takes on the mysteries of orgasms for men and women and explains how they might get more satisfactory, both together and separately. (The voice of an unseen woman talks about women's issues.) Subjects in this volume are masturbation; better orgasms for women and men; how to get a reluctant penis up, keep it up, and not come too soon; how to find a woman's G-spot and what to do about it; where a man's G-spot is and how to stimulate it; mutual orgasm; variety as the spice of sex lives; and the spiritual aspect of sex. Dr. Stanway's message is unfailingly upbeat, and the sex, while explicit, is tastefully shown. It contains useful charts and graphs.

Explicit

Loving Better: A Guide to More Pleasure and Communication in Your Sex Relationship
(a five-volume series)

Moderated by Dr. Sheldon Kule, psychiatrist and sex therapist, former unit chief of psychiatry at Long Island Jewish Hillside Medical Center. Producers: Raffi Bozanian, Sheldon Kule. Director: Sheldon Kule.

These tapes are available through mail order. We ordered them and they arrived, discreetly packaged, within a week, without our paying for rush delivery.

Dr. Sheldon Kule sits behind a desk and acts as our guide for all five volumes. He has a low-key manner that suggests he'd like to help but isn't going to get pushy about it. These tapes are less psychologically oriented than *Ordinary Couples, Extraordinary Sex* and, after a very informational volume 1, less chatty than *Ordinary Couples, Lover's Guides,* and the *Better Sex* series. For that reason, it seems to establish more mood than usual during the lovemaking. And you can turn the sound down on the dreadful chiming chord music without being afraid you're going to miss something. Couples in all the series do the slow, thoughtful thing, not the wild thing. There isn't much sweat, noise, or visible excitement other than erections.

The Basics: Getting Started (vol. 1)

We are introduced to our bodies (male and female) with cutaway drawings and live models. Then we hear about human sexual response and stages of sexual excitement. As a first step to better sex, a couple touches and examines each other's genitals in detail. Dr. Kule also suggests communication exercises, such as writing an advertisement for your partner (for sale or rent, making a list of turn-ons and turn-offs, etc.). Volume 1 is mostly talking, and it's the only video in the series during which the good doctor monopolizes the screen.

Discovery: Communicating through Touch (vol. 2)

A young couple, Chris and Leslie, go through various caressing exercises together, taking turns being the giver and the receiver of pleasure. "The Face" concentrates on their stroking each other's faces. "The Body" concentrates on all parts of the body except the genitals. "The Genital Caress" shows various ways to touch each other, with each partner guiding the other to personal preferences, and demonstrates two techniques for delaying male orgasm. "The Vaginal Caress" has the penis in the vagina with very little movement. Chris and Leslie talk about how they feel as these things happen.

Loving and Caring: Variation in Lovemaking (vol. 3)

In this volume we see a man and a woman masturbating, then a couple whose sexual priority is fitting their lovemaking into the time period of a commercial break on late-night television. After a long view of a better way to make love, including three basic sexual positions, Chris and Leslie put all the things they have learned in their exercises to good use and go on to variations on the three basic sexual positions. The music is annoying, and since the couples aren't speaking on this tape you can turn the sound off until you see Dr. Kule's face appearing on the screen, without missing a single word of wisdom. The exception is the positions portion of the tape, during which Dr. Kule discusses the advantages of each position in a voice-over. Variety is the catsup and mustard on the hamburger of marriage.

Marital Aids and Fantasies (vol. 4)

Toys and their uses, oral sex, the bath, and sexual fantasies. Steve and Renee, the slightly older and more sophisticated couple, show how they use several different vibrators for their mutual pleasure. Then they enthusiastically show their preferred varieties of oral sex. Dr. Kule says that in his work with thousands of patients he has found the most common male fantasies are having two women at the same time, overcoming a woman's objections so that she desires him, and a harem from which they can pick according to their mood. Women's fantasies are more romantic. They imagine a man so inflamed with passion for them that he overcomes their resistance (no, not rape, romance); they imagine a faceless man who removes them from feelings of guilt; they wonder about making love to a woman.

Sexual Problems (vol. 5)

We are told the three steps to sex therapy: proper information, opportunity, permission. We can't correct physical problems in therapy (e.g., blood flow, hormones, senility, response to medicine) but we can deal with psychological issues. These include problems of desire (50 percent of all couples suffer from differing levels of libido between the partners), as well as difficulties with erection, lubrication, penetration, and orgasm. He gives some exercises for couples to start communicating and suggests ways to find competent, accredited professional help for those times when a video is not enough.

Ordinary Couples, Extraordinary Sex

(three volumes)

Dr. Sandra Scantling, sex therapist and clinical psychologist, assistant clinical professor of psychiatry, University of Connecticut School of Medicine, coauthor of Ordinary Women, Extraordinary Sex.

Dr. Culley Carson, certified sex therapist, doctor of urology, cochair of the sexual dysfunction unit, Duke University Medical Center.

We purchased these tapes via credit-card mail-order from advertisements in *Playboy* and the *New York Times* (though some rental places may carry them). They arrived in less a week, without payment of an extra-fast-mail fee, and the packages in no way proclaimed their contents.

Five signals that you may need to spend some time with Dr. Scantling and Dr. Carson:

• You aren't making time for touching and sharing.
• Sex has become a boring and routine chore for you.

- Words of criticism dominate your vocabulary and are more common than words of appreciation and support.
- Attempts to resolve your anger and hurt escalate into arguments.
- You long for connection and sexual closeness and fill yourself with substitutes.

Dr. Sandra Scantling and her colleague Dr. Culley Carson spend as much time on exercises for couples learning to talk and communicate as they do on the mechanics of sex. The five couples who appear throughout the tapes are mostly in their thirties and forties. Their problems range from breast cancer survivor (lumpectomy, apparently), to loss of libido after childbirth, wounds left by a difficult childhood that make nurturing and trust an issue, people in second marriages trying not to make the same mistakes all over again, and so on. Drs. Scantling and Carson provide a voice-over commentary as the couples demonstrate and discuss (also in voice-over) their sexual preferences. The couples also spend more time than is usual in tapes of this description with their clothes on talking to each other and to the doctors, and the language tends to be more psychotherapeutically oriented than most. If both of you are into therapy or some form of self-actualization, these may be the right tapes for you.

One viewer said she didn't feel she needed the tapes herself but wanted to buy them so her husband could hear a few of the communication suggestions coming from a "neutral" third party. She thought the sight of couples coupling might provide enough carrot for the message to stick. We don't know how it worked, but it seemed worth a try.

Discovering Extraordinary Sex (vol. 1)

In volume 1 the seven steps to increasing intimacy are presented and explained, and several of the couples are introduced. The seven steps are as follows (the tapes explore these steps in detail): (1) Assert your needs and respect each other's boundaries. (2) Put away old hurts and angers, starting today. (3) Focus on pleasure, not measure; remember, sex is not an Olympic event. (4) Break old patterns; find new ways to make your loving exciting and fresh. (5) Treat each other like company; don't treat strangers better than your lover. (6) Make time for each other. (7) Practice clear communication.

Getting Creative with Sex (vol. 2)

This volume presents the eighth step to increasing intimacy: Concentrate on all your senses. Suggestions demonstrated include creating beautiful images in your environment, experimenting with fragrances, experimenting with touch, experimenting with sounds, experimenting with taste, and teasing for pleasing or prolonging your lovemaking. Also studied are making sex playful with games, using fantasy exercises to find out new things about each other, asking for what you want, keeping your communication clear, and listening to your partner with an open heart.

Keeping Sex Extraordinary (vol. 3)

Two of the couples meet with Dr. Scantling to further open themselves to extraordinary sex. In guided therapy sessions they work in even more detail on the eight steps (such as putting away old hurts and angers) that will allow them to establish a safe and loving place for passion and heal each other's past hurts. By learning to nurture each other, they improve their sexual relationship.

Dr. Scantling stresses that these tapes are for people with ordinary communication problems. She suggests that individuals and couples with sexual dysfunction or highly conflicted relationships should consult a qualified sex therapist or other credentialed professional. (For information on contacting such professionals, contact the American Association of Sex Educators, Counselors and Therapists, 312-644-0828.)

Index of Videos by Category

About the Business: Fiction

Curious about the world of adult moviemaking? It's one of adult movies' favorite subjects. Get a fictional look at what goes on behind the scenes. The movies in this category will give you the next best thing to getting a job on a set—in front, or behind, the camera.

BLUE MOVIE^{WW}
CHRISTY'S COMEBACK
EXPOSED^{WW}
GREAT SEXPECTATIONS
MAKIN' IT
SEXCAPADES^{WW}
WHERE THE BOYS AREN'T

About the Business: Nonfiction

Professionals in the business instruct and enlighten you in the ways of their business.

DEEP INSIDE . . . SERIES
FANTASY BOOTH
HISTORY OF THE BLUE MOVIE
MY SURRENDER
ONA ZEE'S SEX ACADEMY
ONLY THE BEST: JIM HOLLIDAY, VOL. 1
PERIL OR PLEASURE: FEMINIST PRODUCED PORNOGRAPHY

Alternative Sexuality

Although the focus of this guide is movies specifically aimed for heterosexuals, we did run into a few videos we thought our audience might enjoy.

Bi with Straight Appeal

BI COASTAL

Lesbian with Straight Appeal

BARBARA DARE'S TRUE LOVE

FANTASY DANCER

THINGS CHANGE: MY FIRST TIME

THINGS CHANGE 2: LETTING GO

Straight with Lesbian Appeal

ANNA OBSESSED

PRISON WORLD

SUBURBAN DYKES

Andrew Blake

Andrew Blake's style was entirely his own—until he turned out to be one of the chief influences of the upscale '90s videos. Hard edged, lushly shot with great color, his films have the polished look of high-fashion magazines and almost no dialogue or story. We thought about his work as candy for your eyes and could imagine his movies projected on a huge screen—with the sound turned off.

DESIRE

HIDDEN OBSESSION[WW]

HOUSE OF DREAMS

NIGHT TRIPS

NIGHT TRIPS 2

SECRETS

SENSUAL EXPOSURE[WW]

Best Foreign Feature Releases

Sexy feature releases from France and Japan, as well as erotica from Europe.

BELLE DE JOUR

COUSIN COUSINE

EMMANUELLE (THE SERIES)

FANNY HILL

FELICIA

THE FELINES

HONEY

IN THE REALM OF THE SENSES

JUNGLE HEAT

LE PARFUME DE MATHILDE

LAST TANGO IN PARIS

LIKE WATER FOR CHOCOLATE

THE LOVER

SENSATIONS

SEX FREAKS
SKIN
SKIN TOO
THE STORY OF O (THE SERIES)
TOKYO DECADENCE

Best Scenes

These movies get our nod for having the hottest, most sensuous, and most original scenes. They come closest to having the perfect combination of intimacy and explicitness. This doesn't necessarily mean that the whole movie is great, though some are. Check the reviews.

AMERICAN BLONDE
ANGELS
BABYLON PINK
BARE MARKET
CAT AND MOUSE
CORRUPTION
CRAZY WITH THE HEAT 2
THE DANCERS[WW]
EASY
ENDLESSLY
EXPOSED[WW]
EXSTASY
FELICIA
INSATIABLE[WW]
MY SURRENDER[WW]
OCTOBER SILK[WW]
SHE'S SO FINE
STAIRWAY TO PARADISE
SUZIE SUPERSTAR[WW]
THE TEASE
TROUBLEMAKER
VEIL

Classic Erotica

Fortunately for us, many of the classics from the '70s and '80s have not been lost. These movies have the most original stories, listenable dialogue, and professionally acted performances.

ALICE IN WONDERLAND[WW]
AMANDA BY NIGHT[WW]
ANNA OBSESSED
AUTOBIOGRAPHY OF A FLEA
BABYLON PINK
BARBARA BROADCAST
BEAUTY[WW]

BEHIND THE GREEN DOOR
BLONDE AMBITION[WW]
CAFE FLESH[WW]
CANDY STRIPERS
CORPORATE ASSETS[WW]
CORRUPTION
THE DANCERS[WW]
DEBBIE DOES DALLAS
DEEP THROAT
THE DEVIL IN MISS JONES
THE DEVIL IN MISS JONES 2[WW]
ECSTASY GIRLS[WW]
EVERY WOMAN HAS A FANTASY 1[WW] AND 2[WW]
EXPOSED[WW]
F[WW]
FIRESTORM
FOXTROT
GREAT SEXPECTATIONS
HISTORY OF THE BLUE MOVIE
INSATIABLE[WW]
MIDNIGHT HEAT[WW]
NAKED CAME THE STRANGER[WW]
NAUGHTY VICTORIANS
NOTHING TO HIDE
OCTOBER SILK[WW]
OPENING OF MISTY BEETHOVEN[WW]
OUTLAW LADIES[WW]
PLATINUM PARADISE[WW]
PRIVATE AFTERNOONS OF PAMELA MANN
ROOMMATES
SEXCAPADES[WW]
SEX WORLD[WW]
SLEEPYHEAD
SMOKER
SUZIE SUPERSTAR[WW]
TALK DIRTY TO ME
3 AM[WW]
THE TIFFANY MINX
UP 'N' COMING

Classics Retold

Adding their own fresh and irreverent twists, erotic moviemakers have borrowed without restraint from stories familiar and obscure.

ALICE IN WONDERLAND[WW]
AUTOBIOGRAPHY OF A FLEA
BEAUTY[WW]
BEAUTY AND THE BEAST
CYRANO

DRACULA EXOTICA
FANNY HILL
JUNGLE HEAT
NAUGHTY VICTORIANS
THE PASSIONS OF CAROL
SHERLOCK HOMIE: IN THE MYSTERIOUS CASE OF ISABELLA THE MAN EATER
THE STORY OF O (THE SERIES)

Comedy

You can laugh at them and with them. Often scandalously outrageous, these movies make you smile, chuckle, and even guffaw.

AMERICAN GARTER
AUTOBIOGRAPHY OF A FLEA
BABY FACE
BEAUTY AND THE BEAST
BEHIND THE GREEN DOOR: THE SEQUEL[WW]
BLONDE AMBITION[WW]
CANDY STRIPERS
DEBBIE DOES DALLAS
EXPOSED[WW]
F[WW]
FANTASEX
FOXTROT
THE GRAFENBERG SPOT
HEAVEN'S TOUCH
HOT DALLAS NIGHTS
NAKED CAME THE STRANGER[WW]
NIGHTSHIFT NURSES
THE OPENING OF MISTY BEETHOVEN[WW]
THE OTHER SIDE OF JULIE
OUTLAW LADIES[WW]
PRETTY PEACHES 2
PRETTY PEACHES 3: THE QUEST
SEXCAPADES[WW]
SEX WORLD[WW]
SHERLOCK HOMIE: IN THE MYSTERIOUS CASE OF ISABELLA THE MAN EATER
SHE'S SO FINE
SORORITY SEX KITTENS, PART 1
TALK DIRTY TO ME
WHERE THE BOYS AREN'T

Couples

The couples in these movies face the same hazards to their relationships as the rest of us. Their solutions are innovative and original. This is also a good place to start if you're looking to charm, beguile, or surprise your special someone. Great for taking along on that getaway weekend, they may give you an idea or

two to get through the rough spots of your life or help you give new heat to a
smoldering fire.

ALEXANDRA
ANNA OBSESSED
BEAUTY^{WW}
BRANDY AND ALEXANDER^{WW}
BURGUNDY BLUES
CAT AND MOUSE
THE CATHOUSE
CHRISTINE'S SECRET^{WW}
CORPORATE ASSETS^{WW}
CRAZY LOVE
CRAZY WITH THE HEAT 2
THE DANCERS^{WW}
THE DEVIL IN MISS JONES 2^{WW}
DINNER PARTY
DIRTY BOOKS
ECSTACY GIRLS^{WW}
EVERY WOMAN HAS A FANTASY 1^{WW}, 2^{WW}, AND 3
EXPOSED^{WW}
EXSTASY
FELICIA
THE FELINES
HOUSE OF DREAMS
INSATIABLE^{WW}
MY SURRENDER^{WW}
NAKED CAME THE STRANGER^{WW}
THE OPENING OF MISTY BEETHOVEN^{WW}
THE OTHER SIDE OF JULIE
OUTLAW LADIES^{WW}
RITES OF PASSION
SECRET GAMES 3
SENSUAL ESCAPE
THE SWAP
THE SWAP 2
A TASTE OF AMBROSIA^{WW}
THREE DAUGHTERS^{WW}
URBAN HEAT
THE VOYEUR
X-FACTOR
X-FACTOR: THE NEXT GENERATION

Fantasy

Looking to put a little high drama into your life? Imagine masquerading as a
stripper, dancer, prostitute, or even an innocent ingenue.

BABYLON PINK
CABIN FEVER
CHRISTINE'S SECRET^{WW}

DINNER PARTY
DREAMS OF DESIRE[WW]
EMMANUELLE (THE SERIES)
EVERY WOMAN HAS A FANTASY 1[WW], 2[WW], AND 3
F[WW]
FANTASEX
FANTASY BOOTH
FANTASY DANCER
HIDDEN OBSESSION[WW]
HONEY
THE HOTTEST BID[WW]
MIRAGE 1
MIRAGE 2
NIGHT TRIPS
NIGHT TRIPS 2
PANDORA'S MIRROR
PLATINUM PARADISE[WW]
THE SECRET LIFE OF NINA HARTLEY
SENSUAL ESCAPE
SEX WORLD[WW]
SEXUAL FANTASY, THE VIDEO
SUBURBAN DYKES
A TASTE OF AMBROSIA[WW]
URBAN HEAT

Fashion, Fetish, and Cross-dressing

Exquisite clothes, unusual fixations, and morphing.

AMERICAN GARTER
BEHIND THE GREEN DOOR
BEHIND THE GREEN DOOR: THE SEQUEL[WW]
BLUE MOVIE[WW]
CAFE FLESH[WW]
CONTRACT FOR SERVICE
CORRUPTION
THE DEVIL IN MISS JONES 2[WW]
DINNER PARTY
EVERY WOMAN HAS A FANTASY 1[WW], 2[WW], AND 3
FABULOUS 40'S
LE PARFUME DE MATHILDE
LATEX
NAUGHTY VICTORIANS
OUTLAW LADIES[WW]
PRISON WORLD
SEX 1994
SHE'S SO FINE
SKIN
SKIN TOO
THE STORY OF O (THE SERIES)
SUBURBAN DYKES

280

First Amendment

A persistent concern—and with good reason—of the adult film industry is freedom of expression. This legitimate fear of losing that freedom has become a theme for exploration in erotic movies.

LATEX
PERIL OR PLEASURE: FEMINIST PRODUCED PORNOGRAPHY
REVELATIONS
SEXOPHRENIA

For Beginners

Softer, less in-your-face, these are the perfect videos to watch if you're just getting acquainted with erotic movies. "(s)" indicates simulated sex.

ALEXANDRA
ALICE IN WONDERLAND[WW]
BLONDE AMBITION[WW]
CABIN FEVER (S)
CHRISTINE'S SECRET[WW]
ECSTASY GIRLS[WW]
EVERY WOMAN HAS A FANTASY 1[WW] AND 2[WW]
EXPOSED[WW]
THE HOTTEST BID[WW] (S)
THE MASSEUSE: SHE'LL RUB YOU RIGHT
MY SURRENDER[WW]
NAKED CAME THE STRANGER[WW]
THE OPENING OF MISTY BEETHOVEN[WW]
PLATINUM PARADISE[WW]
RED SHOES DIARIES (THE SERIES) (S)
SECRET GAMES 3 (S)
SENSUAL ESCAPE
SENSUAL EXPOSURE
SEXUAL RESPONSE (S)
SUZIE SUPERSTAR[WW]
THE SWAP
THE SWAP 2
A TASTE OF AMBROSIA[WW]
THREE DAUGHTERS
URBAN HEAT
THE VOYEUR (S)
X-FACTOR
X-FACTOR: THE NEXT GENERATION

Hot Hollywood

Some of our own personal favorites—old and new, demonstrating that you don't need nudity to get turned on. You'll find the whole range, from romance to S/M.

THE BIG EASY
BLACK ORCHID
BLUE SKY
BLUE VELVET
BODY OF EVIDENCE
BULL DURHAM
DON JUAN DEMARCO
THE HUNGER
LAST SEDUCTION
9 1/2 WEEKS
SEA OF LOVE
TEQUILA SUNRISE
THELMA AND LOUISE
WHITE PALACE
WOMEN IN LOVE

Moral Tales

There are lessons to be learned from a life of sin, drugs, and, oh yes, clean living (*The Devil in Miss Jones*).

ANGELS
CHINATOWN
CORRUPTION
THE DEVIL IN MISS JONES
ROOMMATES
SEX 1994
SEX 2: FATE
TOKYO DECADENCE

Musicals

In this list you'll find Broadway-like productions, nightclub acts, and a story about the perils of climbing the ladder of success.

ALICE IN WONDERLAND[WW]
BLACK AND WHITE IN LIVING COLOR
BLONDE AMBITION[WW]
BURGUNDY BLUES
SUZIE SUPERSTAR[WW]
UP 'N' COMING

Noir, Mystery, Suspense, and Thrillers

Makers of erotic movies haven't forgotten the dark side of human nature. Infidelity, double dealing, and murder are all treated in this category.

AMANDA BY NIGHT[WW]
ANGELS

ANNA OBSESSED
BODIES IN HEAT
CHINATOWN
COMPANION 2:
THE DOG WALKER
FOOLPROOF
FOREVER YOUNG
GOIN' DOWN SLOW
LAST SEDUCTION
LUST ON THE ORIENT EXPRESS
MIDNIGHT HEAT[WW]
3 AM[WW]
TROUBLEMAKER

Offbeat

Weird by any standard, these cover the entire range from the jocular to the capricious. A mixed bag, there's something for everyone.

AMERICAN GARTER
BITTERSWEET
CAFE FLESH[WW]
CAT AND MOUSE
CORRUPTION
THE DEVIL IN MISS JONES
THE DEVIL IN MISS JONES 2[WW]
DRACULA EXOTICA
F[WW]
FANTASY BOOTH
FOREVER YOUNG
IMMORTAL DESIRE
LATEX
NAUGHTY VICTORIANS
NIGHTDREAMS
PANDORA'S MIRROR
SEX 1994
SEX 2: FATE
SEX FREAKS
SMOKER
TWO HEARTS
VIRTUAL SEX

Over Forty

Each of these videos features at least one great-looking woman over forty. A great source of inspiration to the rest of us!

AMERICAN GARTER
BABY FACE

CHRISTINE'S SECRET^{WW}
CRAZY WITH THE HEAT 2
FANTASY BOOTH
LE PARFUME DE MATHILDE
NAUGHTY VICTORIANS
THE OTHER SIDE OF JULIE
THREE DAUGHTERS^{WW}
TWO HEARTS
WHITE PALACE

Porn Therapy

Probably not like any therapy you've ever had, but it is therapy.

BAD HABITS
THE CHAMELEON
CLAIR OF THE MOON
CORPORATE ASSETS^{WW}
CRAZY LOVE
LATEX
NIGHTDREAMS
NIGHT TRIPS
NIGHT TRIPS 2
PRETTY PEACHES 2
SEXUAL RESPONSE
SEX WORLD^{WW}

Result is Romance

. . . and they lived happily ever after.

ALEXANDRA
AMANDA BY NIGHT^{WW}
BAD HABITS
BEAUTY^{WW}
BEAUTY AND THE BEAST
BLONDE AMBITION^{WW}
BLUE MOVIE^{WW}
BRANDY AND ALEXANDER^{WW}
BURGUNDY BLUES
CORPORATE ASSETS^{WW}
ECSTASY GIRLS^{WW}
EXSTASY
GREAT SEXPECTATIONS
JUSTINE, OR, NOTHING TO HIDE^{WW}
MY SURRENDER
X-FACTOR
X-FACTOR: THE NEXT GENERATION

Rough Stuff

Boisterous, raucous, rowdy, and raunchy sex.

AMERICAN PIE
BEHIND THE GREEN DOOR
BONNIE AND CLYDE I
BONNIE AND CLYDE II
THE CATHOUSE
THE CATWOMAN
THE CHAMELEON
CHINATOWN
DEBBIE DOES DALLAS
DOG WALKER
DRACULA EROTICA
EASY
EVERY WOMAN HAS A FANTASY 3
LATEX
MASSEUSE 2
NIGHTSHIFT NURSES
NIGHT TRIPS 2
PRETTY PEACHES 2
PRETTY PEACHES 3: THE QUEST
REVENGE OF THE BI DOLLS
SILK STOCKINGS, BLACK WIDOW
SKIN TOO
SORORITY SEX KITTENS, PART 1
SORORITY SEX KITTENS, PART 2
THINGS CHANGE 2: LETTING GO
TOKYO DECADENCE
THE VOYEUR 2

S/M

Most of what you'll find in this category is light bondage and S/M, not for the pain but the fun of it.

BARBARA BROADCAST
BEHIND THE GREEN DOOR
BITTERSWEET
CONTRACT FOR SERVICE
EXSTASY
HONEY
LEARNING THE ROPES (INSTRUCTIONAL)
LOVERS: AN INTIMATE PORTRAIT, 2
9 1/2 WEEKS
PRISON WORLD
SENSATIONS
SKIN

SKIN TOO
THE STORY OF O (THE SERIES)
TOKYO DECADENCE

Safe Sex

We think videos of the '90s should include safe sex, though few do. These make a point of it.

BEHIND THE GREEN DOOR: THE SEQUEL[WW]
THE HOTTEST BID[WW]
SENSUAL ESCAPE
SUBURBAN DYKES
SUZIE SUPERSTAR[WW]
THREE DAUGHTERS[WW]

Sci Fi

Most of these are movies set in the future or the past—a few feature morphing and other out-of-this-world fantasies and hauntings.

CAFE FLESH[WW]
THE CATWOMAN
THE CHAMELEON
CHAMELEONS: NOT THE SEQUEL[WW]
CURSE OF THE CATWOMAN
FOREVER YOUNG
INSIDE OUT (2 AND 3 OF THE SERIES)
LATEX
MAD LOVE
REVELATIONS
SEXOPHRENIA
STAIRWAY TO PARADISE

Settings with Flair and High Style

Romance and sex alfresco, spectacular locations, and extra-special interiors and costumes.

BAD HABITS
DESIRE
DINNER PARTY
FABULOUS 40'S
FIRESTORM
HIDDEN OBSESSION[WW]
HOUSE OF DREAMS
INSATIABLE[WW]
LATEX
LE PARFUME DE MATHILDE

THE LOVER
MIRAGE 1
NIGHT TRIPS
NIGHT TRIPS 2
PANDORA'S MIRROR
PASSION IN VENICE
REVENGE OF THE BI DOLLS
SECRETS
SENSUAL ESCAPE
SENSUAL EXPOSURE
THE STORY OF O (THE SERIES)
URBAN HEAT
VIRTUAL SEX

Simulated

Movies that don't go the whole nine yards or, in the case of these, the whole seven inches, can sizzle and scorch, too.

BLUE VELVET
CLAIR OF THE MOON
CONTRACT FOR SERVICE
COUSIN COUSINE
DON JUAN DEMARCO
EMMANUELLE (THE SERIES)
FANNY HILL
HONEY
THE HOTTEST BID[WW]
THE ITALIAN STALLION
LAST TANGO IN PARIS
THE LOVER
9 1/2 WEEKS
RED SHOE DIARIES (THE SERIES)
SEXUAL RESPONSE
THE STORY OF O (THE SERIES)
THELMA AND LOUISE
THE VOYEUR
WHITE PALACE
WHORE
WOMEN IN LOVE

The Story's the Thing

Having a beginning, a middle, and an end isn't one of the standards of adult movies. The ones you'll find here have a linear order, for all you Virgos and others perplexed by nonlinear narratives.

ALEXANDRA
AMANDA BY NIGHT[WW]
BAD HABITS

BEAUTY AND THE BEAST
BI COASTAL
BLONDE AMBITION[WW]
BURGUNDY BLUES
CABIN FEVER
CHAMELEONS: NOT THE SEQUEL[WW]
CYRANO
DINNER PARTY
EASY
FIRESTORM
THE GODDAUGHTER, PART 1 AND 2
JUSTINE, OR, NOTHING TO HIDE[WW]
LUST ON THE ORIENT EXPRESS
THE MASSEUSE: SHE'LL RUB YOU RIGHT
MIDNIGHT HEAT[WW]
MIRAGE 1
THE NICOLE STANTON STORY 1 AND 2
NOTHING TO HIDE
OCTOBER SILK[WW]
THE OPENING OF MISTY BEETHOVEN[WW]
THE OTHER SIDE OF JULIE
PANDORA'S MIRROR
PRETTY PEACHES 3: THE QUEST
R & R
SHE'S SO FINE
SLEEPYHEAD
SOFT, WARM RAIN
SUSIE SUPERSTAR[WW]
THE SWAP
THE SWAP 2
THINGS CHANGE: MY FIRST TIME
THINGS CHANGE 2: LETTING GO
3 AM[WW]
UP 'N' COMING
VEIL
X-FACTOR
X-FACTOR: THE NEXT GENERATION

Stripping

Take it off, take it all off, with attitude and élan. Master the techniques of removing your bra using a boa for camouflage, and learn to shake your booty like a pro.

ANGELS
THE DANCERS[WW]
LOVERS: AN INTIMATE PORTRAIT, 2
MIRAGE 1
VEIL

Talk a Little Dirty

Because we're so decorous, we haven't used the *F* word in this book, except perhaps in a quote. That doesn't mean we don't or that you shouldn't. The right word at the right time said with feeling can have the desired effect.

AMERICAN BLONDE
AMERICAN PIE
BRANDY AND ALEXANDER[WW]
THE DEVIL IN MISS JONES
DRACULA EXOTICA[WW]
EXPOSED[WW]
FANTASEX
PLATINUM PARADISE[WW]
SORORITY SEX KITTENS, PART 1
SORORITY SEX KITTENS, PART 2
TALK DIRTY TO ME
TROUBLEMAKER
THE VOYEUR 2

Tantric Sex

The secrets of the East revealed. You'll find some specific practices that are easy to incorporate into your sex life. A good place to start, especially if you're a student of yoga.

THE HOTTEST BID[WW] (SIMULATED)
AN INTIMATE GUIDE TO MALE GENITAL MASSAGE (INSTRUCTIONAL)
JEWEL IN THE LOTUS (INSTRUCTIONAL)
RITES OF PASSION
THE TANTRIC GUIDE TO SEXUAL POTENCY

Teaching Tools

You'll find many instructional videos in the "Instructional" and "How-to" sections, but these stories also show how to with a light, carefree touch.

DIRTY BOOKS
THE GRAFENBERG SPOT
THE MASSEUSE: SHE'LL RUB YOU RIGHT
OCTOBER SILK[WW]
ONA ZEE'S SEX ACADEMY
VEIL

Womanly Bodies

What all these videos have in common is at least one main female cast member who has a tummy, full thighs, and a rounder figure than one might expect to see taking it all off. They aren't, by any means, huge—just *womanly*. In general, videos prior to the mid '80s have less-worked-out bodies than those made later.

ALEXANDRA
AMERICAN GARTER
BABY FACE
THE CATHOUSE
CHRISTINE'S SECRET^{WW}
THE DEVIL IN MISS JONES 2^{WW}
EVERY WOMAN HAS A FANTASY 1^{WW}
EXSTASY
SEXUAL FANTASY: THE VIDEO
SEX WORLD^{WW}
SHERLOCK HOMIE: IN THE MYSTERIOUS CASE OF ISABELLA THE MAN EATER
TIFFANY MINX

Women on Top

Videos that have at least one scene in which the woman directs the action.

BABY FACE
BABYLON PINK
BARBARA BROADCAST
BARE MARKET
CANDY STRIPERS
THE FELINES
THE MASSEUSE: SHE'LL RUB YOU RIGHT
MASSEUSE 2
OCTOBER SILK^{WW}
OUTLAW LADIES^{WW}
PRETTY PEACHES 3: THE QUEST
PRISON WORLD
SKIN TOO
SMOKER
SORORITY SEX KITTENS, PART 1
SORORITY SEX KITTENS, PART 2
TWO HEARTS

Index of Leading Performers

Here is an abbreviated list of some of the main performers. Spelling variations are included when known.

Mail-order Sources

The following catalogs come in plain envelopes, so you needn't worry about prying eyes and knowing glances.

CATALOGS

Adam and Eve
P.O. Box 800
Chapel Hill, NC 27515
1-800-765-2326
Catalog for women and men. Toys, videos, some lingerie. Illustrated with full-color, explicit photographs.

After Midnight Collection for Women
1-800-400-6103
c/o Horizon Trading Group, Inc.
P.O. Box 13176
Scottsdale, AZ 83267-3176
Catalog lists videos, books, and toys, chosen with women in mind. Illustrated with line drawings. When asked about the contents of a video, the woman who answered the telephone viewed the film and called back within a day with the information. Excellent service.

Eve's Garden
119 West 57th Street
New York, NY 10019-2383
212-757-8651
A retail store that also has a mail-order catalog of toys, books, and videos. Catalog has line drawings of toys and other merchandise.

Femme Productions
302 Meadowland Dr.
Hillsborough, NC 27278

Good Vibrations
1210 Valencia Street

San Francisco, CA 94110
415-974-8990 (7 A.M. to 7 P.M. Pacific time, Monday through Saturday)
Two retail stores and a mail-order catalog (line drawings). Emphasis is on
women and alternative sexuality. The Sexuality Library (over three hundred
books, magazines, and videos about sex); Video Library (videos only).

Multi-Focus, Inc.
1525 Franklin Street
San Francisco, CA 94109
1-800-821-0514
Distributes educational films, videos, and slides in human sexuality. The
catalog lists educational films for schools, professionals, and couples with
special needs, including hard-to-find topics such as "AIDS, Women and
Sexuality," "Breast Cancer: Adjusting to It," "Don't Tell the Cripples about
Sex," and "Touching" (a paraplegic man and woman explore a satisfying sexual relationship). No illustrations. Many 35-millimeter films. Rental or purchase.

Playboy Catalog
P.O. Box 809
Department 59264
Itasca, IL 60143-0809
1-800-423-9494
Catalog of books, clothes, discreet toys, and videos. Most videos are soft core,
simulated, or cable cut. Illustrated with nonexplicit nudes and other color
photographs.

Video Gold
P.O. Box 8845
Chapel Hill, NC 27515
An adult video club for men and women with books, toys, some lingerie.
This is a PHE club, which means that selections have been evaluated by
therapists. The mailing is illustrated with explicit, full-color photographs.
Once you join, you'll receive a monthly selection unless you tell them not
to send it.

Video Mail
P.O. Box 1550, Madison Square Garden
New York, NY 10159
1-800-846-0555
Catalog of videos, books, and toys. Illustrated with explicit, full-color
photographs.

The Xandria Collection
Department PBO695
P.O. Box 31039
San Francisco, CA 94131
Toys, aids, books, and videos. ($4.00 U.S., $5.00 Canada, check or money
order for catalog, applicable to first purchase.)

DIRECT-MAIL SERIES

The Better Sex Video Series
The Townsend Institute
Department ZP
P.O. Box 8855
Chapel Hill, NC 27515
1-800-888-1900
How-to series.

The Loving Better Videos
Brandon Research
P.O. Box 770336
Coral Springs, FL 33077
1-800-438-8149
How-to series.

Ordinary Couples, Extraordinary Sex
The Sinclair Institute
Box 8865
Chapel Hill, NC 27515
1-800-955-0888
How-to series.

Bibliography and Further Reading

Bakos, Susan Crain. *Kink: The Hidden Sex Lives of Americans.* New York: St. Martin's Paperbacks, 1995.

Barbach, Lonnie. *Pleasures: Women Write Erotica.* New York: Doubleday, 1984.

Bright, Susie. *Sexwise.* Pittsburgh: Cleis Press, 1995.

Delacoste, Frederique and Priscilla Alexander (Eds.). *Sex Work: Writings by Women in the Sex Industry.* San Francisco: Cleis Press, 1987.

Friday, Nancy. *My Secret Garden.* New York: Pocket Books, 1974.

Friday, Nancy. *Women on Top.* New York: Simon and Schuster, 1991.

Holliday, Jim. *Only the Best: Jim Holliday's Adult Video Almanac and Trivia Treasury.* Van Nuys, CA: Cal Vista Publication, 1986.

Janus, Samuel S. and Cynthia Janus. *The Janus Report on Sexual Behavior.* New York: John Wiley and Sons, Inc., 1993.

Keough, Peter (Ed.). *Flesh and Blood: The National Society of Film Critics on Sex, Violence, and Censorship.* San Francisco: Mercury House, 1995.

Kippins, Laura. *Bound and Gagged: Pornography and the Politics of Fantasy in America.* New York: Grove Press, 1996.

Lovelace, Linda with Mike McGrady. *Ordeal.* New York: Berkeley Books, 1981.

Maurer, Harry. *Sex: Real People Talk about What They Really Do.* New York: Penguin USA, 1994.

Reinisch, June M. *The Kinsey Institute New Report on Sex.* New York: St. Martin's Press, 1990.

Riley, Patrick. *The X-Rated Videotape Guide,* vol. 5. Amherst, NY: Prometheus Books, 1995.

Rimmer, Robert J. *The X-Rated Videotape Guide,* vols. 1, 2. Buffalo, NY: Prometheus Books, 1991.

Rimmer, Robert J. and Patrick Riley. *The X-Rated Videotape Guide,* vols. 3, 4. Buffalo, NY: Prometheus Books, 1994.

Stoller, Robert J. *Porn.* New Haven: Yale University Press, 1991.

Stoller, Robert J. and I. S. Levine. *Coming Attractions: The Making of an X-Rated Video.* New Haven: Yale University Press, 1993.

Williams, Linda. *Hard Core: Power, Pleasure and the "Frenzy of the

Visible." Berkeley and Los Angeles, CA: University of California Press, 1989.

Winks, Cathy and Anne Semans. *The Good Vibrations Guide to Sex.* San Francisco: Cleis Press, 1994.

Zacks, Richard. *History Laid Bare: Love, Sex, and Perversity from the Ancient Etruscans to Warren G. Harding.* New York: Harper Collins, 1995.